# LIBRARY OF HEBREW BIBLE/ OLD TESTAMENT STUDIES

## 436

*Formerly Journal for the Study of the Old Testament Supplement Series*

### Editors
Claudia V. Camp, Texas Christian University
Andrew Mein, Westcott House, Cambridge

# SUBVERSIVE SCRIBES
# AND THE SOLOMONIC NARRATIVE

A Rereading of 1 Kings 1–11

Eric A. Seibert

t&t clark

NEW YORK • LONDON

T & T Clark International, 80 Maiden Lane, New York, NY 10038

T & T Clark International, The Tower Building, 11 York Road, London SE1 7NX

T & T Clark International is a Continuum imprint.

Unless otherwise indicated, biblical quotations are from the New Revised Standard Version Bible, copyright 1989, Division of Christian Education of the National Council of the Churches of Christ in the United States of America. Used by permission. All rights reserved

**Library of Congress Cataloging-in-Publication Data**
Seibert, Eric A., 1969-
Subversive scribes and the Solomonic narrative : a rereading of 1 Kings 1-11 / Eric A.
   Seibert.
   p. cm. -- (Library of Hebrew Bible/Old Testament studies ; 436)
Includes bibliographical references and index.
ISBN 0-567-02771-6 (hardcover)
1. Bible. O.T. Kings, 1st, I-XI--Criticism, interpretation, etc. 2. Subversive activities
Biblical teaching. 3. Propaganda--Biblical teaching. I. Title. II. Series.
   BS1335.52.S45 2006
   222'.5306--dc22
                                        2006007654

*Printed and bound in Great Britain by*
*Biddles Ltd., King's Lynn, Norfolk*

06 07 08 09 10      10 9 8 7 6 5 4 3 2 1

*For Elisa*

*best friend, lifelong companion*

# CONTENTS

## Part I
### A THEORY OF SCRIBAL SUBVERSION

Part II
AN INVESTIGATION OF SCRIBAL SUBVERSION
IN 1 KINGS 1–11

Chapter 3
PROLEGOMENA TO READING 1 KINGS 1–11

Chapter 4
PROPAGANDA AND SUBVERSION IN SOLOMON'S RISE TO POWER:

## ACKNOWLEDGMENTS

The completion of a book is a time for great rejoicing! It is also a time to thank the many people who had a part in this project along the way. Since, this book represents a revision of my dissertation (completed May 2002), the first round of thanks goes to the members of my dissertation committee: Herbert B. Huffmon, Jacques Berlinerblau, and Gary N. Knoppers. Each member assisted me with this project in various ways by giving of their time and expertise. Professor Knoppers opened up for me the world of the Deuteronomistic Historian through his many (!) writings on the subject and graciously extended hospitality to me while visiting him at Penn State University. Professor Berlinerblau taught me the value of a good theory and first got me thinking about subversive scribes. Professor Huffmon served as my dissertation advisor and helped bring greater focus to my work. I especially appreciated his very careful reading of my dissertation and the many insightful comments and suggestions he offered which substantially improved its quality. His revisions, along with certain ideas/suggestions from Professors Berlinerblau and Knoppers, were often utilized and/or directly incorporated with no special notation. I am also grateful for the many ways Professor Huffmon invested in me while a graduate student at Drew University. I have benefitted from his classroom instruction and his enthusiasm for all things ancient. Particularly, I wish to thank Professor Huffmon for demonstrating the value of asking many and varied questions of the text without neglecting to take into account the very real historical and social forces that shaped the production of the Hebrew Bible. May his tribe increase!

In April 2004, I gave a paper derived from my dissertation at the Eastern Great Lakes Biblical Society's annual meeting. It was titled "Solomon's Execution Orders (1 Kgs 2:13–46): Political Propaganda or Scribal Subversion?," and has since been published in *Proceedings, Eastern Great Lakes and Midwest Biblical Societies* 24 (2004): 141–52. I am grateful for permission to use that material here.

In various ways, Messiah College has generously supported this writing project. Through the College's Work Load Reallocation Program I was given release time to work on this manuscript. Additionally, two internal grants provided funding for this work. Both the time and resources were helpful in completing the book. My thanks are also due to Dee Porterfield (and staff) who works wonders through the College's Interlibrary Loan Department with unusual speed and grace. Her help in securing resources was indispensable. I was also fortunate to have the assistance of an exceptional student named Brian Hamilton who not only read the entire manuscript and made certain suggestions, but quite capably tackled the thankless job of preparing an initial draft of the indexes.

I would also like to extend my appreciation to the folks at Continuum, particularly Henry Carrigan and Amy Wagner, for assisting me with the details of seeing this manuscript through to publication. When this manuscript was being consideration for publication, an anonymous reader offered helpful suggestions about how to improve the first part of the book. The final product is much better as a result. I would additionally like to acknowledge the fine copy-editing done by Duncan Burns in the final stages of preparing this book for publication.

Finally, I would like to express my sincere gratitude to Elisa, my wife. She has demonstrated great patience with me while I toiled with Solomon and the scribes who wrote about him. Elisa has been a constant support and source of encouragement throughout this long process, and I am deeply grateful for the many sacrifices she has made on my behalf along the way. It is to her this book is affectionately dedicated.

# ABBREVIATIONS

| | |
|---|---|
| AB | Anchor Bible |
| *ASTI* | *Annual of the Swedish Theological Institute* |
| BA | *Biblical Archaeologist* |
| BAR | *Biblical Archaeology Review* |
| BETL | Bibliotheca ephemeridum theologicarum lovaniensium |
| *Bib* | *Biblica* |
| *BibInt* | *Biblical Interpretation* |
| BKAT | Biblischer Kommentar, Altes Testament |
| *BN* | *Biblische Notizen* |
| *BRev* | *Bible Review* |
| BWA(N)T | Beitrage zur Wissenschaft vom Alten (und Neuen) Testament |
| BZAW | Beihefte zur Zeitschrift für die alttestamentliche Wissenschaft |
| *CBQ* | *Catholic Biblical Quarterly* |
| CBQMS | Catholic Biblical Quarterly Monograph Series |
| ConBOT | Coniectanea biblica: Old Testament Series |
| *CQR* | *Church Quarterly Review* |
| FOTL | Forms of the Old Testament Literature |
| GCT | Gender, Culture, Theory Series |
| *HAR* | *Hebrew Annual Review* |
| HBM | Hebrew Bible Monographs |
| *HS* | *Hebrew Studies* |
| HSM | Harvard Semitic Monographs |
| *HTR* | *Harvard Theological Review* |
| *HUCA* | *Hebrew Union College Annual* |
| IBC | Interpretation: A Bible Commentary for Teaching and Preaching |
| ICC | International Critical Commentary |
| *Int* | *Interpretation* |
| *JAAR* | *Journal of the American Academy of Religion* |
| *JAOS* | *Journal of the American Oriental Society* |
| *JBL* | *Journal of Biblical Literature* |
| *JETS* | *Journal of the Evangelical Theological Society* |
| *JSOT* | *Journal for the Study of the Old Testament* |
| JSOTSup | Journal for the Study of the Old Testament: Supplement Series |
| *JSS* | *Journal of Semitic Studies* |
| *JTS* | *Journal of Theological Studies* |
| NCB | New Century Bible |
| NIBCOT | New International Biblical Commentary on the Old Testament |
| NICOT | New International Commentary on the Old Testament |
| OBO | Orbis biblicus et orientalis |
| OBT | Overtures to Biblical Theology |

| | |
|---|---|
| OTL | Old Testament Library |
| PIASH | Proceedings of the Israel Academy of Sciences and Humanities |
| *Proof* | *Prooftexts: A Journal of Jewish Literary History* |
| *RB* | *Revue biblique* |
| SBLDS | Society of Biblical Literature Dissertation Series |
| SBLMS | Society of Biblical Literature Monograph Series |
| SBT | Studies in Biblical Theology |
| ScrHier | Scripta hierosolymitana |
| *SJOT* | *Scandinavian Journal of the Old Testament* |
| SOTSMS | Society for Old Testament Studies Monograph Series |
| *Text* | *Textus* |
| *TynBul* | *Tyndale Bulletin* |
| *VT* | *Vetus Testamentum* |
| VTSup | Vetus Testamentum Supplements |
| WBC | Word Biblical Commentary |
| *WO* | *Die Welt des Orients* |
| *ZAW* | *Zeitschrift für die alttestamentliche Wissenschaft* |

PART I

A THEORY OF SCRIBAL SUBVERSION

Chapter 1

PROPAGANDA, SUBVERSION, AND SCRIPTURE

*Be a craftsman in speech, so that thou mayest be strong,*
*for the tongue is a sword to a man,*
*and speech is more valorous than any fighting.*

—The Instruction for King Meri-ka-re[1]

One of the fundamental challenges facing the interpreter of 1 Kgs 1–11 is determining how to appraise the particulars of Solomon's reign. Traditionally, scholars have divided this material into two sections and have argued that the first part, 1 Kgs 1–10 (or 1 Kgs 3–10), is favorable toward the king while the second, 1 Kgs 11, is not.[2] As Mordechai Cogan uncategorically asserts, "The Deuteronomist's criticism of Solomon begins in 11:1 and not before."[3] This prevailing view has been challenged in a

1. "The Instruction for King Meri-ka-re" (translated by John A. Wilson, *ANET*, 415).

2. So, e.g., John Gray, *I & II Kings: A Commentary* (OTL; Philadelphia: Westminster, 1963), 28–29; Bezalel Porten, "The Structure and Theme of the Solomon Narrative (1 Kings 3–11)," *HUCA* 38 (1967), 93–128 (97–98); J. Liver, "The Book of the Acts of Solomon," *Bib* 48 (1967), 75–101 (90, 96); Burke O. Long, *1 Kings with an Introduction to Historical Literature* (FOTL 9; Grand Rapids: Eerdmans, 1984), 120–22; Gwilym H. Jones, *1 and 2 Kings* (2 vols.; NCB; Grand Rapids: Eerdmans, 1984), 61. This thesis has more recently been defended by Gary N. Knoppers, *Two Nations Under God: The Deuteronomistic History of Solomon and the Dual Monarchies.* Vol. 1, *The Reign of Solomon and the Rise of Jeroboam* (HSM 52; Atlanta: Scholars Press, 1993), 57–168 (57–60); cf. David McLain Carr, *From D to Q: A Study of Early Jewish Interpretations of Solomon's Dream at Gibeon* (SBLMS 44; Atlanta: Scholars Press, 1991), 59–61, and David Jobling, "'Forced Labor': Solomon's Golden Age and the Question of Literary Representation," in *Poststructuralism as Exegesis* (ed. David Jobling and Stephen D. Moore; Semeia 54; Atlanta: Scholars Press, 1992), 57–76 (60), who views chs. 3–10 as a mostly positive portrait which is bracketed by negative appraisals on either side. Jobling does, however, allow for some negativity in ch. 9 (p. 69).

3. Mordechai Cogan, *I Kings* (AB 10; New York: Doubleday, 2001), 189.

number of literary studies[4] which have attempted, in part, to defend and refine Martin Noth's long neglected proposal that criticism of the king actually begins back in ch. 9.[5] Other studies have contested both of these construals by arguing that any attempt to bifurcate the "Solomonic narrative"[6] in this manner is inappropriate.[7] They maintain that praise and criticism run throughout the narrative, thereby allowing both positive and negative elements to coexist simultaneously in ways that stymie efforts to pinpoint precisely where praise stops and criticism begins.[8]

This study seeks, in part, to contribute to the ongoing discussion by investigating the Solomonic narrative through the optics of propaganda and, specifically, subversion. Since previous studies have already given

4. Attempts to locate the first hint of criticism in God's second dream appearance in 1 Kgs 9:1 can be found in Kim Ian Parker, "Repetition as a Structuring Device in 1 Kings 1–11," *JSOT* 42 (1988): 19–27 (22, 25, 27); idem, "Solomon as Philosopher King? The Nexus of Law and Wisdom in 1 Kings 1–11," *JSOT* 53 (1992): 75–91 (86–89); and Amos Frisch, "Structure and Its Significance: The Narrative of Solomon's Reign (1 Kings 1–12.24)," *JSOT* 51 (1991): 3–14 (6). Marc Zvi Brettler ("The Structure of 1 Kings 1–11," *JSOT* 49 [1991]: 87–97 [89, 97]) argues the hostile unit begins at 9:26.

5. Martin Noth, *The Deuteronomistic History* (2d ed.; JSOTSup 15; Sheffield: JSOT Press, 1991), 60; trans. of *Überlieferungsgeschichtliche Studien* (2d ed.; Tübingen: Max Niemeyer, 1957).

6. Though I realize this expression is not entirely satisfactory, for convenience sake, "Solomonic narrative" is used here and throughout this study to refer to 1 Kgs 1–11.

7. For a recent (and extensive!) critique of those who divide the Solomonic narrative into two sections—one favorable toward Solomon and the other not—and for an alternate understanding of the structure of this material, see Jung Ju Kang, *The Persuasive Portrayal of Solomon in 1 Kings 1–11* (Bern: Peter Lang, 2003), 141–212. According to Kang, "The arrangement of 1 Kgs 1–11 does not show a simple characterisation of Solomon, as generally a great king (1–10) who only at the late stage becomes a failure (11). Rather, the repeated units, in a subtle or clear contrast, show the reader that Solomon's disobedience is not an isolated incident in his old age, but his inevitable failure is already implied from his establishment of the kingdom" (p. 203).

8. See especially Jerome T. Walsh, "The Characterization of Solomon in First Kings 1–5," *CBQ* 57 (1995): 471–93; idem, *1 Kings* (Berit Olam: Studies in Hebrew Narrative and Poetry; Collegeville, Minn.: Liturgical Press, 1996), 3–156, and to a lesser degree Marvin A. Sweeney, "The Critique of Solomon in the Josianic Edition of the Deuteronomistic History," *JBL* 114 (1995): 607–22. For a consistently (and excessively) negative evaluation of Solomon, see Lyle Eslinger, *Into the Hands of the Living God* (JSOTSup 84; Sheffield: Almond Press, 1989), 123–81. For "a critical reading of Solomon" based on the structure of 1 Kgs 1–11, see John W. Olley, "Pharaoh's Daughter, Solomon's Palace, and the Temple: Another Look at the Structure of 1 Kings 1–11," *JSOT* 27 (2003): 355–69 (368).

considerable attention to the propagandistic potential of various aspects of the Solomonic narrative, the following investigation will be particularly interested in exploring examples of scribal subversion in 1 Kgs 1–11. Texts which covertly undermine the legitimacy or the legacy of Solomon will be given special consideration. In the process, a serious effort will be made to understand the social context in which scribal subversion was not only possible, but perhaps even necessary. Thus, while "resolving" the particular question about the presence of praise and criticism in the Solomonic narrative is not the primary purpose of this investigation, it is hoped that the focused approach taken here will nevertheless further that conversation.

This book is divided into two major sections. The first part explores the theory of subversive scribal activity. Attention is given to defining subversion, discussing the goals of literary scribal subversion, and exploring various ways this subversive activity was deployed textually. Anticipating some of our conclusions, it will be argued that one of the most effective ways to deploy subversion in ancient literature was in the guise of royal propaganda. The remainder of this chapter is, therefore, devoted to two tasks: (1) developing definitions of propaganda and subversion, and (2) briefly reviewing other studies that have utilized these literary classifications when discussing biblical texts. Chapter 2 contains an extended discussion of the role of scribes in the ancient Near East, with specific attention being devoted to clarifying their social location and relationship *vis-à-vis* the royal establishment. Questions will be raised about how their institutional affiliations affected their behavior and their writings. Did scribes always do what they were told? Were they simply pre-programmed political functionaries who produced on demand (or else!)? Or did these scribes have a mind of their own? Could they express their own opinions, even if these differed from the "party line"? And if so, how?

An important distinction is made in this chapter between "submissive scribes," individuals who wrote what they were told, and "subversive scribes," individuals who did otherwise. Given the fact that many scribes were writing for the very people who paid them, those wanting to engage in subversive literary activity had to do so carefully and—to a certain extent—covertly. Otherwise, they would be detected and exposed. Yet their critique could not be so obscure that none could detect it. There needed to be enough clues to allow like-minded scribes to read the text and appreciate the critique, but not so many that opponents could charge such scribes with sedition. Being aware of the possibility of literary scribal subversion and knowing how to detect it offers new ways of (re)reading many well-known narratives in the Hebrew Bible.

The second section of the book applies this strategy of reading to 1 Kgs 1–11. Various methodological considerations and working assumptions relevant to this portion of the Hebrew Bible are briefly outlined for the reader in Chapter 3. The actual investigation of the Solomonic narrative commences in Chapter 4. This rather lengthy chapter explores elements of both propaganda and subversion in 1 Kgs 1–2 and discusses the implications of their curious coexistence in this portion of the text. Chapter 5 focuses more exclusively on those passages which seem to yield especially promising examples of scribal subversion in the remainder of the Solomonic narrative (1 Kgs 3–11). The final chapter of the book then highlights various conclusions that can be supported from this study while also noting some additional areas for further investigation.

## *Propaganda Defined*[9]

In popular culture, propaganda conjures up images of German swastikas, Communist indoctrination, and political rhetoric. For many, the very word itself elicits a Pavlovian response of suspicion and resistance. Propaganda is believed to be manipulative in the extreme, an attempt to "brainwash" others, resulting in the loss of all critical faculties and the inability to think for oneself. Understood as an attempt intentionally to deceive and distort, propaganda is regarded as dangerous, dishonest, and ultimately destructive. In short, propaganda is perceived as "false."[10]

Given this decidedly negative attitude towards propaganda, it is little wonder that many have been reticent to speak of biblical literature in this fashion. In fact, general discussions of propaganda in the Hebrew Bible are hard to come by. While a brief discussion can be found in Mario Liverani's 1992 entry in the *Anchor Bible Dictionary*,[11] to my knowledge,

---

9.  Literature dealing with the phenomena of propaganda outside of biblical studies has mushroomed in the second half of the twentieth century and is far too vast to be considered here. The classic text is Jacques Ellul, *Propaganda* (New York: Knopf, 1968). Other studies of interest include Oliver Thomson, *Mass Persuasion in History: A Historical Analysis of the Development of Propaganda Techniques* (New York: Crane, Russak & Co., 1977), and A. P. Foulkes, *Literature and Propaganda* (London: Methuen, 1983).

10.  For example, it should be noted that this perception is not solely confined to popular understandings of the term. For example, Dale Patrick and Allen Scult, *Rhetoric and Biblical Interpretation* (JSOTSup 82; Sheffield: Almond Press, 1990), 64, understand propaganda "to mean that the author sacrifices the truth to serve the cause of legitimization."

11.  Mario Liverani, "Propaganda," *ABD* 5:474–77. That this is apparently the first such entry ever to appear in a Bible dictionary/encyclopedia only accentuates the relative scarcity of such discussions.

the only monograph largely devoted to this subject is the volume by Rex Mason titled *Propaganda and Subversion in the Old Testament*.[12] While this splendid treatment is particularly helpful in demonstrating the appropriateness of regarding numerous portions of the Hebrew Bible as being intentionally propagandistic or subversive, it stands alone.

Though many scholars simply ignore the matter altogether, others deem it inappropriate to read the Hebrew Bible from this perspective.[13] Consider, for example, the position taken by John H. Walton. While Walton correctly recognizes that "propagandistic...agendas are readily identifiable in ancient historiography," he curiously excludes this possibility when it comes to ancient Israelite historiography.[14] "With regard to purpose," writes Walton, "Israel...does not evidence anything like the propagandistic intention visible in the royal annals."[15] The reasons given for this anomaly betray two unwarranted assumptions.[16] First, Walton believes that the presence of "negative elements" throughout the "biblical history" demonstrates that these narratives were not primarily intended as propaganda.[17] And secondly, Walton falls into the customary trap of equating propaganda with "intentional falsification."

A more positive assessment is rendered by Paula McNutt, who nevertheless appears unduly cautious when she writes, "It is likely...that in their original social contexts some of the biblical materials *may have been* intended in part as propaganda" and "propaganda is *almost certainly*

12. Rex Mason, *Propaganda and Subversion in the Old Testament* (London: SPCK, 1997). I am obviously indebted to Mason for the title of this present study.

13. This is especially true among many evangelical and "conservative" scholars who espouse high views of biblical inspiration and worry that admitting propagandistic intentions to the writers of these texts necessarily erodes the authority of Scripture. While I fundamentally disagree, a full discussion of this issue is regrettably beyond the scope of this study.

14. John H. Walton, *Ancient Israelite Literature in its Cultural Context: A Survey of Parallels between Biblical and Ancient Near Eastern Texts* (Grand Rapids: Zondervan, 1989), 115.

15. Ibid., 119.

16. Ibid., 118.

17. Yet this fails to take into account the way that such elements could be used propagandistically. Consider, for example, 2 Sam 11–12. Presumably the events associated with the Bathsheba affair were too well known to sweep under the carpet. So instead of ignoring them, the writer records not only the events, but also David's response after being confronted by the prophet Nathan. In this way the propagandist is able to put the deviant king in the most favorable light possible, no mean task given the horrific circumstances! As Mason (*Propaganda and Subversion*, 18) observes, "The report of a humble submission and repentance may itself be a piece of favourable propaganda showing the ideal piety of the king concerned."

present in the Hebrew Bible."[18] Given the ubiquity of propagandistic texts in the ancient Near East and numerous studies suggesting the presence of propaganda in the Hebrew Bible (see below), one suspects such qualifications are unnecessary.

Despite the reluctance of some and the caution of others, several scholars have found propaganda a useful optic through which to understand the meaning and function of certain biblical passages. One of the most important and influential studies which regards a portion of the Hebrew Bible as being intentionally designed as a piece of political propaganda is Leonhard Rost's *Die Überlieferung von der Thronnachfolge Davids*.[19] Rost argues, among other things, that 2 Sam 9–20 and 1 Kgs 1–2 is a unified composition that was written to legitimate Solomon's right to rule. Rost's thesis that this portion of Samuel–Kings be regarded as political propaganda gained widespread acceptance and inspired numerous studies which have adopted and expanded his conclusions.[20]

Several other portions of the Hebrew Bible have similarly been studied as pieces of propaganda. For example, the Abrahamic narratives have been understood as Davidic propaganda,[21] the history of Saul's rise as state propaganda,[22] the history of David's rise as pro-Davidic apologetic,[23] the *original* narrative behind 2 Kgs 9–11 as a "political novella"

---

18. Paula McNutt, *Reconstructing the Society of Ancient Israel* (Louisville, Ky.: Westminster John Knox, 1999), 6–7 (my emphasis).

19. Leonhard Rost, *The Succession to the Throne of David* (trans. Michael D. Rutter and David M. Gunn; Historic Texts and Interpreters in Biblical Scholarship 1; Sheffield: Almond Press, 1982); trans. of *Die Überlieferung von der Thronnachfolge Davids* (BWA[N]T 3/6; Stuttgart: Kohlhammer, 1926).

20. See especially R. N. Whybray, *The Succession Narrative: A Study of II Samuel 9–20; I Kings 1 and 2* (SBT 2/9; Naperville, Ill.: Allenson, 1968), in this regard. A fuller discussion of studies following and modifying Rost's thesis can be found in Chapter 3 of the present study.

21. Ronald E. Clements, *Abraham and David: Genesis 15 and its Meaning for Israelite Tradition* (Naperville, Ill.: Alec R. Allenson, 1967).

22. Marsha White, "'The History of Saul's Rise': Saulide State Propaganda in 1 Samuel 1–14," in *"A Wise and Discerning Mind": Essays in Honor of Burke O. Long* (ed. Saul M. Olyan and Robert C. Culley; Providence, R. I.: Brown University Press, 2000), 271–92.

23. Neils Peter Lemche, "David's Rise," *JSOT* 10 (1978): 2–25; P. Kyle McCarter Jr., "The Apology of David," *JBL* 99 (1980): 489–504; Keith W. Whitelam, "The Defense of David," *JSOT* 29 (1984): 61–87; Marc Zvi Brettler, *The Creation of History in Ancient Israel* (London: Routledge, 1995), 91–111, and in an abbreviated form, "Biblical Literature as Politics: The Case of Samuel," in *Religion and Politics in the Ancient Near East* (ed. Adele Berlin; Bethesda, Md.: University

intended as an *apologia* for Jehoiada,[24] and the majority of the Deuteronomistic History as political propaganda designed to bolster the reforms
of King Josiah.[25] Other studies have investigated entire biblical books,
such as Genesis[26] and Judges,[27] as pieces of political propaganda.

These and other studies raise our suspicions that propaganda is not
only present but prevalent in the biblical text.[28] And while disagreements
will remain about whether this or that particular passage was intended to
be a piece of political and/or religious propaganda, there is no reason to
dismiss such possibilities from the outset. On the contrary, as Liverani
contends, "The Old Testament as a whole can be considered as a huge
propagandistic work and...many texts or passages constitutive of the Old
Testament (or embedded in it) display a more or less clear propagandistic
purpose."[29]

Still, simply establishing that such a reading may be warranted leaves
many questions unanswered. For example, we are often left wondering
who commissioned these propagandistic pieces, and perhaps more tellingly, for whom they were intended. Regrettably, many of the studies
which have been favorable to the notion of propaganda in the Hebrew
Bible are woefully undertheorized. One notable exception, however, has

Press of Maryland, 1996), 71–96; Steven L. McKenzie, *King David: A Biography*
(Oxford: Oxford University 2000), esp. 30–36; cf. Tryggve N. D. Mettinger, *King
and Messiah: The Civil and Sacral Legitimation of the Israelite Kings* (ConBOT 8;
Lund: Gleerup, 1976), 38–41.

24. Lloyd M. Barré, *The Rhetoric of Political Persuasion: The Narrative Artistry
and Political Intentions of 2 Kings 9–11* (CBQMS 20; Washington, D.C.: Catholic
Biblical Association of America, 1988).

25. Frank Moore Cross Jr., *Canaanite Myth and Hebrew Epic: Essays in the
History of the Religion of Israel* (Cambridge, Mass.: Harvard University Press,
1973), 274–89, esp. 284.

26. Gary A. Rendsburg, "Biblical Literature as Politics: The Case of Genesis," in
Berlin, ed., *Religion and Politics in the Ancient Near East*, 47–70. Rendsburg
believes "the author of Genesis was a royal scribe in Jerusalem, who lived during the
reigns of David and Solomon in the 10th century B.C.E., and whose ultimate goal
was to justify the monarchy in general, and Davidic–Solomonic kingship in particular...[t]he book of Genesis thus appears as a piece of political propaganda" (p. 50).

27. Marc Zvi Brettler, "The Book of Judges: Literature as Politics," *JBL* 108
(1989): 395–418. Brettler conceives of the book of Judges as "a political allegory
fostering the Davidic monarchy" (p. 416). Despite his (intentional?) avoidance of the
term "propaganda," his reading of Judges reveals his clear understanding that the
book functioned as such.

28. In light of this, it would seem that Liverani's ("Propaganda," 475) decade-old
pronouncement that "the study of Old Testament passages as 'pieces of propaganda'
has generally won a scarce success" now requires some modification.

29. Ibid.

been the work of Keith W. Whitelam. His article dealing with Davidic propaganda contains many especially relevant and sociologically significant insights regarding the nature of propaganda generally.[30] Moreover, his work signals an advance over previous studies by positing a social location for both the producers and consumers of the text which is congruent with the social dynamics of an agrarian society from which and in which such literature would have functioned. As such, his study raises a number of crucial issues that must be addressed for an adequate understanding of the nature and function of propaganda in general, and its use in biblical texts in particular.

Whitelam repeatedly returns to the question of audience. He rightly understands that propaganda "cannot be divorced from the audience addressed."[31] Similarly, A. P. Foulkes realizes that "if we cannot establish a link between the propagandist and his or her audience, then we cannot speak of 'propaganda.'"[32] Propaganda is always aimed at or directed toward someone, or better, some group or groups.

Given this crucial and necessary connection between propagandist and audience, it may be helpful to coin the phrase "the propaganda process" to describe the larger phenomenon involving both the production *and* consumption of propaganda. It is well known that in Israel and throughout the ancient Near East, scribes were largely responsible for the creation and diffusion of propagandistic texts along with many other kinds of texts as well. Less certain is the identification of the intended audience.[33] While it seems reasonably clear that most biblical texts were written for a "present" rather than a "distant future" audience, is it possible to be more specific about who was on the receiving end of the propaganda process? Whitelam thinks so. He believes the consumers of written propaganda in ancient Israel (and ancient agrarian societies generally) were members of the upper echelon in society, namely, the elite. He writes,

---

30. Whitelam, "The Defense of David." See also his "The Symbols of Power: Aspects of Royal Propaganda in the United Monarchy," *BA* 49 (1986): 166–73.

31. Whitelam, "Defense of David," 66.

32. Foulkes, *Literature and Propaganda*, 9, utilizing Richard Taylor's study of German and Russian film propaganda.

33. Discussing what is meant by the "audience" of a particular text is a complicated matter. An audience may simply refer to a group of individuals who are assembled together in one place on a particular occasion to hear a text. Yet the word might also be used to refer to a select "class" or other carefully circumscribed "group" of people for whom the text might be intended or targeted, which is how I have used the term here. Additionally, considering the fact that the biblical materials would have been utilized in various settings over an indeterminate period of time, it is also helpful to keep more broadly in mind the presence and response of a variety of "audiences" over time.

The elite form the most serious threat or potential threat to the king and royal family and therefore much propaganda is aimed at this elite audience in order to reiterate and reinforce the right of the king to rule and the need to deny counterclaims to the throne. This is particularly true of the written or inscribed material in societies with restricted literacy.[34]

Compare the similar sentiments expressed by Mason:

In a simple society in which many of the masses may not be able to read, the literary presentation of propaganda must be aimed primarily at select inner circles of those who wield power and hold positions of responsibility in the "court," or at administrative officers in political or ecclesiastical hierarchies.[35]

These observations seem fundamentally correct. The elite in ancient Israel would have included the king and royal family—which itself contained many opposing factions as the bloody succession battles make all too clear—and those who had special access to them such as scribes, advisors, priests, certain prophets, and other key court officials and functionaries. Also included among the elite would be merchants, military leaders, and landowners, though many of these individuals would not have been literate. Given the complexity and diversity of this elite stratum in ancient Israel, it is probably best to envision multiple audiences as being on the receiving end of the propaganda process.

It should not be thought, however, that written propaganda was *exclusively* for the elite. It is reasonable to assume that many who could not read these texts for themselves—such as certain elite individuals and the masses generally—periodically heard them read aloud since this practice was normative in the ancient world. As Susan Niditch observes, "Very few people in the culture we are envisioning [i.e. Israel] know written works because they have seen and read them; they have received the works' messages and content by word of mouth."[36] Whether it is possible to identify particular groups of people—elite or otherwise—which were being intentionally targeted in any given instance is an open question

34. Whitelam, "Symbols of Power," 168. See also his "Israelite Kingship: The Royal Ideology and its Opponents," in *The World of Ancient Israel: Sociological, Anthropological and Political Perspectives* (ed. R. E. Clements; Cambridge: Cambridge University Press, 1989), 119–39 (134). The notion of restricted literacy in ancient Israel will be discussed in Chapter 2.

35. Mason, *Propaganda and Subversion*, 172.

36. Susan Niditch, *Oral World and Written Word: Ancient Israelite Literature* (Louisville, Ky.: Westminster John Knox, 1996), 5. Niditch (pp. 1–7) argues for a much closer interplay between orality and the written word in ancient Israel than is commonly granted.

to be explored as we investigate various portions of the Solomonic narrative.

Another important item to consider when constructing a definition of propaganda is to determine the source of its efficacy. Must propaganda address certain "felt needs" in order to be successful, or is the propagandist able to so influence the audience's perception of reality that the propagandist is able to elicit a response which accords with his or her own wishes and desires? In his analysis of propaganda in Egyptian texts, Edward Bleiberg argues in favor of the former. He writes, "For propaganda to be successful, it must appeal to the preconceived ideology of the audience."[37] Likewise, Whitelam believes that "the propagandist must satisfy some deeply felt need within the audience by articulating fundamental beliefs and hopes of the society, beliefs and hopes which he shares, if he is to be successful."[38] Here Mason objects. He concedes that there may be times in which the propagandist is tapping into the felt needs and ideological aspirations of the audience. But his reading of the Hebrew Bible through the lenses of propaganda and subversion leads him to conclude that in certain instances individuals attempt "to foster a new political or religious outlook on the part of others by which they may gain assent to the position and privileges they are claiming for themselves or their group."[39] In this way, the success of the propagandist depends less upon exploiting a "deeply felt need" and more upon persuasive skill and savvy. The propagandist seeks to make his or her vision that of the propagandees'. Whether that vision coincides with the fundamental hopes and beliefs of the target population is ultimately irrelevant from the propagandist's perspective. All that matters is that the audience accept the vision and act accordingly.

These sentiments seem to resonate with many who have attempted a definition of propaganda. According to F. C. Bartlett,

> Practically everybody agrees that propaganda must be defined by reference to its aims. Those aims can, in fact, be stated simply. Propaganda is an attempt to influence opinion and conduct—especially social opinion and conduct—in such a manner that the persons who adopt the opinions and behavior indicated do so without themselves making any definite search for reasons.[40]

---

37.  Edward Bleiberg, "Historical Texts as Political Propaganda during the New Kingdom," *Bulletin of the Egyptological Seminar* 7 (1985–86): 5–13 (6).

38.  Whitelam, "Defense of David," 67.

39   Mason, *Propaganda and Subversion*, 172.

40.  F. C. Bartlett, "The Aims of Political Propaganda," in *Public Opinion and Propaganda* (ed. Daniel Katz et al.; New York: Holt, Rinehart & Winston, 1954),

Mason defines propaganda as "the presentation of material so as to express a particular belief or set of beliefs in such a way as to command assent to it from those to whom it is addressed."[41] Similarly Liverani regards it as "the deliberate (albeit mostly dissimulated) spreading of ideas, information, rumors, etc. in order to support one's own political (or religious) cause, to acquire more proselytes, and in the last analysis to gain more power."[42]

A very careful attempt to define propaganda *vis-à-vis* ideology in the context of ancient Israel is offered by Jacques Berlinerblau. Berlinerblau believes propaganda would be a better term for what most Hebrew Bible scholars seem to mean when they speak of ideology. Berlinerblau's "voluntaristic conception" of ideology (i.e. propaganda) is defined as

> (1) the existence of (usually dominant) groups or classes across Judahite and/or Israelite time and space who, (2) conscious of their own political and theological interests, (3) formulated an ideology to express these interests (4) and sought to persuade others by inscribing them (overtly or covertly) in this or that biblical text.[43]

The foregoing definitions share several things in common. First, they all attempt to define propaganda functionally, in terms of what it does. Consequently, each one recognizes the role persuasion plays in the deployment of propaganda. Additionally, they share a recurring emphasis that propaganda contains a strong element of self-interest. Based on these observations and the foregoing discussion, I would propose defining propaganda as a form of persuasion consciously deployed with the intention of convincing others to see things from the point of view of the propagator, regardless of whether that perspective resonates with the particular desires, concerns, and/or ideological affinities of the audience(s).

It should be recalled that I began my discussion of propaganda by deeming inadequate any simplistic equation of propaganda with deception. It should be clear from my definition that this was not, however, meant to suggest that the propagandist is engaged in presenting either a dispassionate or a disinterested construal of events. As Liverani insight-

---

463–70 (464). This definition is cited by both Whitelam, "Defense of David," 66, and Mason, *Propaganda and Subversion*, 171.

41. Mason, *Propaganda and Subversion*, 170. Much of the advertising we see, hear, and read is basically propaganda.

42. Liverani, "Propaganda," 474.

43. Jacques Berlinerblau, "Ideology, Pierre Bourdieu's *Doxa*, and the Hebrew Bible," in *The Social World of the Hebrew Bible: Twenty-Five Years of the Social Sciences in the Academy* (ed. Ronald A. Simkins, Stephen L. Cook, and Athalya Brenner; Semeia 87; Atlanta: Scholars Press, 1999), 193–214 (198).

fully remarks, "Even though the common meaning as 'forgery,' 'false-hood,' or the like is certainly inaccurate, it is true that *propaganda is more interested in effectiveness than in correctness*, and its informations are biased as a result of unfair selection, cunning deformation, and subtle connotation."[44] Clearly propaganda is intended to persuade, even if that means resorting to a rather narrow, highly invested, and ideologically charged presentation of things. The propagandist does this not in order to deceive but in order to convince the intended audience that his or her perspective is the right one. As applied to the biblical text, I concur with Norman C. Habel who states, "Most biblical texts push a point. They seek to win over the minds of the implied audience and persuade those who hear the message that the beliefs announced in the texts are authoritative and true."[45] This is the power and persuasive potential of propaganda.

### *Subversion Defined*

One should be cautious about drawing too sharp a distinction between propaganda and subversion.[46] In fact, sometimes there seems to be very little which distinguishes one from the other. To illustrate this point, a contemporary example may be helpful. Suppose I felt the payment of federal income taxes was immoral. I might choose to stop filing tax returns—or even generating income—and attempt to persuade others to see things from my perspective by distributing pamphlets and making speeches to that effect. Given our definition of propaganda—a form of persuasion consciously deployed with the intention of convincing others to see things from the point of view of the propagator, regardless of whether that perspective resonates with the particular desires, concerns, and/or ideological affinities of the audience(s)—my actions would cer-tainly qualify as being propagandistic. On the other hand, my tax evasive efforts and my missionary fervor could equally be understood as being

44.  Liverani, "Propaganda," 474 (my emphasis).
45.  Norman C. Habel, *The Land is Mine: Six Biblical Land Ideologies* (OBT; Minneapolis: Fortress, 1995), 10.
46.  Consider, for example, the relationship between propaganda and subversion in Ellul's (*Propaganda*, 70–74) discussion of the "propaganda of agitation," which he describes as "subversive propaganda." It should be noted, however, that Ellul's concept of subversion differs markedly from my use of the term. According to Ellul, propaganda of agitation is deployed by openly inciting hatred of a common enemy and is thought to be most effective among the least educated. The kind of subversion we will be interested in detecting in the Solomonic narrative is far more subtle and was probably most effective among the educated elite. This perspective is developed more fully in the remainder of this chapter and the following chapter.

highly subversive since they constitute an intentional attempt to under-mine the operations of the government. One might say that my *effort* (distributing pamphlets) is propagandistic while the intended *effect* of that effort (causing people to stop paying taxes) is subversive. In other words, I am using propaganda for subversive ends.[47]

For the purposes of this study, I am proposing that we consider subversion to be a subset of propaganda since both activities seek to per-suade.[48] As such, subversion may be understood as a particular kind of propaganda. Put another way, we might say that all subversion is propa-gandistic, although not all propaganda is subversive.

The Oxford English Dictionary defines a subversive as "one who wishes to overthrow a political regime."[49] Such a definition reflects a common understanding of subversion which frequently associates it with the efforts of certain renegades seeking power for themselves or their cause. But subversion can be understood much more broadly than that, especially when the art of literary subversion is under consideration.[50] This wider usage is suggested, for example, in the Oxford English Dic-tionary's fourth definition of subversion as "overthrow" or "ruin" when it is applied "in immaterial senses" to certain laws, conditions, and persons.[51]

Shifting the focus from "overthrowing" to "undermining," Bruce Lin-coln, in his monograph *Authority: Construction and Corrosion*, coins the phrase "corrosive discourse" to represent "all those sorts of speech which are not only nonauthoritative, but downright antithetical to the con-struction of authority, given their capacity to eat away at the claims and pretensions of discourses and speakers who try to arrogate authority for themselves."[52] Of course, whether or not something is perceived as being

47. The effectiveness or ineffectiveness of the effort does not change the subver-sive intention of the act. An act should be classified as subversive on the basis of what it intends to do, not on the basis of whether is succeeds or fails.

48. Depending upon the particular intentions of the scribe in question, there may be some instances in which this "persuasive" element is less prominent in certain subversion activities. See the section in Chapter 2 entitled "The Aims and Possibi-lities of Literary Subversion" (pp. 65–66).

49. The *Oxford English Dictionary*, 2nd ed., *s.v.* "subversive."

50. For studies of subversion outside biblical studies, see, e.g., Jack Zipes, *Fairy Tales and the Art of Subversion: The Classical Genre for Children and the Process of Civilization* (New York: Routledge, 1991), and Rosemary Jackson, *Fantasy: The Literature of Subversion* (London: Methuen, 1981).

51. The *Oxford English Dictionary*, 2nd ed., *s.v.* "subversion."

52. Bruce Lincoln, *Authority: Construction and Corrosion* (Chicago: University of Chicago Press, 1994), 78.

subversive or corrosive depends, in part, on the perspective of the reader/listener. Lincoln rightly observes that "there are multiple audiences for any speech or action, and different groups (or fractions [*sic*] within a group) are capable of responding in quite different ways."[53]

With these introductory remarks in hand, we might now offer a *provisional* definition of subversion which can be refined later. For now, let us consider subversion to be a form of propaganda whose persuasive efforts are directed towards undermining, criticizing or otherwise "corroding" an ideology, institution, or individual. These persuasive efforts which seek to subvert may be initiated by those in power and by those outside the circles of power. Moreover, whether such subversive efforts are regarded as positive or negative will largely depend upon the evaluator's perspective and whether his or her interests coincide with that of the subverter or the subverted. As Mason puts it,

> Just as we have to remember that not all propaganda is "bad," so we have to realize that not all subversion is necessarily good. Subversion may be as mixed in motive and as questionable in its results as the power claims of any established order. People may challenge the power of others because they themselves want their own hands on power in order to make it serve their ends.[54]

*Concealed Subversion*

In order to expand upon our provisional definition of subversion, it will be helpful to differentiate between two fundamentally different ways in which subversion is deployed. I will describe these as "concealed subversion" and "conspicuous subversion."[55] Extending this a bit further, we might say that concealed subversion is deployed by a "secretive subversive" while conspicuous subversion designates the method used by a "shameless subversive."

Concealed subversion, as the term suggests, is subversion deployed covertly. It is disguised and hidden. One might even call it underground propaganda. The "secretive subversive" launches his or her calculated critique in such a way that seeks to avoid open detection without totally obscuring the message. In other words, such an individual wants to get the message out, but does not want to be "blamed" for it by those who

---

53. Lincoln, *Authority*, 86.

54. Mason, *Propaganda and Subversion*, 166.

55. Cf. Yairah Amit's (*Hidden Polemics in Biblical Narrative* [trans. Jonathan Chipman; Leiden: Brill, 2000], 44–45, 93–94) distinction between hidden polemics and explicit polemics, which is functionally similar to my distinction between concealed and conspicuous subversion.

find it offensive and who could easily take steps to retaliate. Obviously, there is an element of risk inherent in such subversion and the ever present fear of being exposed.

Presumably, concealed subversion is used most commonly by subversives who lack the power (or will) openly to critique some dominant entity. For example, a royal scribe who wants to use "commissioned" writing to critique royal ideology would need to exercise great caution or risk detection and possibly death! The covert nature of concealed subversion would be just the right way to proceed. Of course, this suggestion immediately raises the very practical question of how such subversion was "hidden" in the text in the first place and how it can now be extracted. These issues will be addressed at some length in the following chapter.

*Conspicuous Subversion*
Conspicuous subversion, on the other hand, is subversion deployed overtly. As such, it is obvious and openly recognizable. If concealed subversion could be regarded as underground propaganda, conspicuous subversion might be thought of as open-air propaganda. Such subversion is transparent and easily detectable. In literary texts, conspicuous subversion is inscribed on the surface of the text and no effort is made to disguise it. The "shameless subversive" launches a frontal assault and has little or no fear of the consequences of being directly associated with his or her subversive efforts. The risks are negligible or at least calculated. But who would engage in this form of subversive activity? What kind of person can critique major ideologies, institutions, or individuals with impunity? Presumably, one who enjoys some distance—be it historical, sociological, geographical, or otherwise—between themselves and the object of critique.

This point has been emphasized by Berlinerblau in his study of "official religion."[56] As one of several options for understanding the perplexingly conspicuous critique of the monarchy in the pages of the Hebrew Bible, Berlinerblau posits a temporally distant locus. He writes, "The antimonarchic impulses of the Old Testament could be explained as a consequence of textual editing that took place at another period in time.

---

56. The phrase "official religion" has been used rather carelessly in biblical studies. For a brief evaluation of the current state of affairs and a helpful corrective, see Jacques Berlinerblau, "Preliminary Remarks for the Sociological Study of Israelite 'Official Religion,'" in *Ki Baruch Hu: Ancient Near Eastern, Biblical, and Judaic Studies* (ed. R. Chazan, L. Schiffman, and W. Hallo; Winona Lake, Ind.: Eisenbrauns, 1999), 153–70.

Thus, the critique found in the Old Testament was leveled from a period far removed from the events described—from a 'critical distance,' so to speak."[57] Following the lead of Morton Smith, Berlinerblau argues that Yahwistic intellectuals, who were in the minority during the period of the monarchy, rose to power in the Persian period (or later) and at *that* time "composed texts harshly critical of non-Yahwistic 'official religions' past."[58] If correct, this would certainly provide a reasonable explanation for the presence of overt monarchical critique in the Hebrew Bible. Regardless of whether or not one accepts Berlinerblau's particular construal, it seems quite reasonable to conclude that much of the conspicuous subversion in the Hebrew Bible can be attributed to later periods of production.

Still, it also seems quite possible that some overt subversion may have been contemporaneous if it was produced at some institutional distance. Consider, for example, a royal scribe working under the watchful eye of the king (or at least under the watchful eye of other scribes loyal to the king). Such an individual could hardly hope successfully to subvert the hegemonic apparatus overtly and would be foolish to use anything other than the most subtle literary conventions to critique the king or royal establishment. On the other hand, it is much easier to envision a critique of the king coming from temple scribes who worked with considerably more freedom *vis-à-vis* the palace.[59] Again, it is the scribe's "distance" from the object of critique that seems to dictate whether or not conspicuous subversion is possible or prudent.

Admittedly, the foregoing distinction between concealed and conspicuous subversion is not entirely satisfactory. This is especially the case regarding what I have described as concealed subversion since an element of conspicuousness is inherent in the very nature of this kind of subversion. In other words, whether a particular feature of the text is perceived as being a conspicuous critique or a concealed critique depends,

---

57. Ibid., 168.

58. Ibid., 169. One of Berlinerblau's alternative hypotheses which suggests that this minority group, part of a Yahwistic "opposition party" *vis-à-vis* the non-Yahwistic state-controlled apparatus, "produced texts that expressed their disdain of the monarchy and the non-Yahwistic 'official religion' that it advocated" *during* the monarchic period, seems rather problematic (p. 168). Who would have trained such individuals in the art of reading and writing? If they were not part of the ruling elite, when would they have had the time or the opportunity to learn such highly specialized skills? And who would have paid them to do so? These questions will be taken up in the next chapter as we explore the social location of scribes in monarchic Israel/Judah.

59. See Chapter 2 of this study for a discussion of royal and temple scribes.

in part, upon the vantage point of the reader/hearer. What is hidden from one person may be glaringly obvious to another. The crucial question again becomes that of audience. Who is reading/hearing this text? *From whom* would this potentially subversive element be concealed and *to whom* would it be conspicuous, or at least detectable? Given this nuanced understanding of concealed subversion, perhaps it would be more accurate to speak of it as *potentially* concealed subversion or even *partially* concealed subversion, obscured from some, obvious to others. It is this kind of covert critique we are interested in exploring in our study of the Solomonic narrative.

With that in mind, I am now ready to fill out my earlier provisional definition of subversion. This definition is intended as a guide for the reader to indicate the kind of subversion which interests me in this study. It is not, therefore, a definitive explication of the meaning of this rich term. Functionally speaking, covert literary subversion can be defined as that which subtly undermines, criticizes, or "destroys" an ideology, institution, or individual that is often, though not always, connected with or representative of a dominant power structure. In what follows, we will have opportunity to investigate numerous examples of *concealed* subversion situated in the Solomonic narrative. Our interest will be in detecting these more subtle and less discernable critiques "hidden" throughout the narrative rather than commenting on passages like 1 Kgs 11 which openly condemn Solomon for his transgressions.

### *Previous Studies Exploring Subversion in the Hebrew Bible*

If discussions on propaganda in the Hebrew Bible have "won a scarce success," discussions on subversion may seem to have fared even worse. To my knowledge, no Bible dictionary, Bible encyclopedia, or similar reference work has ever included an entry under the heading "subversion." Likewise, the term almost never appears in the subject indexes of books relating to either the ancient Near East generally or the Hebrew Bible specifically. On this basis alone, one might think that few scholars have found subversion to be a useful category for describing the nature and function of certain passages in the Hebrew Bible. This is misleading. There are, in fact, numerous studies which identify subversive tendencies in various biblical books and passages. What makes these studies difficult to locate is a lack of uniform terminology. Many of these works use a rubric other than "subversion" to describe the corrosive effects particular texts are thought to exhibit. When this consideration is taken into account, the apparent lack of subversive studies is partially mitigated. By reviewing several of these works, we will be able to determine where other scholars have located subversion in the Hebrew Bible and to note the kind of subversion they have identified.

The following review is construed rather broadly, allowing for an exploration of both overt and covert subversion in the biblical text. While our particular interest resides with the latter variety, it is helpful to consider a wider range of studies at the outset. The review is intended to be representative rather than exhaustive and is designed to be more descriptive than evaluative, though some assessments will be made. It should also be noted that some of the works included in this discussion have been selected because they demonstrate a potentially subversive way of reading biblical texts, even if that approach is not the one advocated by the author. Finally, while no guiding principle dictates the arrangement of this review, it is loosely topical (e.g. examples of feminist subversion are discussed together).

We begin with one of the more substantial treatments of subversion in the Hebrew Bible, namely, the second half of Mason's monograph *Propaganda and Subversion in the Old Testament.* Here Mason considers the subversion of the Deuteronomists, prophets, visionaries (i.e. apocalypticists), and universalists. Many key passages and helpful examples are produced throughout Mason's study which illustrate various expressions of subversion in ancient Israel.[60] Though Mason never explicitly discusses how he identifies a subversive text, the examples he cites would seem to suggest that he is primarily—if not exclusively—looking for what I have described as conspicuous subversion.

Since extended treatments of subversion in the Hebrew Bible are not abundantly forthcoming, one is hesitant to be overly critical of the deficiencies of Mason's treatment, especially given the enormous benefit derived from it for the purposes of this present study! Nevertheless, I would mention three appreciable shortcomings which detract from an otherwise excellent piece of work. First, unlike his treatment of propaganda in the ancient Near East in the opening chapter of the book, Mason produces no similar parallels of subversive literature. Also disappointing is the all too brief[61] attention given to a discussion of what constitutes subversion, not to mention the virtual absence of any comment on the social location of subversives or the way in which subversive literature may have functioned in ancient Israel. In all fairness, I must acknowledge that some of these issues are addressed in the nearly one hundred

---

60. While it would be impracticable to list all the passages Mason considers, some of the most significant ones include, 1 Sam 8; Jer 7:1–15; Joel 2:28–32; Amos 3:1; 9:7; Mic 3:1–3; 4:1–4; Zeph 2:3; 3:12–13; Zech 10:1–3a; 11:4–17; 13:7–9.

61. Less than a single page (p. 174) of his *Propaganda and Subversion.*

pages Mason has devoted to subversion in the Hebrew Bible. Still, given the dearth of treatments on this topic, it seems that a more systematic discussion of these and related issues would have enhanced the value of his study immensely. Third, Mason's understanding of subversion as overthrow seems unnecessarily narrow.[62] He writes, "The aim of the criticism of political and ecclesiastical propaganda...is to bring that power to an end, not merely to reform it."[63] While this is certainly one aspect of subversion, I have suggested that the aims and purposes of literary subversion are far broader than this understanding allows. Finally, since the stated audience of the book is the non-specialist in biblical studies, Mason has chosen to include only a minimal number of footnotes and bibliographic references. More often than not, these point to important treatments of the prophets or of apocalyptic literature but seldom direct the interested reader to other specific discussions of subversion in the Hebrew Bible, furthering the difficulty of cross-referencing other studies with related interests.[64] These shortcomings notwithstanding, Mason's study remains nonetheless an excellent treatment of what we have called conspicuous subversion.

Published the same year as Mason's study, Jonathan Magonet's monograph *The Subversive Bible* represents a full book-length treatment of subversion in the Hebrew Bible.[65] This book is divided into two major sections, the first of which explores the subversive potential of selected segments and themes of the Hebrew Bible including the Abrahamic narrative, the Exodus traditions, the notion of Israel as the "chosen people," and the book of Jonah. The second part of the book consists of a compilation of short sermons given by Magonet which he describes as "a way of exploring the subversive nature of the Bible in a more public context."

Despite its promising title, Magonet's work is rather disappointing to someone hoping for a clear and extensive discussion of subversion in the Hebrew Bible. The material in the first section of the book—which is where one would expect the most concentrated investigation of subver-

---

62. Curiously, Mason's own discussion of certain subversive passages (e.g. Deut 17:14–20) requires a broader understanding of the term than his definition would seem to allow. See particularly his comments on the Deuteronomistic subversion of the monarchy in this regard (*Propaganda and Subversion*, 75–85).

63. Ibid., 174.

64. The singular exception being a reference to J. P. M. Walsh, *The Mighty from their Thrones: Power in the Biblical Tradition* (OBT 21; Philadelphia: Fortress, 1987), a work in which Mason (*Propaganda and Subversion*, 175 n. 6) believes Walsh "dealt forcefully with the idea of Israelite subversion of established orders in the name of Yahweh."

65. Jonathan Magonet, *The Subversive Bible* (London: SCM Press, 1997).

sion to be found—seems rather unfocused. These chapters contain a mixture of Magonet's comments on the particular biblical stories he has chosen to investigate and earlier Jewish interpretations of the same. Yet the reader is often left wondering exactly how the particular texts being considered function subversively even though this would seem to be the major focus of his study. This difficulty is compounded by a regrettable lack of any significant discussion about what constitutes subversion, an especially strange omission given the title and apparent focus of the book.[66]

Much more promising is Yairah Amit's monograph *Hidden Polemics in Biblical Narrative*. Like our study, Amit is especially interested in detecting *concealed* subversion—or "hidden polemics" as she calls it—in Hebrew narratives. For Amit, "the description of a biblical text as polemical indicates its attitude toward an issue that lies at the center of some ideological struggle: one which generally—in one way or another—has some bearing upon reality."[67] Although Amit examines three kinds of polemic in the Hebrew Bible—open (explicit) polemics, indirect polemics, and hidden polemics—her main interest is in detecting those polemics which are hidden.[68] According to Amit,

> A polemic is hidden when its subject is not explicitly mentioned, or when it is not mentioned in the expected, conventional formulation. Through various hints, the reader is left with the feeling that a double effort has been made within the text: on the one hand—to conceal the subject of the polemic, that is, to avoid its explicit mention; on the other—to leave certain traces within the text (referred to…as "signs") that through various means will lead the reader to the hidden subject of the polemic.[69]

In a review of Amit's work, David Marcus says

---

66. Magonet (ibid., 6) briefly discusses what he means by subversion in the following paragraph: "I do not want to get into definitions of what is 'subversive.' This book is an exploration rather than a formal thesis, but it may be helpful to think in terms of two aspects of the Bible's subversive power—what we may call extrinsic and intrinsic ones. The former is typically the prophetic attack on the policies of a king or on the activities of his contemporary priests and prophets, or on the people's practice of idolatry. These are situations where the Bible itself openly addresses some aspect of Israelite society and calls a recognizable group of people to account. The 'intrinsic' aspect has more to do with the presuppositions with which the Hebrew Bible operates and the way it views the world. By its very nature, by the stand it takes against the conventions of its own world, it subverts the power structures or gender definitions or religious presuppositions of its own times."

67. Amit, *Hidden Polemics*, 7.

68. Ibid., 44.

69. Ibid., 93.

covert polemics are akin to an allegorical mode of interpretation. The characters and place names that appear in the stories are only stand-ins for the intended characters and place names. The true characters and place-names can be discovered by the aid of clues which Amit believes are discernible in the text.[70]

There are four "clues" or criteria Amit develops for detecting a hidden polemic which she summarizes as follows:

Refraining from explicit mention of the subject, which the author is interested to condemn or to advocate.

The evidence of other biblical materials regarding the existence of a polemic on the same subject.

The presence of a number of signs by whose means the author directs the reader toward the polemic so that, despite the absence of explicit mention of the polemical subject, the reader finds sufficient landmarks to uncover it.

Reference to the hidden subject of the polemic in the exegetical tradition concerning the text in question.[71]

With these criteria in hand, Amit methodically investigates what she believes are four examples of hidden polemic in the Hebrew Bible: (1) a polemic against Bethel in Judg 2:1–5 and Judg 17–18, (2) a polemic against Jerusalem—a place alluded to but never explicitly mentioned in the Torah—in Gen 14:18–20 and Deut 33:12, (3) a polemic against Saul in Judg 19–21, and (4) a polemic against, and in support of, the Samaritans, in Gen 34 and the book of Chronicles, respectively.[72]

Unfortunately, Amit's theoretical discussion of why a writer would use a hidden polemic is brief and not particularly well developed.[73] She offers two basic reasons. First, Amit sees rhetorical advantages in using hidden polemic. She believes it enhances the persuasive power of the argument being made. Second, Amit believes hidden polemic was sometimes necessary when the subject being polemicized was especially sensitive, making overt critique unwise and dangerous. As Amit puts it, "Hidden polemic also serves the needs of 'censorship.' At certain times, due to the special sensitivity of the subject of the polemic and the fear of a hostile atmosphere, the polemic 'went underground' and became hidden."[74]

---

70. David Marcus, review of Yairah Amit, *Hidden Polemics in Biblical Narrative*, *BibInt* 12 (2004): 324–26 (324).

71. Amit, *Hidden Polemics*, 96–97. See pp. 93–97 for a fuller discussion.

72. Ibid., 99–217.

73. Amit does say more about the function of these hidden polemics in connection with each of the hidden polemics she describes in the second part of the book.

74. Ibid., 97–98.

To illustrate Amit's methodology, let us take a closer look at the polemic against Saul which she detects in Judg 19–21. Amit's first criterion for discovering a hidden polemic, "refraining from explicit mention of the subject," is clearly met since Saul is never mentioned by name in any of these chapters.[75] Amit also highlights the presence of numerous anti-Saul elements in the Hebrew Bible (e.g. 1 Sam 13:13–15; 15:11, 36), thus fulfilling her second criterion.[76] A significant part of Amit's discussion of Judg 19–21 is devoted to identifying the various "signs" she believes allow the reader to detect the hidden polemic against Saul in Judg 19–21. She discusses these under five headings: "Places Names," "The Levite," "Motifs Related to War," "Hospitality in Bethlehem of Judah," and "Jerusalem as an Alternative."[77] Here Amit highlights a number of key similarities to the story of Saul, such as the frequent reference to Gibeah, Saul's hometown, the Levite's cutting of the concubine and Saul's cutting of the oxen's yoke to call people to war, "the use of an exaggerated number of warriors (Judg 20:1; 1 Sam 11:7), the contrast between Bethlehem's hospitality and Gibeah's, and the reference to Jebus as a place were the Levite could have spent the night had he chosen to do so rather than making the fateful journey to Gibeah. These are just a few of many "signs" Amit discusses in this section. Finally, Amit briefly notes that scholars since the nineteenth century have regarded the final chapters of Judges as polemical, thus fulfilling her fourth and final criterion.[78]

At the end of her treatment of Judg 19–21, Amit offers some rationale for why it was necessary for this polemic to be hidden. She conjectures that after Zedekiah's rebellion and Babylon's change of attitude toward Judah, some Benjaminites hoped that the house of Saul would return to power and once again exercise leadership. Based on this conjecture, Amit, believes "the polemic...was written by supporters of the Davidic house, who feared at this stage to openly express their outlook."[79] She also believes that this polemic, situated at the end of Judges, was intended to influence negatively the way readers evaluated Saul when reading stories about him in the book of Samuel.[80] Although one may dispute the

75. Ibid., 96, 178.

76. Ibid., 171–78.

77. Ibid., 179–84.

78. Ibid., 184. Brettler ("The Book of Judges," esp. 412–15), should be added to her list since he also believes these chapters contain "an anti-Saul polemic" (p. 412).

79. Amit, *Hidden Polemics*, 186.

80. Ibid., 186–87. Amit writes, "From the perspective of biblical historiography, there were those who were disturbed by the literary fashioning of the Book of Samuel, that fosters understanding, compassion and even appreciation for Saul. This later

*Sitz im Leben* Amit proposes for this particular passage and might question whether all the "signs" she posits are really indicative of covert polemics, her reading seems fundamentally sound. There do seem to be subversive undercurrents running throughout Judg 19–21 which do not bode well for Saul.

One of the ways my investigation of concealed subversion will fundamentally differ from Amit's involves where such "hidden polemics" may be found. This present study does not limit concealed subversion only to places where the subject of the polemic is not explicitly mentioned. Thus, Amit's first criterion for finding hidden polemics is too restrictive in my estimation. We will discover that concealed subversion can be deployed against people even in texts explicitly written about them and even in texts which may, at least on the surface, seem favorable toward them.

A rather different kind of work which also explores certain subversion elements in the Hebrew Bible is Walter Brueggemann's provocative book, *The Prophetic Imagination*.[81] His major thesis suggests that the task of prophetic ministry is to nurture, nourish and evoke an alternative consciousness and perception from that of the dominant culture.[82] "Prophets" accomplish this both by criticizing and by energizing. As Brueggemann describes it, criticizing involves delegitimizing the present order while energizing directs people toward what they can and should be.[83] In my estimation, Brueggemann's understanding of prophetic criticism seems rather close to Mason's discussion of subversion, since the prophet is, in part, a destabilizing element.[84] He writes, "It is the vocation of the prophet to keep alive the ministry of imagination, to keep on conjuring and proposing alternative futures to the single one the king wants to urge as the only thinkable one."[85] Brueggemann focuses particularly on the pathos of the prophet Jeremiah[86] which he regards as a wake-up call

---

editor decided to attempt to tip the scales by planting anticipatory materials, in whose light what is told in Samuel may be interpreted in a different manner" (p. 186).

81. Walter Brueggemann, *The Prophetic Imagination* (Philadelphia: Fortress, 1978).

82. Ibid., 14. Cf. Magonet's definition of extrinsic subversion quoted above.

83. Brueggemann's concern with prophetic criticism is, of course, different from our primary interest in detecting subversive *scribal* activity, a concept that will be developed with some care in the following chapter.

84. For this notion of the prophet as a "destabilizing" element, see Walter Brueggemann, "The Prophet as a Destabilizing Presence," in *The Pastor as Prophet* (ed. Earl E. Shelp and Ronald H. Sunderland; New York: Pilgrim, 1985), 49–77 (51–54).

85. Brueggemann, *Prophetic Imagination*, 45.

86. One might also consider other actions of Jeremiah—such as calling for surrender to the Babylonians—as overtly subversive from the perspective of the king

to the "royal community."[87] The prophet's prominent grief over Jerusalem suggested that things were not good, thereby subverting the royal ideology by highlighting the dangers of simply maintaining the *status quo*.[88]

In his more recent *Theology of the Old Testament*, Brueggemann's discussion of "Israel's countertestimony" also reveals certain subversive tendencies in the Hebrew Bible.[89] Here Brueggemann explores Israel's witness to Yahweh's hiddenness, abusiveness, contradictory character, unreliability, negativity, and violence. These images of Yahweh challenge Israel's core testimony and present a different and rather uncomplimentary view of the deity. Yet according to Brueggemann, *"Israel as witness knows that if Yahweh is not endlessly criticized and subverted, Yahweh will also become an absolute, absolutizing idol, the very kind about which Moses aimed his protesting, deconstructive work at Sinai."*[90]

David Penchansky also finds subversive tendencies in this so-called dark side of God. He examines six narrative passages which he believes contain "sinister" images of God.[91] These negative construals of God, he contends, are intentionally seditious, providing a counter voice to widely held assumptions about the benevolence of the deity. Though he (wisely) resists assigning the production of these texts to a particular individual or group, he clearly regards their function as subversive and believes these texts to be perfectly suited to destabilizing the dominant power structure. Based upon his investigation of these passages, Penchansky draws the following conclusion:

and the pro-independence party. In fact, such efforts were perceived as being seditious, not merely subversive, and nearly cost the prophet his life on more than one occasion (e.g. Jer 26:11; 38:4).

87. Ibid., 52.

88. Brueggemann's highly suggestive article, "'Vine and Fig Tree': A Case Study in Imagination and Criticism," *CBQ* 43 (1981): 188–204, further explores the central thesis of *The Prophetic Imagination* by applying it to two particular biblical texts, namely, Mic 4:1–5 and 1 Kgs 4:20–5:8 (Eng. 4:20–28). Brueggemann regards Mic 4:1–5 as "a practice of knowing, subversive political imagination" (p. 194), while arguing that we cannot finally determine whether the passage in Kings "is a serious statement of state policy or if it is heavy-handed propaganda or if it is subtle, critical irony" (p. 198).

89. Walter Brueggemann, *Theology of the Old Testament: Testimony, Dispute, Advocacy* (Minneapolis: Fortress, 1997), 317–403.

90. Ibid., 332 (emphasis in original).

91. David Penchansky, *What Rough Beast? Images of God in the Hebrew Bible* (Louisville, Ky.: Westminster John Knox, 1999). The six passages are Gen 3; Exod 4:24–26; Lev 10; 2 Sam 6; 24; 2 Kgs 2:23–25.

Politically, I have suggested that these stories, by undermining the most basic theological verities (the goodness and reliability of God), undermine as well the structures of power within the society that tells them. I called these stories seditious because they suggested that things were not fair and orderly—that the cult was not a reliable way to protect oneself against God; neither was a pure heart. Awful things just happened, regardless of one's behavior. They depended on the erratic moods of an inconstant, often hostile, deity. So the strictures to obedience and submission to the divinely ordained authorities were all called into question. *These would be ideal stories to be told by a group that wanted to overthrow a king or topple a political priesthood.*[92]

Beyond studies dealing with specific books or passages, some attention has been given to exploring certain *genres* of biblical literature as subversive. Particularly noteworthy in this regard is the apocalyptic material found in the Hebrew Bible which is sometimes regarded as resistance literature. After citing two studies which connect the writing of apocalyptic literature with the economically advantaged,[93] McNutt offers a description of these writers: "These individuals may have been scribes, government officials, and/or others with similar status within Jerusalem society, perhaps with a lesser status and prestige than those who employed them, who were frustrated and dissatisfied in some way both with the system of leadership and with the distribution of wealth."[94] McNutt says that for this perspective the literature produced by such individuals represents a "rhetoric of desperation," though one might argue that a more accurate description might be a "rhetoric of subversion."

For the past several decades, feminist critics have engaged in various readings of the biblical text which are clearly subversive. These studies remind us that ideologies (like patriarchy) can be undermined as well as individuals. Feminist scholars have taken a variety of approaches which are helpfully classified by Eryl Davies in his recent book *The Dissenting Reader: Feminist Approaches to the Hebrew Bible.*[95] Davies identifies five ways feminist biblical scholars attempt to subvert the patriarchy of the biblical text. These are the evolutionary approach, cultural relativism, the rejectionist approach, the "canon-within-a-canon" approach, and the holistic approach. While some of these approaches critique patriarchy

---

92. Ibid., 93 (my emphasis).

93. Jon L. Berquist, *Judaism in Persia's Shadow: A Social and Historical Approach* (Minneapolis: Fortress, 1995), 177–92; Philip R. Davies, "The Social World of the Apocalyptic Writings," in Clements, ed., *The World of Ancient Israel*, 251–71.

94. McNutt, *Reconstructing*, 212.

95. Eryl W. Davies, *The Dissenting Reader: Feminist Approaches to the Hebrew Bible* (Hants, UK: Ashgate, 2003), 17–35.

from a place outside the text (e.g. the rejectionist approach), others do so from within (e.g. canon-within-a-canon approach). Davies recognizes that "despite the patriarchal emphasis of the Hebrew Bible, the biblical tradition also contains narratives which either overtly reject or implicitly undermine the patriarchal structures which ostensibly appear to dominate the text."[96] Since efforts to locate liberating moments within the text itself seem most suggestive for the present study, I begin here.

According to Davies, the work of feminist scholar Phyllis Trible could be described as "a more refined version of the 'canon-within-a-canon' approach."[97] Trible believes the seeds of subversion *vis-à-vis* patriarchy are contained in the biblical text itself. According to Trible,

> The Bible can be redeemed from bondage to patriarchy; that redemption is already at work in the text... To bring together the self-critique that operates in the Bible with the concerns of feminism is to shape an interpretation that makes a difference for all of us—an interpretation that begins with suspicion and becomes subversion, but subversion for the sake of redemption, for the sake of healing, wholeness and well-being.[98]

Trible believes there is a "depatriachalizing principle at work in the Hebrew Bible" which she regards as "a hermeneutic operating within Scripture itself."[99] In her groundbreaking work, *God and the Rhetoric of Sexuality*, Trible offers several examples of narratives which subvert the patriarchy of the biblical text, namely, Gen 2–3, the Song of Songs, and the book of Ruth.[100] Contrary to many interpretations of Gen 2–3 which regard the woman as subordinate or inferior, Trible understands the text to be claiming something quite different. For her, the woman is portrayed as being a fully equal partner with the man.[101] This then becomes "the

96.   Ibid., 98–99.

97.   Ibid., 26.

98.   Phyllis Trible, "Eve and Miriam: From the Margins to the Center," in *Feminist Approaches to the Bible* (ed. Hershel Shanks; Washington D.C.: Biblical Archaeological Society, 1995), 5–24 (8).

99.   Phyllis Trible, "Depatriarchalizing in Biblical Interpretation," *JAAR* 41 (1973): 30–48 (48).

100.   Phyllis Trible, *God and the Rhetoric of Sexuality* (OBT 2; Philadelphia: Fortress, 1978), 72–199.

101.   Referring to her reading of Gen 2–3, Trible ("Eve and Miriam," 15) writes, "If the structural, verbal and grammatical ambiguities of this ancient story yield interpretations that defy patriarchy and open up other possibilities for interpreting the story and for appropriating it in new ways, the text thereby encourages us to look even further within the Bible, to listen for other accents and other voices that subvert patriarchy." Trible does this when reading about Miriam in the Hebrew Bible (see her "Eve and Miriam," 15–24, and "Bringing Miriam Out of the Shadows," *BRev* 5:1 [1989]: 14–25, 34).

hermeneutical key" which guides her interpretation of other texts, such as the Song of Songs.[102] Regarding the Song she writes, "Of the three speakers [woman, man, daughters of Jerusalem], the woman is the most prominent. She opens and closes the entire Song, her voice dominant throughout. By this structural emphasis her equality and mutuality with the man is illuminated."[103] Trible describes the book of Ruth as one in which the women's story is predominant. She regards the actions of Naomi and Ruth as bold and decisive, and believes the narrative refuses to let patriarchal concerns overshadow or coopt this perspective.[104] Trible believes that the interaction between a "feminist perspective" and a "rhetorical-critical methodology…reveal[s] countervoices within a patriarchal document."[105]

Other feminist scholars, including Ilana Pardes, have also identified "countervoices" in the Hebrew Bible. In her monograph titled *Countertraditions in the Bible: A Feminist Approach*, Pardes investigates "the tense dialogue between the dominant patriarchal discourses of the Bible and counter female voices which attempt to put forth other truths."[106] These include the voices of Eve, Rachel, Zipporah, the "idyllic revisionism" in the book of Ruth, the Shulamite in the Song of Songs, and Job's wife. Her project attempts "to illustrate the diversity of antithetical texts and voices which call into question the predominately patriarchal base of monotheism."[107] Like Trible, Pardes finds evidence of subversion within the text itself.

Many feminists have launched a critique of biblical patriarchy from a place outside the text. Regarding the text as hopelessly androcentric, they position themselves against it. Cheryl Exum, for example, in her study titled *Fragmented Women: Feminist (Sub)versions of Biblical Narratives*, attempts "to subvert the men's stories…by stepping outside the androcentric ideology of the biblical text."[108] She is what Davies refers to

102. Trible, *God and the Rhetoric of Sexuality*, 144–65 (144).

103. Ibid., 145.

104. Trible (ibid., 196) writes, "As a whole, this human comedy suggests a theological interpretation of feminism: women working out their own salvation with fear and trembling, for it is God who works in them. Naomi works as a bridge between tradition and innovation. Ruth and the females of Bethlehem work as paradigms for radicality. All together they are women in culture, women against culture, and women transforming culture."

105. Ibid., 202.

106. Ilana Pardes, *Countertraditions in the Bible: A Feminist Approach* (Cambridge, Mass.: Harvard University Press, 1992), 4.

107. Ibid., 144.

108. J. Cheryl Exum, *Fragmented Women: Feminist (Sub)versions of Biblical Narratives* (Valley Forge, Pa.: Trinity, 1993), 9.

as a "dissenting reader" engaged in a conscious critique of the ideology of the text. This also seems to be Trible's intention in her monograph *Texts of Terror*. Unlike her earlier work, this study is not concerned with looking for redeeming elements within the text. Instead, she "recounts tales of terror *in memoriam* to offer sympathetic readings of abused women."[109] Looking at four stories, those of Hagar, Tamar, an unnamed woman (the Levite's concubine), and Jephthah's daughter, Trible emphasizes the violence and tragedy which befell each of these women. She highlights the horror of these stories, refusing to pass over their pain and suffering in silence. Trible hopes that by reading these sickening stories anew our senses will shocked, encouraging us to make theologically appropriate responses to the pain and suffering these women—and many like them—have borne. Ideally, we as readers would repent and determine that such things never happen again. By critiquing and thereby undermining the patriarchal abuse of power which oppresses, dominates, and destroys, Trible's readings are subversive.

Davies believes feminist critics will find deconstruction to be a useful way of reading biblical texts. According the Davies, when deconstruction "is applied to the Hebrew Bible it becomes evident that some biblical passages, while ostensibly affirming the value of the patriarchal system, manage, at the same time, to disavow the hierarchical ordering of the sexes. Such passages indicate the difficulty of maintaining patriarchy in the face of strong counter-currents which affirmed the role and importance of women."[110] He believes that "by drawing attention to attitudes and viewpoints in the narrative which appear to run against the main drift of the story, deconstructionists aim to reveal the covert and potentially subversive ideology latent in the text."[111]

In many ways, this seems to be what Mieke Bal does in her much praised work *Death and Dissymmetry*.[112] Here Bal engages in a subversive reading of the book of Judges by employing a reading strategy she refers to as countercoherence. Bal recognizes "the political coherence" which appears to hold the book together and which many commentators

109. Phyllis Trible, *Texts of Terror: Literary–Feminist Readings of Biblical Narratives* (OBT 13; Philadelphia: Fortress, 1984), 3.

110. Davies, *Dissenting Reader*, 97.

111. Ibid. For a feminist reading that deconstructs certain aspects of the Solomonic narrative by exploring certain ambiguities in its portrayal of wisdom and strangeness, see Claudia V. Camp, *Wise, Strange and Holy: The Strange Woman and the Making of the Bible* (JSOTSup 320; GCT 9; Sheffield: Sheffield Academic Press, 2000), 144–86.

112. Mieke Bal, *Death and Dissymmetry: The Politics of Coherence in the Book of Judges* (Chicago: University of Chicago Press, 1988.

follow in their approach to this material.[113] But instead of following suit, Bal considers other portions of the book, those which have been suppressed and/or neglected. She takes as her starting point the conviction that all parts of the book of Judges are important, not just those which serve a reading of political coherence. Accordingly, she chooses to explore women's stories rather than men's in Judges and she begins with loss and victimization rather than conquest and strength.[114] In this way, she brings what is ostensibly the background into the foreground. While Bal does not claim that such stories were included as intentional acts of subversion, she at least allows that their inclusion is not wholly accidental. She writes,

> This study is, as a whole, an argument for the idea that the composers of the book were to some extent sensitive to the issues I will be raising. It is my contention that the awareness of social history as the background—or foreground—of political history made the composers include the women's stories, as did the presence of these stories in the primarily oral culture.[115]

A rather different application of subversion to "biblical" texts is advanced by André LaCocque's monograph, *The Feminine Unconventional: Four Subversive Figures in Israel's Tradition*, in which he explores how the stories of Ruth, Esther, Susanna, and Judith can be understood subversively.[116] LaCocque believes these four writings belong to "the Second Commonwealth subversive literature in Israel."[117] He reads these stories as a response to the oppressive policies toward women reflected in the books of Ezra–Nehemiah. As such, these writings may be classified as "protest literature."[118]

113. Ibid., 12–16.
114. Ibid., 16–18 (esp. 17).
115. Ibid., 257 n. 20. For a rather different reading of the book which could also be considered subversive, see Adrien Janis Bledstein's bold proposal that the author of Judges was a woman in "Is Judges a Woman's Satire of Men Who Play God?," in *A Feminist Companion to Judges* (ed. Athalya Brenner; The Feminist Companion to the Bible 4; Sheffield: JSOT Press, 1993), 34–54. Bledstein believes that when "read as a woman's satirical narrative, the book of Judges is a trenchant criticism of human (most often male) arrogance" (p. 54).
116. André LaCocque, *The Feminine Unconventional: Four Subversive Figures in Israel's Tradition* (Minneapolis: Fortress, 1990). He is followed by Alice Ogden Bellis, *Helpmates, Harlots, and Heroes: Women's Stories in the Hebrew Bible* (Louisville, Ky.: Westminster John Knox, 1994), 206–26, in a chapter entitled, "Subversive Women in Subversive Books: Ruth, Esther, Susanna, and Judith."
117. LaCocque, *Feminine Unconventional*, xiii.
118. Ibid., 1–6. Cf. Katherine Doob Sakenfeld's chapter titled "Vashti and Esther: Models of Resistance," in her book *Just Wives? Stories of Power and Survival in the Old Testament and Today* (Louisville, Ky.: Westminster John Knox, 2003), 49–67.

Another example of protest literature, though pre-exilic and not directed against patriarchy per se, is noted by Alicia Winters in an essay titled "The Subversive Memory of a Woman." Winters finds subversive possibilities in Rizpah's behavior in 2 Sam 21.[119] Like many commentators, Winters recognizes the ostensible propagandistic intentions of the story of David's slaughter of the remaining sons of Saul.[120] "The text seems to want to defend David by showing that the execution of the seven was not capricious or malicious, but a just restitution that the king felt obliged to demand from those who carried the guilt for violating a solemn oath sanctioned by Yahweh."[121] Yet Winter points out that Rizpah's actions sit uncomfortably in this narrative. Rizpah's lengthy vigil raises questions about the propriety of David's deeds and potentially unsettles more positive construals of David which the text seems to be promoting on the surface. Winters rightly observes that these corrosive aspects of Rizpah's actions are not often noted by commentators. Many are content to regard Rizpah's vigil as little more than "a beautiful illustration of maternal tenderness."[122] Yet for Winters, it is an act of resistance. She writes, "There can be no doubt that the action of Rizpah in the desert had political, even subversive, implications. Her presence at the side of the dead kept their memory alive for all the Benjaminites and all Israel, putting in question the right of David to occupy the throne and his means of staying in power."[123] When viewed in this way, this ostensibly propagandistic text takes on a whole new meaning.[124]

Gender subversion is another form of corrosive discourse some scholars have identified in the Hebrew Bible.[125] In his article, "Gender Subversion in the Book of Jeremiah," Herbert Huffmon examines three passages (or sets of passages) which, he maintains, illustrate gender

---

119. Alicia Winters, "The Subversive Memory of a Woman," in *Subversive Scriptures: Revolutionary Readings of the Christian Bible in Latin America* (ed. and trans. Leif E. Vaage; Valley Forge, Pa.: Trinity, 1997), 142–54.

120. P. Kyle McCarter Jr. (*II Samuel* [AB 9; New York: Doubleday, 1984], 445) refers to this text (21:1–14 + 9:1–13) as an "apologetic document."

121. Winters, "Subversive Memory," 152. See Josh 9:15, 19–20 for the oath in question.

122. Winters, "Subversive Memory," 143.

123. Ibid., 145. Cf. also Gerald West, "Reading on the Boundaries: Reading 2 Samuel 21:1–14 with Rizpah," *Scriptura* 63 (1997): 527–37 (530).

124. We will return to this idea (that propaganda could be used to cloak subversion) repeatedly throughout this study.

125. See, e.g., Erin Runions, "Zion is Burning: 'Gender Fuck' in Micah," in *In Search of the Present: The Bible through Cultural Studies* (ed. Stephen D. Moore; Semeia 82; Atlanta: Scholars Press, 1998), 225–46.

subversion.[126] The passages selected deal with Jeremiah's celibacy (16:1–2), the circumcision of the heart (4:4; 9:24–25; 31:33), and the perplexing text about a woman encompassing a man (31:22). According to Huffmon, these examples illustrate performative subversion, ideological subversion, and enigmatic subversion, respectively. Huffmon writes,

> These subverting texts do not attack the gender categories in a frontal assault, they undermine them. These texts—and the associated behavior—are not an attempt to directly overthrow the established gender traditions, nor do they articulate the addition of a "Third Gender" category, but rather they operate from within the culture in such a way, whether immediately intentional or not, as to stimulate the redefinition of the traditionally constructed gender categories. Subversion involves, instead of specifically opposing the traditions of the "real" world, problematizing reality, opening up alternative possibilities. The effect is to subvert unitary visions and to introduce confusion and alternatives, thereby violating the traditional gender roles and preparing the way for new configurations.[127]

Like feminist criticism, Huffmon's treatment of gender subversion provides yet another example of the breadth and power of subversion.

A number of studies have emphasized the presence of ambiguity and irony in biblical texts, and while some of these studies do not explicitly raise the notion of scribal subversion, their work opens the door for potentially subversive readings to emerge. David Gunn, for example, has offered close readings of selected biblical narratives which seem to me potentially subversive. In his monograph *The Story of King David*, Gunn explores a variety of ambiguities related to the actions and motivations of certain key players in the Succession Narrative, particularly Joab and David. For example, Gunn detects "a curious ambivalence" to David's reaction to the assassination of Ishbosheth (2 Sam 4:9–12).[128] While Gunn believes David's "refusal to countenance the violence done to his rival" reflects positively on him, he recognizes there is "more than a hint of a public relations exercise in his dramatic despatch of the bringers of the gift."[129] This complicates the characterization of David. Does it portray him favorably, as a king who refuses to take the kingdom by

126. Herbert B. Huffmon, "Gender Subversion in the Book of Jeremiah," in *Sex and Gender in the Ancient Near East—Proceedings of the 47th Rencontre Assyriologique Internationale, Helsinki, July 2–6, 2001* (ed. Simo Parpola and R. M. Whiting; Helsinki: Neo-Assyrian Text Corpus Project, 2002), 245–53.

127. Ibid., 246.

128. David M. Gunn, *The Story of King David: Genre and Interpretation* (JSOTSup 6; Sheffield: JSOT Press, 1978), 95.

129. Ibid.

force? Or does it betray a certain royal relief—and perhaps even complicity—in Ishbosheth's death? While Gunn does not pursue this line
of questioning, his reading leaves both possibilities open. Similarly,
Gunn perceives an ambivalence in David's gift of land to Mephibosheth
(2 Sam 9). Though ostensibly about showing kindness (*ḥesed*) to Mephibosheth for the sake of Jonathan, David's actions may be far less salutary. As Gunn points out, giving this land to Mephibosheth costs David
nothing, generates "a healthy subsidy for the court," and allows the king
to keep a close eye of this last surviving member of Saul's house.[130]
Uncertainties about David's motivations once again complicate any
assessment of his character.

In these and other episodes, Gunn believes this narrative ambivalence
is related to the skill and artistry of the author. He writes,

> The author...is continually exploring the range of perspectives open to
> the participants in, and the interpreters of, the situations that constitute the
> stuff of his story. We find in the narrative no simple *Tendenz* or moraliz-
> ing but rather a picture of the rich variety of life that is often comic and
> ironic in its contrasting perspectives and conflicting norms.[131]

For Gunn, this author is a consummate storyteller, one who refuses sim-
plistically to portray characters in absolute ways. Instead, he believes the
writer creates complex characters whose motives remain elusive. This
allows various perspectives to emerge and interact. Though Gunn explicitly rejects the idea that this narrative was the work of a propagandist—
and says nothing directly about the possibility of it functioning subversively—this kind of openness, ambiguity, and multivalence which leads
to contrasting portrayals of David reflects the kind of writing one might
expect from the hand of a subversive scribe.

In his subsequent monograph, *The Fate of King Saul*, Gunn continues
to explore this reading strategy. He regards the story of Saul (1 Sam
8–31) as tragedy and classifies it as "serious entertainment."[132] The ambiguity and openness Gunn discerns in this narrative allows him to propose
readings which are much more sympathetic toward Saul than those typically generated by most commentators. Gunn argues that the precise
nature of Saul's sin in 1 Sam 13 and 15 is shrouded in uncertainty. In
1 Sam 13, a question arises concerning Saul's obedience to Samuel's
instructions to wait seven days (1 Sam 10:8). As Gunn observes,

---

130. Ibid., 96–97 (97).
131. Ibid., 111.
132. David M. Gunn, *The Fate of King Saul: An Interpretation of a Biblical Story*
(JSOTSup 14; Sheffield: JSOT Press, 1980), 11–12.

> The instruction to "wait" is ambiguous with regard to time. On Samuel's interpretation Saul has not waited as instructed, for he should have waited until the prophet came and issued further instructions; as Saul sees it he has waited precisely the required time, seven days, before being at liberty to take action himself.[133]

There is no way to decide conclusively in favor of one reading or another. Both possibilities linger. Similarly, there are ways of understanding Saul's supposed lack of obedience regarding the slaughter of all Amalekites and their livestock which cast the king in a far more positive light than typically assumed. Such a reading takes seriously Saul's claim that he *had* obeyed God's command (1 Sam 15:13), at least insofar as he understood it. Saul may have allowed the people temporarily to spare the best animals for the purpose of sacrificing them. Saul may have believed such a sacrifice was fully compatible with the initial divine directive to destroy everything. Likewise, despite the fact that Agag had not been killed on the field of battle, it is possible that Saul had every intention of killing him later. But no matter. God and Samuel seem hellbent on condemning Saul. If this narrative was originally intended to support the Davidic dynasty by demonstrating Saul's unsuitability to rule, and yet readers leave with the impression of "Saul as essentially an innocent victim of God," then this text clearly functions subversively.[134] Although Gunn's interests do not move in this direction, his reading nicely illustrates the subversive possibilities of this story.

Unlike Gunn, Lyle Eslinger speaks openly of subversive possibilities in various passages in the Deuteronomistic History. In his monograph *Into the Hands of the Living God*, Eslinger is particularly interested in exploring the role of irony in various passages in this corpus. He contests the prevailing view that the Dtr's voice is heard via "the great orations," arguing instead that these speeches are quite dissonant from their surrounding context.[135] He explains why so few have recognized this:

> Readers have failed to hear the narrator's subtle insurgent voice because they are so attuned to hear and accept the clamorous pieties of the human characters of the Bible, with whose existential predicament and religious sentiments they can so easily identify. With regard to the great orations in the Dtr narrative, this means that readers have been disposed to hear the narrative in the light of the orations rather than to read the orations in the light of their existing narrative context.[136]

133. Ibid., 39.
134. Ibid., 123.
135. Eslinger, *Into the Hands*, 3.
136. Ibid., 229.

According to Eslinger, "Nowhere is there more discongruity between narrator and character, between the ideology of one of the great orations and that of its larger narrative context, than in the case of King Solomon's prayers in 1 Kgs 8."[137] To illustrate, Eslinger examines both the preceding and the subsequent literary context in which this prayer is set. He believes this reveals that Solomon's agenda is quite at odds with the pieties and platitudes voiced in the temple prayer. It is this context which allows readers to detect "a powerful hidden agenda underneath the pious overtones" of the prayer.[138] As Eslinger sees it, Solomon is trying to countermand the curses of Deut 28 by forcing God to honor "the eternal aspects" of the covenant made with David in 2 Sam 7, a covenant God subsequently made conditional on obedience (1 Kgs 3:14; 6:12–13; cf. 2:4).[139] Thus, rather than echoing Deuteronomistic pieties, this prayer actually undermines them when read against its larger narrative background. As Eslinger puts it, "That is exactly why this narrative is so subversive of the ideology presented in the character's gushing evaluative discourse."[140]

Eslinger also believes "explicit evaluation" in the Dtr narrative should be read ironically. He demonstrates how these narratorial evaluations, like the great orations, are at odds with the larger narrative context. For example, a careful reading of the book of Joshua reveals that the entire land of Canaan was not subdued despite claims to the contrary such as Josh 21:43–45:

> Thus the LORD gave to Israel all the land that he swore to their ancestors that he would give them; and having taken possession of it, they settled there. And the LORD gave them rest on every side just as he had sworn to their ancestors; not one of all their enemies had withstood them, for the LORD had given all their enemies into their hands. Not one of all the good promises that the LORD had made to the house of Israel had failed; all came to pass.

Yet this passage is at odds with many others in the book which suggest a considerable amount of the "promised land" remained in non-Israelite hands (e.g. Josh 12:8; 13:1–6, 13; 15:63; 16:10; 17:13). While many scholars resort to source theories to explain this, Eslinger pushes for a more integrated reading. He suggests the author has given voice to these alternate perspectives via the narrator only for the purpose of subverting them. He writes,

137. Ibid., 123.
138. Ibid., 156.
139. Ibid., 159–63.
140. Ibid., 177–78.

> If…the narrator's evaluations in 21:43–5 are ironic then the consensus of scholarly opinion about the book's promotion of a successful conquest is a simple but serious case of naive misreading of irony. Instead of accepting the subversion given in the narrator's description of events… readers have mistaken the proffered ironic evaluations for straightforward assertions.[141]

If Eslinger is right, his reading demonstrates how ancient authors could use irony for subversive ends.

Eslinger's reading of Joshua makes generous use of Robert Polzin's work titled *Moses and the Deuteronomist*. In this work, Polzin distinguishes between two voices in the Deuteronomistic History. One is the voice of "authoritarian dogmatism" while the other is "critical traditionalism."[142] The former voice heard on the surface of the text makes absolute statements undermined by the latter. Eslinger regards this latter voice as "narratorial subversion."[143]

Another effort to discern various voices in Hebrew narrative can be found in Keith Bodner's recent book *David Observed: A King in the Eyes of His Court*.[144] Here, Bodner applies Mikhail Bakhtin's notion of *pseudo-objective motivation* to his reading of the Abner's assassination in 2 Sam 3.[145] Bodner describes this "literary technique" as follows:

> What appears to be an authorial utterance in narration is actually the presentation of a commonly held opinion by a given general population. On the surface, such an utterance looks like a comment by the narrator (and thus looks like the implied author's opinion), but in fact it is the opposite: the viewpoint of the collective citizens. Instead of an authoritative utterance, there is actually a tension between the "belief" as stated and the author's actual opinion of the matter at hand.[146]

In the case of 2 Sam 3:36–37, Bodner contends that "the narrator" is "refracting a piece of 'public opinion'" and not representing the author's own views on the matter.[147] Though these verses appear to defend David

---

141. Ibid., 28.

142. Robert Polzin, *Moses and the Deuteronomist: A Literary Study of the Deuteronomistic History*. Part One, *Deuteronomy, Joshua, Judges* (New York: Seabury Press, 1980), 59, 67, 205–6, et passim.

143. Eslinger, *Into the Hands*, 186 n. 5.

144. Keith Bodner, *David Observed: A King in the Eyes of His Court* (HBM 5; Sheffield: Sheffield Phoenix Press, 2005).

145. For a convenient introduction to Bakhtin's life, thought, and application for biblical studies, see Barbara Green, *Mikhail Bakhtin and Biblical Scholarship: An Introduction* (Atlanta: Society of Biblical Literature, 2000).

146. Ibid.

147. Ibid., 42.

from charges of wrongdoing, applying Bakhtin's notion of pseudo-objective motivation raises certain nettlesome questions about David's complicity in the death of Abner. It is not difficult to see how a literary technique like this would have been especially useful to a scribe wanting to launch a covert critique. By enabling a scribe to say one thing on the surface of the text while believing—and hinting at—something quite different, this device would allow a scribe to subvert "the powers that be" with relative impunity.

In assessing the characterization of David, Bodner also appeals to Bakhtin's notion of direct utterance being double-voiced. As Bodner summarizes, "For direct discourse to be double-voiced…there are at least two levels of meaning: one meaning in the immediate context that the speakers and hearers readily understand, and a second meaning that is directed toward a larger theme or ideological component of the author's literary work."[148] Once again, this literary technique holds subversive potential. Bodner believes the principle is at work in the well known saying in 1 Sam 16:7. He writes,

> One could argue that 1 Sam. 16.7 ("for humanity sees according to the eyes, but the LORD sees according to the heart") is a prime example of a double-voiced utterance. On the one hand, this divine statement intimates that a person's inner nature is more important than the normal human signs of success and means of victory. On the other hand (or rather, at the same time), it could be suggested that God's words have an "authorial" accent—they become a thematic vehicle in the narrative, and serve to undermine or destabilize the notion of Samuel as an impartial prophet and kingmaker in a reader's mind.[149]

While Bodner recognizes the critique of Samuel as being overt in this instance,[150] it is not difficult to imagine how this technique could have been utilized more stealthily. The possibility of direct utterances being double-voiced seems to indicate yet another way in which literary subversion could have been intentionally deployed.

Finally, we turn to a recent article by J. Daniel Hays which bears numerous similarities to the present study. The article is tellingly titled, "Has the Narrator Come to Praise Solomon or to Bury Him? Narrative Subtlety in 1 Kings 1–11."[151] In contradistinction to those who bifurcate the Solomonic narrative into two parts, one positive and one negative,

148. Ibid., 15.
149. Ibid., 16.
150. Ibid., 16 n. 18.
151. J. Daniel Hays, "Has the Narrator Come to Praise Solomon or Bury Him? Narrative Subtlety in 1 Kings 1–11," *JSOT* 28 (2003): 149–74.

Hays believes the narrator critiques the king throughout this portion of 1 Kings. Despite the positive portrayal of Solomon one might derive by taking the text at face value, Hays detects negative undercurrents which challenge this ostensibly favorable assessment:

> On the surface of the text, especially when read out of context, the narrator does seem to heap praise after praise on Solomon and the realm that he built. However…there are numerous clues that suggest to us that perhaps the narrator is playing literary games with his readers. He may be openly and overtly praising Solomon on the surface, but he does not tell the story with a straight face, and if we look closely, we see him winking at us.[152]

According to Hays, the key to detecting critical connotations in 1 Kgs 1–11 involves reading in context, which for him means reading 1 Kgs 1–11 in light of Deuteronomy and 1–2 Samuel. Hays believes this critique will be obvious "to those who hold Deuteronomy in their hands as they listen," describing it as "narrative subtlety, or perhaps irony."[153] In this way, "the negative Deuteronomistic critique running through 1 Kgs 3–10 *subverts* (quietly and only through irony) the positive."[154]

Hays finds methodological justification for his approach to 1 Kgs 1–11 in what he believes is an obvious—though subtle—critique of Solomon's numerous horses and wealth in 1 Kgs 10. When this chapter is read in light of Deut 17:14–20, it is clear that Solomon is being severely indicted.[155] By Hays' own reckoning, this is methodologically crucial:

> This observed subtlety is important because it establishes in a clear text that the narrator does indeed employ this type of subtle critique as a literary style. Therefore, we can justify the approach of going back into the first ten chapters of the Solomon narratives and looking for other subtle hints of covenant violation or of impropriety on the part of Solomon and his "glorious" kingdom.[156]

Hays spend very little time with 1 Kgs 1–2 and focuses most of his attention on a variety of items scattered about chs. 3–10. In numerous instances, Hays rightly detects a critique hovering just below the surface of the text. There are critical undertones in those passages describing Solomon's conscription of laborers (1 Kgs 5:27–32 [Eng. 5:13–18]), his divestment of land (9:10–14), and Bathsheba's words of praise (10:6–9), and I will have more to say about these and other features at a later point. Here I would simply note a few weaknesses of Hays' study.

152. Ibid., 154.
153. Ibid., 155.
154. Ibid., 151 n. 3 (emphasis in original).
155. Ibid., 155–57.
156. Ibid., 157; cf. 174.

To begin, one might question whether "finding" a subtle critique of Solomon in 1 Kgs 10 based on reading it from the vantage point of Deut 17 really "justifies" going back through the Solomonic narrative in search of similar critiques based on Deuteronomy and 1 and 2 Samuel. Second, Hays sometimes fails to demonstrate how the critique he sees is subtle. For example, when discussing 1 Kgs 3:1, which reports Solomon's marriage to an Egyptian princess, he seems to regard this as being totally negative. He writes, "the statement in 3.1 should explode like a bomb-shell in the reader's mind."[157] If that is the case, it is hardly a covert critique! Third, some of the supposed critiques cited by Hays seem rather strained. For example, when discussing 1 Kgs 8, he contrasts Solomon's behavior to David's in 2 Sam 6 and finds Solomon wanting in every way. David dances, Solomon does not. David is humble, Solomon is arrogant. Hays argues that this contrast reflects negatively on Solomon, though one suspects Hays is overreading at this point.

What I find most curious about Hays' study is his apparent lack of interest in the question of narratorial motivation and literary function. Assuming Hays is right, why would a narrator intentionally choose to write in a way that appears to praise the king but actually subtly criticizes him? Why would this two-faced approach have been used throughout most of the narrative only to be disbanded at the end? What purpose would such a literary strategy serve, and in what socio-historical circumstances might such a strategy have been regarded as necessary or desirable? These questions are not even broached, let alone addressed, in Hays' article. Yet they seem exactly like the kind of questions his investigation naturally raises. They are questions that are of special interest to me in this study, and I will have the opportunity to begin exploring them in the next chapter as I consider scribes and scribal subversion.

## Conclusion

At the outset of this chapter, I briefly recapped the current debate about how—and even if—the Solomonic narrative can be divided into two separate parts. I noted that while the primary focus of this study is not intended to settle that particular debate, it is hoped that the specific approach to the Solomonic narrative taken here will, nevertheless, further that conversation. The reading strategy that will be employed in this study considers reading the Solomonic narrative through the lenses of propaganda and subversion, with a special emphasis on exploring passages

---

157. Ibid., 161.

which demonstrate subversive tendencies. To the end, I established working definitions for "propaganda" and "subversion," thus laying some initial groundwork for my exploration of 1 Kgs 1–11.

The second part of this chapter comprised a review of biblical scholarship which has utilized the language of propaganda and subversion, or similar terms/categories. This review demonstrated that others have found these helpful categories for understanding the nature and function of certain biblical texts and books. Although it was relatively easy to locate studies which regard certain portions of the Hebrew Bible as propagandistic, it was somewhat more difficult to identify works which employed the language of subversion. This was due, in part, to the diverse language used by scholars to speak about subversive or corrosive tendencies in the biblical text. While some of the studies I identified focused on conspicuous subversion, others explored various ways in which a covert critique might have been deployed in the text. Since my primary interest in this book is exploring examples of concealed subversion in the Solomonic narrative, these studies prove most suggestive for my purposes. They demonstrated various ways in which authors could inscribe a covert critique in the texts they produced. I will have much more to say about these "techniques" in the following chapter and will give special attention to issues of textual indeterminacy, ambiguity, and scribal intentionality. But first, I must turn my attention to a consideration of the nature of scribes in ancient Israel, particularly to the kind of scribes who might have been responsible for producing propagandistic and/or subversive texts in connection with Solomon.

Chapter 2

## SCRIBES AND SCRIBAL SUBVERSION

*Clients usually assume the world view and values of their patrons;*
*to do otherwise would be risky.*

—Mark Sneed[1]

*Behold, there is no profession free of a boss—*
*except for the scribe: he is the boss.*

—ancient Egyptian scribe[2]

In order to better understand the nature and character of propagandistic and subversive literature in the ancient Near East generally and Israel specifically, we must attempt to get inside the minds of the scribes who produced it. Such a task is immediately complicated by the fact that our knowledge of scribes is largely confined to the writings they left behind, writings which often *explicitly* reveal little, if anything, about their author. Anonymity was typical of ancient writers, and even where colophons have been appended the information provided is typically laconic and unspectacular.[3]

Developing a profile of an ancient "scribe" is further complicated by the fact that the Hebrew Bible has no special vocabulary to distinguish between our modern notions of authors, redactors, secretaries, and "mere" copyists.[4] Because ancient scribes were clearly not a homogeneous lot,

1. Mark R. Sneed, "A Middle Class in Ancient Israel?," in *Concepts of Class in Ancient Israel* (ed. Mark R. Sneed; South Florida Studies in the History of Judaism 201; Atlanta: Scholars Press, 1999), 53–69 (64).

2. "The Satire on the Trades" (translated by John A. Wilson, *ANET*, 434).

3. See, for example, C. B. F. Walker, "Cuneiform," in *Reading the Past: Ancient Writing from Cuneiform to the Alphabet* (J. T. Hooker et al.; New York: Barnes & Noble, 1998), 46–48, who cites three common pieces of information in Assyrian colophons—the scribe's name, the date, the place of origin—none of which provides much insight into the nature and character of ancient scribes.

4. This issue is briefly touched upon in Gary N. Knoppers, "Is there a Future for the Deuteronomistic History?," in *The Future of the Deuteronomistic History* (ed. Thomas Römer; BETL 147; Leuven: Leuven University Press, 2000), 119–34 (127).

it becomes difficult to make generalized statements about them.[5] For instance, while some were very close to the establishment, others appear to have been less institutionally connected and some may have even engaged in what amounts to "free-lance" work. Even within a particular institution, such as the state or palace, where numerous scribes were employed, there was an undeniable hierarchy, with some holding more prestigious posts and wielding considerably more power than their less fortunate (or less trained) counterparts.

Ancient scribes are further differentiated by the type of writing that occupied their time. While some used their considerable talents to do mathematics, others directed their energies to writing and reading omen texts, drafting letters, producing political propaganda, or perhaps engaging in astrological study. Such specializations would have clearly distinguished one kind of scribe from another. In terms of sheer mass, it is safe to assume that the majority of ancient scribes would have been primarily involved in routine administrative assignments. Far fewer would have had the freedom—or perhaps even the skill—to produce complex literary works like the Solomonic narrative. Yet it is precisely this cadre of individuals which particularly interests us. While modern notions of authorship cannot fully capture the work of such scribes, given their frequent dependency upon oral traditions, archival records, and other pre-existent sources in the production of their texts, these individuals clearly functioned at a higher and more influential level than the common administrative scribe who simply kept the bureaucracy going. Presumably, these highly skilled scribes were creative writers who took on the roles of author, redactor, compiler, revisionist, and the like.[6] In these capacities, they had the potential to use their considerable abilities to support and/or subvert their patrons and the dominant institutions of power they served in a variety of ways.[7]

Given the diverse functions of ancient scribes and scribal activity, and considering the scope of the present study, my primary objective will be to describe the nature and social location of Israelite/Judahite scribes during the monarchic period.[8] I will be working on the assumption that

5. The heterogeneity of the scribal guild is also apparent when one makes allowance for regional differences as well as the changing role of the scribe over hundreds, and in some cases, thousands of years.

6. See Michael Fishbane, *Biblical Interpretation in Ancient Israel* (Oxford: Clarendon, 1985), 23–88.

7. See the discussion of scribal submission and subversion below.

8. For the purposes of this study, I am using the phrase "monarchic period" to designate the time from the reign of Saul to the Fall of Jerusalem in 586 BCE.

nearly all of the material in 1 Kgs 1–11 is best understood as being created, redacted, and assembled during that particular period or time.[9] Unfortunately, our knowledge of these scribes and their practices during the monarchic period is extremely limited.[10] Apart from the biblical texts and a handful of non-biblical letters,[11] there are virtually no epigraphic remains of a distinctly *literary* quality that yield much insight into the scribal persona.[12] For this reason, I will occasionally draw upon comparative data from the ancient Near East to help fill out the scribal portrait desired in this chapter. It goes without saying that such comparisons need to be used cautiously lest one mistakenly assume that the situation in one context is necessarily analogous to the situation in another.

The following discussion is roughly divided into three major sections. The first part deals with several preliminary matters, namely, scribal self-perceptions, literacy, and scribal schools. The second section then explores three dichotomies which are presented as heuristic devices. Of these three—tethered and untethered, royal and temple, submissive and subversive—considerable attention will be given to the final pair since it is crucial to our thesis and will provide a rationale for our distinct approach to reading the Solomonic narrative. Moreover, by looking at ancient scribes through these lenses, we will ultimately be in a better position to assess the organizational attachments, institutional affiliations, and literary intentions of those scribes who contributed to the production of the Solomonic narrative. The final section of this chapter deals with a variety of issues related to the practice of scribal subversion. Here we explore the aims and possibilities of scribal subversion, discuss subversive scribal techniques, consider issues of textual indeterminacy and ambiguity, and suggest some indicators for detecting intentional literary subversion.

---

9. My focus on this particular time period is not meant to imply that my findings are only applicable to monarchic scribes in Israel. There are undoubtedly many points of continuity between the scribal activity of the pre-exilic period and that which follows.

10. For a brief assessment of the biblical data, see Joseph Blenkinsopp, *Sage, Priest, Prophet: Religious and Intellectual Leadership in Ancient Israel* (Louisville, Ky.: Westminster John Knox, 1995), 28–32.

11. Dennis Pardee, *Handbook of Ancient Hebrew Letters: A Study Edition* (Chico, Calif.: Scholars Press, 1982).

12. Giovanni Garbini, *History and Ideology in Ancient Israel* (New York: Crossroad, 1988), 16–19. Garbini speaks of "the virtually complete absence of Hebrew epigraphy that can be described as historical in the strict sense" (p. 17).

## Scribal Self-Perceptions

In the ancient world, scribes seem to have had a very high view of their vocation and the work in which they engaged. There is considerable evidence that they regarded their profession as far superior to a wide range of other occupations and worked hard to inculcate this perspective in their scribal trainees. This emphasis is a recurring motif in Egyptian literature and is especially noteworthy in "The Satire on the Trades."[13] By describing the accompanying misery associated with the work of common laborers and artisans, especially the long hours and extremely unpleasant physical rigors, "The Satire on the Trades" effectively denigrates other vocations.[14] The intended result was to persuade scribes in training that the scribal profession was unsurpassed and extremely advantageous.[15] "But if thou knowest writing, then it will go better with thee than in these professions which I have set before thee."[16] That such persuasion was deemed necessary testifies to the immense difficulties facing the apprentice learning to read and write.[17] Corporeal punishment by the scribal teacher was also utilized to "encourage" trainees to learn this exacting craft.[18]

13. "The Satire on the Trades," translated by John A. Wilson (*ANET*, 432–34).

14. While Ben Sira similarly discusses a series of trades in contrast to the scribal profession (Sir 38:24–39:11), the tone is much more amicable. His concern is to demonstrate how other trades, though necessary and significant, consume so much of a person's time and energy that there simply is no opportunity for the pursuit and acquisition of wisdom at the end of the day. According the Ben Sira "the wisdom of the scribe depends on the opportunity of leisure" (Sir 38:24a).

15. By way of contrast, A. Leo Oppenheim ("The Position of the Intellectual in Mesopotamian Society," *Daedalus* 104, no. 2 [1975]: 37–46 [44 n. 1]) notes an absence of this emphasis on "the social advantages of being an expert scribe" in Mesopotamian literature.

16. "The Satire on the Trades" (translated by John A. Wilson, *ANET*, 434).

17. Apparently, some scribal trainees lacked the discipline necessary to perfect their craft and abandoned it for more agreeable types of work. Such was the case of Pentawere, an Egyptian scribe, whose deviation from the scribal profession occasioned this disapproving response from Amunemone in "Reminder of the Scribes Superior Status," translated by William Kelly Simpson (*The Literature of Ancient Egypt: An Anthology of Stories, Instructions, and Poetry* [ed. William Kelly Simpson; new ed.; New Haven: Yale University Press, 1973], 343–44): "I have been told that you have abandoned writing and that you reel about in pleasures, that you have given your attention to work in the fields, and that you have turned your back on hieroglyphs. Do you not remember the condition of the field-hand in the face of the registration of the harvest-tax, the snake having taken away half of the grain and the hippopotamus having eaten the remainder?... There is no taxing of the work of the scribe. He does not have dues. So take note of this."

18. Anthony J. Saldarini, "Scribes," *ABD* 5:1012–16 (1012).

Obviously, "The Satire on the Trades" exaggerates the hardships and afflictions of those working outside the scribal profession. Moreover, it should be kept in mind that the intent of this and similar texts was to persuade scribal trainees to remain at their posts! Hence, its value for revealing what scribes really thought about people involved in other trades is suspect. Still, it seems relatively certain that scribes did consider their occupations as superior to those of the vast majority of the population. According to C. B. F. Walker, fully trained Mesopotamian scribes "were members of a privileged élite who might look with contempt on their fellow citizens."[19]

Unfortunately, the Hebrew Bible has not preserved any direct witness to scribal self-perceptions, making it difficult to determine how analogous the situation was in ancient Israel. Considering the relative smallness of Israel and Judah *vis-à-vis* the imperial powers, it seems reasonable to conclude that the monarchic bureaucracy there was considerably less complex than elsewhere. This may suggest more frequent contact and interaction with average Israelites living in and around the administrative power centers. As a result, the chasm between scribe and commoner in Israel, though quite substantial, may have not been nearly so wide and antagonistic as the foregoing analysis would suggest.

## *Literacy*

Discussions of literacy in ancient Israel are immediately complicated by a lack of precision in defining exactly what is meant by literacy.[20] For example, must a person be able to both read *and* write in order to be considered literate or does the ability to do just one of these activities register as literacy? Furthermore, what degree of proficiency is necessary to classify a person as "literate?" If someone could produce the alphabet, write their own name, or even compose a rudimentary letter, should they be considered literate? Or should the term be exclusively reserved for those able to understand and produce literary narratives or texts such as those we find in the Hebrew Bible? After briefly examining the notion of literacy (variously understood) in the ancient Near East and Israel, I will offer a more precise definition of how the term will be understood in this study.

It is widely agreed that literacy in the ancient Near East was restricted to a very elite group of individuals. As Trevor Bryce observes, "Reading

19. Walker, "Cuneiform," 43.
20. For a helpful discussion, see William V. Harris, *Ancient Literacy* (Cambridge, Mass.: Harvard University Press, 1989), 3–24 (3–8).

and writing in the ancient Near East was a highly specialized occupation, and scribes may well have been the only literate members in their society."[21] Commenting on the Egyptian situation, Bleiberg expands the circle of the literati to include "members of the royal family, nobles, priests, and the scribal class of bureaucrats itself."[22] Even so, this still indicates that relatively few people in the ancient world could read or write with any level of proficiency. In fact, according to his impressive study of literacy in ancient Egypt, John Baines concludes that "in most periods" the literacy rate was below 1 per cent.[23] The same could be said of other major imperial powers throughout the ancient Near East such as the Hittite empire, and both the Assyrian and Babylonian empires.

But is this notion of restricted literacy equally applicable to ancient Israel? The situation in Israel was by no means completely analogous since the alphabetic system used to write Hebrew was far less cumbersome than the highly complex cuneiform and hieroglyphic systems used in Mesopotamia, Anatolia, and Egypt. Logically, one might assume that a simpler writing system would result in higher levels of literacy. Yet, as Crenshaw duly notes, "The simplicity of the Hebrew alphabet encouraged literacy, although no correlation between a simple script and mass literacy has been established."[24] Similarly, Menahem Haran believes

> There should be no doubt that the invention of the alphabet facilitated the learning of reading and writing, for it is much easier to master alphabetic writing than pictographic or syllabic writing. Nevertheless, it cannot be assumed that the emergence of this invention was accompanied by the removal of writing from the possession of professional scribes, turning it into a popular phenomenon.[25]

Even in ancient Greece, with the use of an alphabetic script, literacy levels apparently did not exceed 10 per cent.[26] Given this evidence, it is

---

21. Trevor Bryce, *The Kingdom of the Hittites* (Oxford: Clarendon, 1998), 418.

22. Bleiberg, "Historical Texts as Political Propaganda," 7–8.

23. John Baines, "Literacy and Ancient Egyptian Society," *Man* 18/3 (1983): 572–99 (584).

24. James L. Crenshaw, *Education in Ancient Israel: Across the Deadening Silence* (New York: Doubleday, 1998), 39.

25. Menahem Haran, "On the Diffusion of Literacy and Schools in Ancient Israel," in *Congress Volume: Jerusalem, 1986* (ed. J. A. Emerton; VTSup 40; Leiden: Brill, 1988), 81–95 (82). Sean Warner ("The Alphabet: An Innovation and its Diffusion" *VT* 30 [1980]: 81–90) also compellingly argues against the notion that the invention of the alphabet promoted the widespread diffusion of literacy. See also William M. Schniedewind, *How the Bible Became a Book: The Textualization of Ancient Israel* (New York: Cambridge University Press, 2004), 38, 92–93.

26. Harris, *Ancient Literacy*, 61.

reasonable to conclude that widespread literacy should *not* be assumed in Israel (or other small states such as Edom, Moab, or Ammon) simply because their writing system was simpler. As Haran puts it, "It is not the complexity or multiplicity of signs of a given writing system, or, alternatively, its relative simplicity when alphabetic, that can account exclusively for its distribution. Alongside this factor there is always in operation a complex of additional factors, social, economic and political."[27]

Alan R. Millard, arguably the most vocal advocate of widespread literacy in ancient Israel, has challenged the notion of restricted literacy on the basis of numerous archaeological discoveries.[28] He cites a number of "formal documents" such as ostraca, seals, and bullae along with "occasional documents" consisting of graffiti, proper names, and other information of marginal significance which have been discovered at a couple dozen sites. Millard believes several of these documents were written by persons other than professional scribes for two reasons. First, the widespread distribution of these documents—many of which were discovered away from the capital cities of Jerusalem and Samaria where professional scribes presumably operated—would suggest that they originated from private individuals. Second, the (often peripheral) content of these documents, particularly the occasional documents, is not indicative of the kind of thing professional scribes were known to write. On the basis of such evidence, Millard believes that "there can be no question that writing was possible in Israel throughout the period of the Monarchy."[29]

While I have no quarrel with this conclusion, I am far less comfortable with what Millard implies when he states: "Where there was writing there was certainly the possibility of literature, and of reading it. We may conclude that few ancient Israelites were out of reach of the written word."[30] It seems reasonably true to say that ancient Israelites were not "out of reach of the written word" if by the written word one means writing a name on a jug handle or inscribing a decorative abecedary around the lip of a bowl. But are we to believe that the majority of Israelites had access to longer, more complicated texts like those we find in the Bible? Is it plausible to imagine that the common laborer, agriculturalist, or artisan possessed the ability to read and comprehend such complex texts?

27.  Haran, "Literacy and Schools," 83.

28.  Alan R. Millard, "An Assessment of the Evidence for Writing in Ancient Israel," in *Biblical Archaeology Today, Proceedings of the International Congress on Biblical Archaeology, Jerusalem, 1984* (ed. Janet Amitai; Jerusalem: Israel Exploration Society, 1985), 301–12.

29.  Ibid., 306.

30.  Ibid., 307.

While many Israelites may have been capable of the mechanics of writing in its most basic form, surely few possessed the requisite skill necessary to produce the kinds of sophisticated texts preserved in the Hebrew Bible.[31] It seems prudent, therefore, when speaking of literacy, to make a distinction between the ability to write something and the ability to produce literature. Put differently, we might distinguish between rudimentary writing and refined writing. Rudimentary writing would include the ability to write one's own name, to record basic receipts of goods received, and perhaps even to engrave words on a seal or other object. Refined writing, by contrast, would be restricted to a particular social group and would result in the production of highly complex texts demonstrating great learning and skill in the artful use of repetition, direct discourse, rhetorical patterning and the like. For the purposes of this study, I consider literate those Israelite who either produced or consumed refined writing. To borrow language from William V. Harris, this can be referred to as "scribal literacy" over against "craftsman's literacy"[32] or those who might only be "signature-literate." Given this understanding of literacy, it is clear that the vast majority of Israelites in the monarchic period were most certainly illiterate. This is hardly surprising since, as sociologist Gerhard E. Lenski reminds us, "In agrarian societies *limited literacy* was the rule."[33]

In this context, the vast majority of Israelites would have had no access to the Solomonic narrative by reading it. It is possible, however, that the general populace may have heard it read aloud since there were occasions in which covenant, ritual, and legal texts were read publically.[34] It is reasonable to assume the same situation may have prevailed for historical texts. Still, if we hope to understand the production and primary mode of consumption of this narrative, it behooves us to focus our attention on the scribal elite,[35] noting their training and exploring both their relationship to, and their attitude toward, the centers of power located in the temple and palace.

---

31. The kindergarten child who is able to write her own name is not capable of reading, let alone producing something like J. R. R. Tolkien's *The Lord of the Rings.* Many years of education and practice would be required before that could become a possibility.

32. Harris, *Ancient Literacy*, 7.

33. Gerhard E. Lenski, *Power and Privilege: A Theory of Social Stratification* (New York: McGraw–Hill, 1966), 208.

34. See, e.g., Deut 31:10–13; Neh 8:1–12.

35. By "scribal elite" I mean all those who would be considered professional scribes, as well as those who could read and write more complex narratives but did not do so as their primary vocational.

## Scribal Schools

As Michael Fishbane opines, "Regrettably, no biblical sources describe the training of ancient Israelite scribes."[36] There is, of course, no explicit mention of schools in the biblical record.[37] The specific question of whether scribal schools[38] existed in monarchic Judah has been a subject of considerable debate and one which we can only briefly comment upon here.[39] The answer one gives to this question is largely contingent upon the degree of bureaucratic complexity envisioned at various stages in pre-exilic Israel.[40] While not demonstrating a high degree of complexity, the administrative lists which recount various state officials and their positions during the reigns of David and Solomon (1 Kgs 4)[41] suggest

36.  Fishbane, *Biblical Interpretation*, 25.

37.  G. I. Davies, "Were there Schools in Ancient Israel?" in *Wisdom in Ancient Israel* (ed. John Day, Robert P. Gordon, and H. G. M. Williamson; Cambridge: Cambridge University Press, 1995), 199–211 (199–200), suggests 2 Kgs 6:1 refers to "a place of instruction" and finds circumstantial evidence for teachers and schools in references such as Prov 4:7; 5:13; 13:14; 15:7; 17:16; 23:23; Ps 119:99; Isa 8:14, 16; 1 Chr 25:8.

38.  I follow Philip R. Davies' (*Scribes and Schools: The Canonization of the Hebrew Scriptures* [Louisville, Ky.: Westminster John Knox, 1998], 76) use of this term to refer to "an educational institution and not a group of like-minded scribes."

39.  See, e.g., E. W. Heaton, *The School Tradition of the Old Testament* (Oxford: Oxford University Press, 1994); André Lemaire, *Les Ecoles et la formation de la Bible dans l'ancien Israël* (Fribourg: Editions Universitaires, 1981), and idem, "The Sage in School and Temple," in *The Sage in Israel and the Ancient Near East* (ed. John G. Gammie and Leo G. Perdue; Winona Lake, Ind.: Eisenbrauns, 1990), 165–81. Davies (*Scribes and Schools*, 79) dubs Lemaire "the most enthusiastic" proponent of an extensive systems of scribal schools in monarchic Judah. A critique of Lemaire's reconstruction is offered by James Crenshaw, "Education in Ancient Israel," *JBL* 104 (1985): 601–15; cf. also his monograph (*Education in Ancient Israel*, 85–113) in which he finds the epigraphic evidence for schools in Israel from the eighth century onward particularly convincing, though not to the extent envisioned by Lemaire. The minimalist view is represented by Haran, "Literacy and Schools," 81–95; D. W. Jamieson-Drake, *Scribes and Schools in Monarchic Judah: A Socio-archaeological Approach* (JSOTSup 109; Sheffield: Almond Press, 1991), and Davies, *Scribes and Schools*, 74–88, who consigns the emergence of scribal schools to the Persian period (p. 77). For a balanced assessment of the question, see Davies, "Were there Schools in Ancient Israel?," 199–211.

40.  It seems prudent to avoid extremes in either direction. While von Rad's burgeoning bureaucracy flourishing during the "Solomonic Enlightenment" has been rejected by most scholars, nihilistic attempts to deny there ever was a Solomon (not to mention a Solomonic kingdom) seem far more exaggerated.

41.  Following Richard S. Hess ("The Form and Structure of the Solomonic District List in 1 Kings 4:7–19," in *Crossing Boundaries and Linking Horizons:*

that some system of training was in place for scribes in monarchic Judah. Whether this system should be described as a "school" and whether it is beneficial to compare the situation in Judah to the well attested scribal schools in Egypt and Mesopotamia is debatable. The epigraphic evidence has been cited both for[42] and against[43] the evidence of schools. We need not enter that debate since our interests are more in the social location of the producers of these texts. Regardless of whether there were schools in ancient Israel, the fact remains that very few individuals were formally trained in the art of writing, particularly in the art of writing literary texts. As McNutt suggests, "Whatever form their training took, scribal activity was most likely sponsored and controlled by government [and temple!] authorities."[44] It is this dynamic of state sponsorship that now occupies our attention as we explore various relationships between scribes and the powers that be.

We are now ready to direct our attention to a more focused profile of the scribe in ancient Israel. For this effort I will utilize a series of dichotomies in an effort to draw out several broad characteristics of scribes in the monarchic period. These, in turn, will provide a framework for understanding the socio-political context out of which these scribes operated and from which propagandistic and subversive texts emerged.

## *Tethered and Untethered Scribes*

To begin, it is important to differentiate between those scribes who were organizationally attached and those who were not. In order to do so, I am borrowing the notion of a "tether index" from Berlinerblau who has developed it in response to Philip R. Davies' essay, "Is there a Class in

---

*Studies in Honor of Michael C. Astour on His 80th Birthday* [ed. Gordon D. Young, Mark W. Chavalas, and Richard E. Averbeck; Bethesda, Md.: CDL Press, 1997], 279–92) and contra Paul S. Ash ("Solomon's? District? List," *JSOT* 67 [1995]: 67–86), I would argue that these administrative lists provide us with a reasonable picture of the actual constituency of the Israelite court.

42. E.g. Davies, "Were there Schools in Ancient Israel?," 199–211.

43. Stuart Weeks, *Early Israelite Wisdom* (Oxford Theological Monographs; New York: Oxford University Press, 1994), 137–53. Cf. also Haran ("Literacy and Schools," 85–95) who does not believe abecedaries provide evidence for scribal schools but rather assigns them to artisans who produced them for various reasons: practice texts, a guide for their engraving, decorative purposes, or possibly just for the "thrill" of it. This thesis has much to commend it since it explains why these abecedaries were often carved on stone (an odd medium for school exercises) and also accounts for the total absence of any corrective marks which would be expected if these were written in an instructional context.

44. McNutt, *Reconstructing*, 167.

this Text?"[45] Berlinerblau observes the distinction Davies makes "between 'scribes in the service of the state' and scribes who maintain varying degrees of autonomy from royal power."[46] He proposes we designate members of the former group "tethered intellectuals" and members of the latter group "less tethered" or "untethered." While Berlinerblau extends these categories by including some discussion of a scribe's loyalty to his patron, I have chosen to restrict Berlinerblau's "tether index" to refer solely to a scribe's degree of *attachment to* or *autonomy from* the royal/temple establishment.[47]

The basic principle of the tether index is simple: the tighter the tether, the stronger the attachment, thereby resulting in lesser scribal autonomy from the employing institution. The opposite is equally true: the looser the tether, the weaker the attachment which resulted in greater scribal autonomy. Viewed along a continuum, every scribe can be classified as being more or less tethered, or in some instances as being untethered. But this needs to be worked out more carefully. To do so, it is helpful to differentiate two separate though not completely unrelated strands of the tether, one related primarily to economics and power, the other to levels of supervision.

Regarding economics and power, the tether index works like this: the greater the scribe's dependence upon the royal establishment for financial security and social position, the tighter the tether, and vice versa. For example, a scribe who not only works for, but is fully employed by, the state or temple can be said to be much more tightly tethered than a scribe who has only occasional contact with these institutions or is only partially

45. Philip R. Davies, "Is there a Class in this Text?," in Sneed, ed., *Concepts of Class in Ancient Israel*, 37–51.

46. Jacques Berlinerblau, "The Present Crisis and Uneven Triumphs of Biblical Sociology: Responses to N. K. Gottwald, S. Mandell, P. Davies, M. Sneed, R. Simkins and N. Lemche," in Sneed, ed., *Concepts of Class in Ancient Israel*, 99–120 (108).

47. Berlinerblau ("The Present Crisis," 108) believes tethered intellectuals "faithfully give literary expression to the state's ideological agenda" while untethered intellectuals "can modify, *or even subvert*, the themes which their patrons (who might be illiterate or too unsophisticated to notice textual nuances) wish to stress" (my emphasis). In my estimation, the issue of whether a scribe supported or subverted his patron cannot be predicated solely on the basis of his attachment to, or autonomy from, an institution. While organizational attachments would have surely impacted a scribe's literary loyalties, these attachments alone cannot be considered determinative of how that scribe might use his literary abilities *vis-à-vis* his patron. Many additional factors must also be weighed and considered. For that reason, I have chosen to treat the issue of a scribe's allegiance separately. See my discussion of submissive and subversive scribes below.

supported by them. Untethered scribes would refer to those individuals who worked independently, receiving no compensation from the major institutions of power. Whereas tethered scribes had tight institutional connections and may be considered part of the royal establishment, untethered scribes were institutionally unconnected, working instead for an individual or individuals. These two general categories of scribes are succinctly delineated by Aaron Demsky who writes: "Scribes of various degrees of competence were attached to all government and temple offices. Apparently there were also independent scribes who either served the public or were in the employ of men of means."[48] By and large, most scribes in the ancient world were of the former variety, that is, they were tethered.[49] This is due, in part, to the highly specialized nature of writing itself and the limited demand for scribal services. As Davies aptly notes, "Writing is an economically supported activity, requiring the specialized knowledge of writing and, not least, a purpose."[50] Since learning to read and write required both leisure time and surplus resources, we can surmise that those who were trained for such tasks were trained by the elite and were, therefore, often obliged to serve the royal/temple establishment in some capacity in return for their training.

Given these economic considerations and the notion of restricted literacy in Israel, it seems doubtful that many untethered scribes could have arisen in that context. Where would such individuals have learned the requisite skills vital to their trade and who would have paid them to write? Indeed, examples of institutionally unconnected or independent "scribes for hire" are not forthcoming from the pages of the Hebrew Bible.[51] The most celebrated, albeit the *only* biblical example, is Jeremiah's amanuensis Baruch (Jer 36:4).[52] Thus, when speaking of

48. Aaron Demsky, "Scribe," *Encyclopaedia Judaica* 14:1041–43 (1042).
49. Schniedewind (*How the Bible Became a Book*, 37) regards all early scribes this way. He writes, "The scribes were not independent, but served at the discretion of the ruling groups who brought them into existence, provided for their sustenance, and controlled their access to the public."
50. Philip R. Davies, *In Search of "Ancient Israel"* (2d ed.; JSOTSup 148; Sheffield: Sheffield Academic Press, 1995), 101.
51. Of course, the absence of evidence in this regard is hardly conclusive. In the Mesopotamian context, Oppenheim ("Intellectual in Mesopotamian Society," 41) speaks of diviners as "scholar-scribes" whom he describes as "unattached professionals who live solely by their learning…without institutional support." While such individuals may clearly be classified as untethered scribes, there seems to be no functional analogy in ancient Israel.
52. Attempts to link Baruch (and his brother Seriah) with the royal court (William L. Holladay, *Jeremiah 2: A Commentary on the Book of the Prophet Jeremiah Chapters 26–52* [Hermeneia; Minneapolis: Fortress, 1989], 215), are unconvincing.

scribes in Palestine during the monarchic period, perhaps it is best simply to regard the vast majority of them as being more or less tethered to
the institutions which nurtured and sustained them.

But there is another dimension of the tether index we have yet to consider which is related to the degree of "supervision" a scribe experienced.
For this strand of the tether, the basic principle is as follows: the most
tightly tethered scribe is the most closely monitored one. Tightly tethered
scribes were highly attached to, and very carefully controlled by, the
palace and temple administration. Such scribes operated on a short leash,
so to speak. Their work would have been subject to a considerable
amount of scrutiny and supervision by their patrons or those loyal to
them. Less-tethered scribes, on the other hand, experienced less direct
supervision and therefore enjoyed more freedom insofar as their writing
endeavors were concerned. Presumably, all institutionally attached
scribes were more or less tethered in this supervisory sense.

Regrettably, we are never apprised of the degree of scribal supervision
exerted in ancient Israel, making it is impossible to know with any degree
of certainty which scribes were more or less closely monitored in any
given situation. One might imagine that scribes of a more senior rank
were given quite a bit more freedom while their junior partners were
more closely monitored. On the other hand, it is equally possible that the
most senior scribes were watched especially closely due to the sensitive
nature of much of their work. We lack information. Furthermore, while
certain projects might have required extensive oversight and control,
many others would have been far less critical and may have been completely unregulated. And finally, there is the question of how much
"manpower" these institutions could spare for such supervisory tasks.

In short, the amount of supervision exerted over a scribe's literary
endeavors would have varied considerably in accordance with the task
assigned, the scribe involved, and the particular resources of the institution. It will be important to keep in mind the reality of this element of
potential vigilantism as we proceed. Such surveillance would necessitate
any unauthorized critique to be undertaken with the utmost care and
stealth. Otherwise, the dissatisfied scribe crafting it might find himself
without more than just his job! But here I am getting ahead of myself.

### Royal Scribes and Temple Scribes

In light of the foregoing discussion, we may now consider two particular
"varieties" of institutionally tethered intellectuals. Since "there can be
little doubt that much of the literature composed during the period of the

Monarchy was the work of either the royal or the priestly [i.e. temple] scribes,"[53] it is imperative to consider the nature, role, and activity of these individuals. As alluded to earlier, this task is impeded by the paucity of information preserved in the Hebrew Bible about such individuals.

There are basically only two terms used to describe writing professionals in ancient Israel: *sōpēr* and *mazkîr*.[54] The term *sōpēr*, usually translated as "scribe" or "secretary," would seem to include a broad range of individuals occupied with various writing *and* non-writing functions in both temple and palace. The role of the *mazkîr* ("recorder") is largely a mystery.[55] The following discussion explores both the assignments and affiliations of these writing professionals whom I shall refer to by the descriptive designations "royal scribes" and "temple scribes," designations which denote the institution to which these individuals were tethered.

## Royal Scribes

Royal scribes[56] were members of an elite class[57] which consisted of aristocrats, retainers, court administrators, and other fortunate individuals who enjoyed the special privileges accompanying those who were part of the royal establishment.[58] Royal scribes did not, however, all enjoy the

53. R. N. Whybray, "The Sage in the Israelite Royal Court," in Gammie and Perdue, eds., *The Sage in Israel and the Ancient Near East*, 133–39 (137).

54. The situation is quite different in the bureaucratically more complex Mesopotamian setting, where the Proto-Lu list yields no less than "eighteen varieties" of scribes. See Ronald Sweet, "The Sage in Mesopotamian Palaces and Royal Courts," in Gammie and Perdue, eds., *The Sage in Israel and the Ancient Near East*, 99–107 (103).

55. The relationship between the *sōpēr* and the *mazkîr* is unclear. A. D. Crown ("Messengers and Scribes: The ספר and מלאך in the Old Testament," *VT* 14 [1974]: 366–70) contends that *sōpēr* should be understood as "royal messenger" and speculates that the *mazkîr* might be understood as his "official interpreter," though his argument is rather unconvincing.

56. E. Lipiński, "Royal and State Scribes in Ancient Jerusalem," in Emerton, ed., *Congress Volume: Jerusalem, 1986*, 157–64; and Whybray, "The Sage in the Israelite Royal Court," 133–39.

57. The debate about what constitutes a "class" or whether the concept of class is useful in the study of pre-industrial societies lies outside the scope of this study. I am primarily using the term in traditional Weberian fashion to refer to a group of individuals who share a similar economic status. For a relatively recent collection of essays on the subject, see Sneed, ed., *Concepts of Class in Ancient Israel*, esp. pp. 53–57 of Sneed's contribution, "A Middle Class in Ancient Israel?" which provides an account of the problems and possibilities involved in addressing "the question of class in ancient Israel" (p. 53).

58. See McNutt (*Reconstructing*, 167–68) for a discussion of these and other groups of individuals who had special access to the center of royal power.

same level of privileges[59] and it may be useful to differentiate between scribes belonging to the core elite and those who may be considered part of the sub-elite.[60] The core elite includes those royal scribes who appear to have held an office analogous to that of modern day Cabinet Secretaries in the United States, having responsibilities only remotely related to the clerical duties we often associate with "secretaries" today. Such senior officers are occasionally listed among the highest ranking members of the king's "cabinet."[61] Examples include Seraiah/Sheva (read Shausha[62]) under David (2 Sam 8:17; 20:25),[63] his sons Elihoreph and Ahijah under Solomon (1 Kgs 4:3), Shebnah under Hezekiah (2 Kgs 18:18), an unnamed scribe under Jehoash (2 Kgs 12:10//2 Chr 24:11),[64] and Shaphan under Josiah (2 Kgs 22; 2 Chr 34:8–18). As this list suggests, there is some evidence that the royal cabinet scribal positions were passed down from father to son and thus kept in the family. It is clear that these individuals were among the king's most trusted officials, serving the king in a variety of capacities ranging from Secretary of State to military conscriptionist.[65] They, along with other senior advisors, were the king's closest counselors and the people to whom he turned when making major decisions. They were also involved in the highest levels of diplomacy

59. Cf. the remarks of Bryce, *Kingdom of the Hittites*, 418: "No doubt there was a clear hierarchy within the scribal class, ranging at the bottom from persons engaged in mechanical tasks such as copying texts to those at the top who were amongst the most important consultants to the king."

60. These designations are Crenshaw's (*Education in Ancient Israel*, 40–41), though my use here differs since I consider the possibility that scribes may be part of both the core *and* the sub-elite whereas Crenshaw consigns all scribes to the latter category. In this regard, I concur with the conclusions of Sneed ("A Middle Class in Ancient Israel?," 64) who argues that "priests and scribes were patronized by the master class and constitute a broader social category, intellectuals, that should be viewed as an appendage of this class, not as distinct or independent of it. In fact, many of this layer were probably also members of the master class."

61. Fishbane (*Biblical Interpretation*, 25) speculates that the "scribe" listed in the administrative lists "was the overseer of a diversified scribal network," though this is impossible to ascertain for the monarchic period in ancient Israel.

62. Following McCarter (*II Samuel*, 254, 433) who cites the evidence for reading both proper names as *šawšā'* (Shausha) which suggests one, not two individuals are in view.

63. Cf. 1 Chr 27:32, which mentions Jonathan, an otherwise unknown uncle of David, as "a man of understanding and a scribe."

64. This is the only individual in the Hebrew Bible designation as *sōpēr hamme-lek*. Shaphan appears to function in a similar capacity in 2 Kgs 22.

65. Examples include an unnamed scribe (2 Kgs 25:19//Jer 52:25) and Jeiel who was part of Uzziah's administration (2 Chr 26:11).

and functioned as the king's representatives.[66] Moreover, there is no question that some of these high ranking scribes could wield considerable power and were a force to reckon with.[67] Though undoubtedly literate and often multilingual,[68] it is unclear how much actual writing these "court scribes" were required to perform.

Scribes of lesser standing, who were absolutely indispensable to the efficient maintenance of the state, may be regarded as part of the subelite. These "scribes of more humble station"[69] presumably shouldered the bulk of the writing assignments necessary for the monarchical bureaucracy to operate effectively. While some of these assignments were meaningful, many were probably quite menial, what we might call "grunt work." Still, their ability to read and write, and their association with king and court, gave them a privileged standing which elevated them among their compatriots and set them apart.[70]

Second, as previously alluded to, royal scribes were clients of the king.[71] They were employed by and financially dependent upon the state.[72] In his study on scribes in the Mesopotamian context, Ronald Sweet observes that "the leisure…necessary for scholarship required patronage as much in ancient Mesopotamia as it has in later ages and in other lands, and the palace was better able to supply patronage than were private individuals or even the temples."[73] Such a connection surely influenced

66. This is especially striking in the Assyrian crisis during Hezekiah's reign when the Rabshakeh calls for the king and the following three individuals emerge: Eliakim, who was over the palace ( *'al habbāyit*), Shebna the scribe (*sōpēr*), and Joah the recorder (*mazkîr*) (2 Kgs 18:18//Isa 36:3). It is clear that such individuals were part of the king's inner circle and had direct access to him (2 Kgs 18:37; 19:2//Isa 36:22; 37:2).

67. Consider, for example, the activities of the Shaphan family whose support of the prophet Jeremiah stymied Jehoiakim's efforts to eliminate him (Jer 36:1–26). See also the notorious case of Yatarmu, the Ugaritic scribe who rebelled against the king in A. F. Rainey, "The Scribe at Ugarit, His Position and Influence," *PIASH* 3 (1969): 126–47 (145–46).

68. The scribe Shebna(h), along with Eliakim and Joah, was at least conversant in both Hebrew and Aramaic (2 Kgs 18:26//Isa 36:11).

69. Blenkinsopp, *Sage, Priest, Prophet*, 30.

70. More will be said shortly about the particular kinds of writing assignments such scribes were given.

71. Regarding the situation in Mesopotamia, Sweet ("Sage in Mesopotamian Palaces," 104 n. 17) believes "it is reasonable to assume that they [i.e. the *ummânus*] were close to the king and that the literary works attributed to them were written under royal patronage."

72. Rainey ("Scribe at Ugarit," 142–46) discusses grants of real estate given to loyal subjects of the king, including scribes.

73. Sweet, "Sage in Mesopotamian Palaces," 107.

both what royal scribes wrote and why they wrote it. It comes as no surprise then to discover that their literary productions typically reflected the interests and concerns of the ruling class which they served.[74] Working from within the establishment, royal scribes had a vested interest in maintaining (or increasing!) the power and prestige of the royal establishment. As noted in one of the epigraphs to this chapter, "Clients usually assume the world view and values of their patrons; to do otherwise would be risky."[75] Presumably, they would have been cautious about criticizing the state, at least openly.

Third, royal scribes were responsible for the production and preservation of a wide variety of written texts necessary for the effective administration of a state bureaucracy. E. Lipiński's study regards these royal scribes as "compilers of royal annals, writers of state letters, collectors of proverbs and other items, and authors who diffused the Davidic ideology and the royal propaganda."[76] They would have been responsible for keeping a written record of goods exchanged, tribute received, and taxes collected. Royal scribes maintained diplomatic correspondence and drew up legal documents which represented a broad range of topics: boundary lists, marriage contracts, court decisions, political treaties, and the like. These scribes kept the royal archives, which included organizing, classifying, preserving, and retrieving important state documents.[77] Finally, and of particular interest to us, these scribes produced political propaganda.[78] Such tendentious writing was created for a variety of reasons

---

74. Cf. J. A. Brinkman, "Through a Glass Darkly: Esarhaddon's Retrospects on the Downfall of Babylon," *JAOS* 103 (1983): 35–42 (41), who argues that the royal scribes writing Esarhaddon's Babylon Inscriptions "were reflecting the interests of their patron."

75. Sneed, "A Middle Class in Ancient Israel?," 64.

76. Lipiński, "Royal and State Scribes," 157.

77. See especially Davies, *Scribes and Schools*, 15–36 et passim; Fishbane, *Biblical Interpretation*, 23–43.

78. Schniedewind (*How the Bible Became a Book*, 64–90), who argues that "biblical literature began to flourish in the late eighth century" (p. 64), regards prelate eighth century Israelites scribes as bureaucratic functionaries who engaged in rather mundane administrative assignments (see, e.g., pp. 40–41, 61). While scribes obviously did this type of work, this assessment seems unnecessary restrictive. For example, Schniedewind fails to appreciate the important role such scribes played in producing *literary* propaganda—not just monumental inscriptions. Schniedewind claims "it is difficult to assume that royal or temple scribes [in the employ of some of Israel's first kings] would have engaged in the composition of large literary works" (p. 63). But why? It is not at all difficult to imagine a royal scribe(s) during the reign of Solomon being commissioned to produce a text like 1 Kgs 1–2 in the king's defense. Such a text would be most necessary when Solomon's irregular

such as defending a king against claims of illegitimacy, demonstrating his divine approval, and generally enhancing his reputation.[79] In short, royal scribes engaged in every aspect of writing necessary to keep the bureaucracy running smoothly.

*Temple Scribes*[80]

It is well known that temples in the ancient Near East were complex bureaucracies which required considerable personnel to operate effectively. The temple administration would have had its own group of scribes who would have functioned (semi-)independently from those residing in the palace. Like royal scribes, temple scribes were part of an elite class who may have been partly supported by the king and who were similarly concerned about preserving their privileged positions of power and authority. One also suspects that certain aspects of the temple scribe's training would have been similar to that of their royal counterpart. From what we can tell, they often shared similar duties and responsibilities, such as the collection of tithes, offerings, or taxes, and the maintenance of economic records. Given these similarities, what distinguishes a royal scribe from a temple scribe?

To begin, it seems safe to say that temple scribes were less concerned with the political maneuverings associated with the palace than were their royal counterparts. While certainly not uninterested nor oblivious to what happened around the throne, their concern was more religious and less political, though one must be cautious not to draw too great a distinction here as the priestly overthrown of Athaliah makes abundantly clear (2 Kgs 11)! Additionally, though it is difficult to prove, one suspects that temple scribes were, generally speaking, less politically powerful than the highest ranking royal scribes. Temple scribes were not at the forefront of international diplomacy and presumably did not enjoy the

accession was most recent, not a couple hundred years later. Thus, while Schniedewind rightly emphasizes the important connection between scribes and kings (p. 40), he mistakenly limits the scope of their literary activity.

79. In the Assyrian context, enhancing the king's reputation by recounting (with no little embellishment!) the sovereign's great military exploits was quite common. See the discussion by Hayim Tadmor, "Propaganda, Literature, Historiography: Cracking the Code of the Assyrian Royal Inscriptions," in *Assyria 1995: Proceedings of the 10th Anniversary Symposium of the Neo-Assyrian Text Corpus Project, Helsinki, September 7–11, 1995* (ed. Simo Parpola and Robert M. Whiting; Helsinki: Helsinki University Press, 1997), 325–38.

80. By temple scribes, I mean those individuals who served in the temple during the monarchy. They are to be distinguished from the priestly writers (P) who are active in the post-exilic period and thus are not the focus of my discussion.

same kinds of opportunities for advancement as did scribes in the royal employ.

Although the king often co-opted the temple to serve state interests, it would be misguided to view the temple as little more than a tool of the state. While it seems reasonable to conclude that the activities of the Jerusalem temple were more closely monitored than those of outlying sanctuaries, geographical proximity should not be taken to suggest ideological unanimity. Despite the close connection between palace and temple in Jerusalem,[81] there were clearly tensions and sharp ideological differences between these two powerful institutions. In the context of frequent and sometimes bitter disagreements, it is not difficult to imagine that temple scribes occasionally might use their writings as a means to indicate their favor or displeasure with the king and his politics. Moreover, even if temple scribes were paid in part by the king, it seems reasonable to assume that some of them enjoyed a relative measure of freedom from the king's direct control.

The religious interests of temple scribes, such as concern for the correct preservation of rituals and the proper maintenance of the cult, had a direct and obvious impact upon what they wrote. Temple scribes fastidiously kept genealogical records, composed liturgical texts, and recorded laws and general instructions relating to the temple service. As R. N. Whybray observes, "Psalms, laws, and other cultic material are probably of priestly origin, although the lack of information provided by the texts themselves about their authorship makes it impossible to draw a sharp distinction."[82] Additionally, it is also possible that some scribes had the responsibility of teaching the law to the general population,[83] though it is difficult to know how much of this took place during the monarchic period.

With these admittedly general profiles of royal and temple scribes, we are still left with several nagging questions. For instance, how loyal were tethered scribes to their patrons? Did they always write what they were told? And how might they have registered a protest against the state when their ideas clashed with those of the ruling class? My attempt to address these questions leads me to posit a distinction between those scribes who submitted to the will of the king/temple authority, and those subverted it.

---

81. Ibid.
82. Whybray, "Sage in the Israelite Royal Court," 137.
83. Cf. the concept of Levitical Torah teachers in Max Weber, *Ancient Judaism* (trans. and ed. Hans H. Gerth and Don Martindale; Glencoe, Ill.: The Free Press, 1952), 176–79.

## Submissive and Subversive Scribes

Whereas "royal" and "temple" describe the institutional affiliations of scribes, "submissive" and "subversive" describe their literary intentions. As such, every royal and temple scribe can be further characterized as being at times either submissive or subversive. As I am using it, the designation "submissive scribes" refers to those temple/palace scribes who used their considerable literary talents in accordance with the wishes and desires of their patrons. "Subversive scribes," on the other hand, refers to those individuals who choose *not* to do so, opting instead to launch an attack or critique of some sort against their patrons and the institutions they served. Additionally, scribes may be considered subversive if their literary product is destabilizing even if that writing has been commissioned by their patron. For example, a temple scribe who writes a covert critique of the state at the behest of his temple patron is acting subversively regarding the king even though his efforts may not conflict with the will of his patron.

Presumably, individual scribes would vacillate between submission and subversion, depending in part upon the nature of the assignment and the degree to which their own ideological agenda may or may not have corresponded to that of their patron. Submission and subversion, therefore, differentiate between two fundamentally different *modi operandi* of tethered intellectuals which function at the *intentional* level. While both engage in writing projects paid for and sponsored by the royal/religious establishment, a submissive scribe would dutifully reproduce the ideology of the palace/temple whereas a subversive scribe might find some way to undermine it.

Max Weber's concept of ideal types proves especially beneficial for exploring this dichotomy between submissive and subversive scribes. As Joseph Blenkinsopp reminds us,

> An ideal type is a construct based on abstraction and conceptualization that has the purpose of guiding inquiry back into the mass of available data. Weber's ideal types were not intended to be normative. They served as a means of provisional classification, allowing for some preliminary understanding of the phenomenon, creating and testing hypotheses, distinguishing between constants and variables, and identifying deviations.[84]

---

84. Blenkinsopp, *Sage, Priest, Prophet*, 116.

Weber himself helpfully utilized the notion of ideal types to identify two general categories of prophets—ethical and exemplary.[85] This allowed him to compare and contrast the various associations, characteristics, beliefs, and goals of these two rather distinct categories of prophets which in turn further clarified the nature and mission of the prophets described in the pages of the Hebrew Bible. I will use a similar approach in my investigation of the literary intentions of royal and temple scribes.

### Submissive Scribes

Submissive scribes were loyalists. Satisfied to write on behalf of the king or palace, these scribes used their intellectual powers to support, maintain, and advance the cause of the royal establishment through their literary endeavors. Working under the aegis and patronage of the establishment, submissive scribes did what they were told. They were the "Yes Men" of the kingdom or temple. These scribes were "either constrained, or perfectly content, to put their literary talents in the service of the powers that be."[86]

Submissive scribes were particularly needed in both palace and temple administrations in order to produce, promote, and perpetuate royal ideology. Their texts were designed to foster consensus among diverse elements of the realm by legitimating the king and supporting his divine right to rule. This was especially necessary given the volatile political climate of agrarian states. In these socio-political hotspots, control of power was frequently up for grabs among disparate factions of the ruling elite. As Lenski notes, "the internal struggles for power, both violent and nonviolent, which plagued most agrarian states…[w]ere struggles between opposing factions of the privileged class, each seeking its own special advantage."[87] Simply gaining the throne was no guarantee of remaining there. In order to maintain control and stay in power, the king had to establish his rule through a mixture of force and consent. Consent rather than coercion was deemed the most prudent way to consolidate royal power since "the use of force was too costly and on the whole inefficient in maintaining royal power."[88] Indeed, "the genius of the hegemonic

85. See Max Weber, *The Sociology of Religion* (Boston: Beacon, 1963), 46–59 (55–59), and *Ancient Judaism*, 312–15.

86. Berlinerblau, "The Present Crisis," 108. Cf. Davies' (*In Search of "Ancient Israel"*, 103) comment, made in reference to Second Temple scribes but equally true of submissive scribes writing during the monarchic period: "These scribes write what their paymasters tell them to, or allow them to, which means generally that they write to safeguard or increase the power and prestige of the monarch or the temple."

87. Lenski, *Power and Privilege*, 211.

88. Whitelam, "Israelite Kingship," 121.

apparatus is precisely this ability to make allies, as opposed to enemies who, ultimately, require costly and complex coercive responses."[89] This "ability to make allies" and to create consensus came about with significant help from submissive scribes who were commissioned to produce various pieces of propaganda and who willingly complied.

Since religion is one of the most important consensus-creating mechanisms available to the state, it is natural to expect submissive scribes to foster the religious preferences and beliefs of the ruling elite, a symbolic system we might refer to as "official religion." The submissive scribes "employed by the monarchy were responsible for the creation, dissemination and maintenance of this 'official religion.'"[90] By using their considerable writing talents to promote and perpetuate this official religion, submissive scribes legitimated the king's right to rule by demonstrating his divine approval and support.

*Subversive Scribes*
According to Lloyd M. Barré, narratives such as 2 Kgs 9–11 along with "politically motivated works such as the Yahwist's Epic, the Succession Narrative, [and] the History of David's Rise, show that kings of Judah were well aware of the power of the word, and that the royal scribes of the Judean court stood ready to devote their mastery of rhetoric to the interests of the state."[91] While this is certainly true in many respects, as the foregoing discussion suggests, one wonders whether all scribes "stood ready to devote their mastery of rhetoric to the interests of the state" at all times. Certainly there were scribes who at times felt some personal snub or that the "party line" was immoral, not in their best interests, or otherwise objectionable.[92] Were these scribes always so servile? Was it even possible for scribes to act subversively and to incorporate a critique of the king in the very texts they were commissioned and paid to pro-

---

89. Berlinerblau, "The Present Crisis," 104. These insights are derived from his reading of Antonio Gramsci's *Selections from the Prison Notebooks*.

90. Jacques Berlinerblau, *The Vow and the "Popular Religious Groups" of Ancient Israel: A Philological and Sociological Inquiry* (JSOTSup 210; Sheffield: Sheffield Academic Press, 1996), 30.

91. Barré, *Rhetoric of Political Persuasion*, 142–43. He believes that "this genre of literature is typically the product of royal scribes who were commissioned to use their literary skills to defend a regime that had come to power through the use of violence" (p. 140).

92. This is obvious given the numerous critiques of the king, his policies, and sometimes even the very institution of kingship itself found in the Hebrew Bible. It seems likely, however, that many of these overt criticisms of the king stem from a later post-monarchic period.

duce? Some scholars think not. "In all of our historical texts," writes
Bleiberg in his study of Egyptian New Kingdom texts, "the official point
of view is communicated."[93] Was it so in Israel? Was a tethered scribe
always a loyal mouthpiece for the royal establishment? Did a scribe
always faithfully reproduce the dominant ideology? I think not.

I am suggesting that subversive scribes not only could but did resort to
subversive tactics when they became dissatisfied with the actions and/or
attitudes of the king or the ruling class. It is not hard to imagine a tethered
scribe finding himself at odds with his colleagues and the (other) members of the ruling class for any number of reasons, such as objections to
specific military policies, foreign alliances, or the "official" religious
position. A scribe's dissatisfaction could also stem from something as
mundane as a lack of personal recognition or the failure to be given the
more important assignments. Davies believes that "the necessity of
serving rulers to whom they may have regarded themselves as intellectu-
ally superior no doubt instilled in the scribes the techniques of satire and
ambiguity: the ability to inscribe on the surface of a political text their
own traces."[94] Whatever the reason, rather than turn a blind eye, subversive scribes went into action. No longer content simply to reproduce
royal ideology *ad nauseam*, these scribes challenged the *status quo*,
criticized the king, and undermined the dominant ideological assumptions through their writing.

But what king would stand for that? Even though the king himself was
probably not able to read these texts,[95] his literate supporters would surely
have brought any subversive or otherwise unfavorable documents to his
attention, resulting in swift punishment of those responsible. As a case in
point, consider the actions of King Jehoiakim who dispatched a posse to

---

93. Bleiberg, "Historical Texts as Political Propaganda," 5. It should be emphasized that Bleiberg is *only* considering New Kingdom texts here, leaving open the
possibility that he might hold a different view of other Egyptian texts.

94. Davies, *Scribes and Schools*, 19. It is these "traces" we shall be interested in
identifying as we explore the Solomonic narrative for evidence of subversion.

95. Although several Mesopotamian kings claimed to be able to read and write,
most of these claims are highly suspect, Ashurbanipal being a notable exception.
The only king in the Hebrew Bible who is explicitly said to read something is, oddly
enough, an unnamed Israelite king, possibly Jehoram (2 Kgs 5:7). Jehu, the military
officer turned king, is described as writing several (deadly!) letters in order to
consolidate his power (2 Kgs 10:1–3, 6–7), thereby implying that he too could both
read and write. The same is also true of Jezebel (1 Kgs 21:8–10). One cannot,
however, rule out the possibility that these kings made use of "submissive" scribes
not otherwise mentioned. If so, then it is not possible to speak of these kings being
literate in the sense in which I am using the term.

arrest Baruch and Jeremiah upon hearing (and incinerating!) the document Baruch had written at Jeremiah's dictation (Jer 36:20–26). If a
royal scribe wished to be subversive, and hoped to keep his job—and his
head—he needed to be extremely careful.

Since subversive (as well as submissive) scribes worked under the
auspices of the palace and temple, it stands to reason that they were
under the "control" of the primary power brokers within each of these
institutions. Still, as was noted above, it would be naive to assume that
the literary activity of each scribe received exactly the same level of
administrative oversight. Therefore it is not difficult to imagine differing
levels of freedom and constraint. Some scribes may have enjoyed considerable "autonomy" from the watchful eye of those in power while
others attracted the closest scrutiny. As observed earlier, the level of
watchfulness may have also been linked to the nature of the task
assigned. Those projects deemed most sensitive would have generated
special supervision while more menial scribal activities would have gone
largely unchecked. Still, any scribe attempting to write subversively was
engaging in risky behavior and needed to do so with the utmost caution.
It is only natural to assume these scribes would have taken every
precaution to minimize the risk of getting caught.

These preliminary remarks about the activities of subversive scribes
implicitly raise certain questions about the aims and possibilities of
literary subversion. Why did ancient writers produce subversive literature, and what did they hope to accomplish by it?

### *The Aims and Possibilities of Literary Subversion*

The aims and possibilities of literary subversion are, understandably,
rather diverse and any systematic treatment of the issue extends well
beyond the scope of this study. Here I must confine my remarks to some
brief provisional comments pertaining to literary subversion in the
Hebrew Bible. First, it seems relatively clear that overt literary subversion in the Hebrew Bible often reflects a desire seriously to diminish, if
not completely dismantle, the ruling apparatus.[96] Obviously, such sentiments were especially troublesome to the ruling elite since they called
for a totally new and completely reorganized set of power relations in
society.

In the case of covert subversion, which is the focus of our investigation, the situation seems more subdued and less radical. Concealed

96. See Mason, *Propaganda and Subversion*, 75–163.

subversion could be deployed for a variety of reasons.[97] For example, it might be intended to erode the legitimacy of a particular ruler(s) or to express criticism of ruling policies and/or practices. In some instances, it may have been hoped that such efforts would actually effect real social change, though it is difficult to determine whether this was the anticipated outcome. At other times, the secretive subversive may have simply been attempting to persuade others to adopt his particular point of view about some matter while having no particular "political" agenda. Most people enjoy being around others who think like they do and who share their values and perspectives. Presumably, subversive scribes were no different. Additionally, covert subversion might reflect a sophisticated way of griping and expressing discontent with prominent policies, practices, or persons. Alternatively, it might simply be an expression of ridicule, intended to belittle or otherwise disparage those who are or were in power. As such, its function might have been to provide entertainment— not to mention consensus and cohesion—for like-minded insiders. In any case, whatever the reason, the hope was that some would detect the cleverly disguised critique while others, especially those who would have found it threatening, would remain oblivious to it.

## *Subversive Scribal Techniques*

Assuming that many subversive scribes worked under the watchful eye of their patrons, it is natural to wonder how such individuals could register a critique of the royal/temple establishment and get away with it. How do such carefully monitored persons effectively engage in subversive activities? What techniques did they have at their disposal that would assist them in writing a compelling critique of the powers that be while escaping the consequences such "bad press" could easily elicit?

Admittedly, this clandestine critique is somewhat difficult to detect since subversive scribes were not in the habit of leaving their calling cards! The very nature of their work required them to disguise their subversive efforts, keeping them hidden from the watchful eye of those loyal to the palace/temple officials. Moreover, one assumes that the craftier the scribe the more difficult it may be to detect subversive elements. Still, if their work was to have its intended effect, it could not be so heavily camouflaged as to preclude everyone from appreciating it. This gives us

---

97. Specific examples will be provided in the following chapter and throughout my study of the Solomonic narrative. The nature of the discussion at this point is general and theoretical.

hope that such subversive encoding in literary texts is still recognizable and recoverable.

Enormous gains have been made in the last two decades in our understanding of the literary artistry, or poetics, of Hebrew narrative. A number of studies appearing in the early 1980s[98] discussed a variety of techniques scribes had at their disposal when crafting such texts. These and subsequent works have demonstrated how the biblical writers carefully and intentionally utilized such things as the art of reticence, repetition, direct dialogue, naming, and point of view to assist them in the act of communicating their message through narrative art. Of course, such techniques were not the sole property of scribes writing submissively. Subversive scribes would have also exploited these techniques to their own advantage when they felt it to be in their best interests.

In an attempt to demonstrate how surreptitious subversion may have been inscribed in the text, I will now explore a variety of subversive scribal techniques. The examples given below are intended to be illustrative and programmatic. Moreover, since our primary interest here is to suggest the *potential* mechanics of scribal subversion, it is not necessary to defend or refute the validity of each of the particular examples offered below.

*Camouflaged Character Critiques*
It is widely recognized that many biblical texts primarily reflect the interests of their producers. This means that even though such texts may (or may not) yield some reliable "historical" information about the people, places, and events to which they refer, they do reveal important clues about the socio-historical setting and concerns of those responsible for their production. Thus, when reading stories about Abraham or Joseph, rather than first asking what these might teach us about conditions in Palestine or Egypt during the second millennium BCE, we might begin by asking what these stories reveal about the attitudes and circumstances of their writers, presumably during the period of the monarchy.[99]

---

98. Some of pioneering studies include Shimon Bar-Efrat, *Narrative Art in the Bible* (Tel Aviv: Sifriat Poalim, 1979; repr., JSOTSup 70; Sheffield: Almond Press, 1989); Robert Alter, *The Art of Biblical Narrative* (New York: Basic Books, 1981); Adele Berlin, *Poetics and Interpretation of Biblical Narrative* (Bible and Literature Series 9; Sheffield: Almond Press, 1983; repr., Winona Lake, Ind.: Eisenbrauns, 1994); Meir Sternberg, *The Poetics of Biblical Narrative: Ideological Literature and the Drama of Reading* (Bloomington: Indiana University Press, 1985).

99. In this regard, note the following two monograph-length attempts to read portions of the Hebrew Bible as political allegory: Joel Rosenberg, *King and Kin: Political Allegory in the Hebrew Bible* (Bloomington: Indiana University Press,

While there were many ways the past could be used to address present concerns, one especially intriguing method was to use an ancient character as a foil or cipher for someone in the present.[100] By cloaking the present in the words and deeds of characters from the past, it would be possible to deliver a critique of contemporary persons and practices with some degree of impunity.

As one example, consider Gary A. Rendsburg's reading of Gen 38.[101] Rejecting the documentary hypothesis, Rendsburg nonetheless contends that much of Genesis was written in the tenth century, during the reign of King David. He believes that the author of Gen 38 intentionally designed the story so that the characters there match "personalities from David's circle." In this way, the story of Judah and Tamar, ostensibly a story about Israel's ancestors, is really a story about David and his family. Without pressing for exact parallels, Rendsburg sets forth a clever case by examining seven correspondences between Judah's family and David's family.[102] Rendsburg believes this very carefully crafted tale was written "to poke fun at the royal family" and believes it to be "mocking the king and his court."[103] This kind of covert critique, utilizing the patriarchal period, is just the sort of thing we would expect from a subversive scribe. As Rendsburg astutely observes, "By setting the story in Israel's distant past, the author can plead innocent if ever accused of directly insulting the royal family."[104] Placing this story in the distant past

1986), and David S. Sperling, *The Original Torah: The Political Intent of the Bible's Writers* (New York: New York University Press, 1998).

100. As with all these methods, the same technique could be used for propagandistic purposes. For just one example, see Richard D. Nelson, "Josiah in the Book of Joshua," *JBL* 100 (1981): 531–40.

101. Gary A. Rendsburg, "David and his Circle in Genesis XXXVIII," *VT* 36 (1986): 438–46.

102. Judah = David; Hirah = Hiram; the daughter of Shua = Bathsheba; Er = deceased firstborn son of David and Bathsheba; Onan = Amnon; Shelah = Solomon; Tamar = Tamar.

103. Rendsburg, "David and His Circle," 444 and 445, respectively. For a propagandistic reading of the patriarchal narratives, consider Robert L. Hubbard, Jr., *The Book of Ruth* (NICOT; Grand Rapids: Eerdmans, 1988), 39–42. Hubbard argues that the book of Ruth has been intentionally modeled after the patriarchal traditions which he believes were politically intended to support and legitimate David.

104. Rendsburg, "David and His Circle," 445. Intriguingly, Rendsburg recognizes the propagandistic potential of Gen 38 which might have been intended to excuse the considerable familial strife experience within David's household. He writes (p. 445 n. 19), "The story might be an apologia for the royal family, stating in a sense that the clan has always suffered from familial problems." My thesis, which suggests that propaganda was one of the most effective means of disguising subversion, would allow both possibilities to exist simultaneously, not making it an either/or.

mitigates some of the dangers inherent in such subversive writing. This is exactly the kind of covert creation a subversive scribe working under the watchful eye of royal administrators could write and get away with.

A somewhat different, though not altogether dissimilar approach, is offered in a brief study by Knut Holter, which, if correct, would yield another very interesting example of how the past might be used to critique the present.[105] This time the primary vehicle of critique is an animal rather than a person. Holter believes the serpent in Gen 3 should be regarded as a metaphoric symbol for "Israel's political neighbours/enemies."[106] Assigning this text to the Yahwist writer, and assuming a tenth-century date for its composition, Holter contends "there is an *undertone* of criticism in the account, a criticism against the open internationalism in Solomon's foreign policy."[107] He attempts to establish this claim, in part, by examining the careful deployment of the *leitmotif ʿāśā* in Gen 2–3 *vis-à-vis* the women and the serpent and by citing other biblical passages in which *nḥš* may be regarded as a metaphor for Israel's enemies.[108]

Holter is not alone is sensing a Solomonic critique in this story. He cites the works of both Mandfred Görg[109] and W. von Soden[110] who similarly regard this text as containing a concealed critique against Solomon. "Von Soden and Görg both emphasize that J's criticism of the Solomonic policy is, and had to be, rather disguised."[111] Once again, this is consistent with our understanding of the nature and *modus operandi* of a subversive scribe who only partially conceals his critique so that some would "get it" without giving so much away that others could prove it behind a doubt. In sum, the contributions of both Rendsburg and Holter are especially intriguing—whether correct or not—since they illustrate the possible presence of subversive scribal activity in the Hebrew Bible

---

105. Knut Holter, "The Serpent in Eden as a Symbol of Israel's Political Enemies: A Yahwistic Criticism of the Solomonic Foreign Policy?," *SJOT* 1 (1990): 106–12.

106. Ibid., 106.

107. Holter, "Serpent in Eden," 107.

108. Isa 14:29; Jer 8:17; 46:22.

109. Manfred Görg, "Die 'Sünde' Salomos: Zeitkritische Aspekte der jahwistischen Sündenfallerzählung," *BN* 16 (1981): 42–59. See also his "Das Wort zur Schlange (Gen 3,14 f.): Gedanken zum sogenannten Protoevangelium," *BN* 19 (1982): 121–40. Here Görg contends that Gen 3:14–15 is post-Yahwistic and carries a "concealed criticism against the foreign policy of Hezekiah" (as cited in Holter, "Serpent in Eden," 111 n. 9).

110. W. von Soden, "Verschlüsselte Kritik an Salomo in der Urgeschichte des Jahwisten?," *WO* 7, no. 2 (1974): 228–40.

111. Holter, "Serpent in Eden," 111.

and also demonstrate how this might have been accomplished, namely, by using the past to critique the present.[112]

### Redactional Recasting

Redaction criticism has taught us that texts can be reshaped and adapted to new situations by recontextualizing them and allowing new emphases to emerge. It is also quite possible that in the process of recasting a text, certain themes and ideas present within (or implied by) the *Vorlage* may be subverted.[113] As one example of this process, we will take another look at Gen 2–3. David Carr argues that "Genesis 2–3 is an anti-wisdom story *that depends for part of its effect* on its artful subversion of an early creation account now contained in much of Genesis 2."[114] Carr's redactional analysis isolates an earlier creation story in Gen 2:4b–5, 7–8, 15bβ, 18–24 to which 2:6, 9–15abα, 16–17, 25 and the majority of ch. 3 has been added.[115] He believes that the original creation story, which emphasized "gender connectedness" and which could be construed as offering a positive portrayal of wisdom given the orderliness of the created order, has been radically reoriented by the inclusion of a crime and punishment story contained in ch. 3. Observing the dense concentration of wisdom language in this additional material, Carr concludes that the redactional recasting of Gen 2–3 "is polemicizing against the wisdom tradition— more specifically, against the kind of independent human determination of good and evil characteristic of that tradition."[116] This, in Carr's estimation, accounts for the conflicting interpretations regularly advanced for Gen 2–3. Those who focus on elements from the original story find it liberating while others, concentrating on the later recasting, experience it as oppressive.[117] Might a similar explanation account for the diverse range

---

112. For a much broader discussion of this technique, see Amit, *Hidden Polemics*, 93–217. Amit believes a broad range of narrative elements (e.g. place names, themes), not just characters, could function as ciphers. See the previous chapter for my discussion of her proposal to find a "hidden polemic" against Saul in Judg 19–21.

113. Cf. the remarks of David M. Gunn and Danna Nolan Fewell (*Narrative in the Hebrew Bible* [Oxford: Oxford University Press, 1993], 56) who make a similar point, albeit it from a literary-critical perspective. Referring to Genesis–2 Kings, they believe that "we could conceive of the story as a story told by various narrators, now the one, now another, intruding without warning—none wholly reliable because always subject to subversion by another."

114. David Carr, "The Politics of Textual Subversion: A Diachronic Perspective on the Garden of Eden Story," *JBL* 112 (1993): 577–95 (577).

115. Ibid., 581–82.

116. Ibid., 589–90.

117. Ibid., 593–94.

of opinions about whether certain portions of the Solomonic narrative are praising or criticizing the king? Perhaps.

*Prophetic Fronts*
Davies argues that all (!) scribal critique in the Hebrew Bible is mediated through the use of prophetic "fronts" which allowed the scribe the freedom overtly to criticize while remaining anonymous. He writes,

> These scribes not only work for the governing institution; they are also part of it, by being a rather privileged élite. That does not prevent them from criticizing their own régime. There are texts in the Bible that contain quite trenchant denunciation. *But this is always expressed in the words of an earlier prophet, so that no direct criticism of the current authorities is explicit.*[118]

By placing this critique on the lips of past prophetic figures, these scribes could subtly criticize contemporary rulers and power structures with impunity. But one wonders if these critiques must always have been offered "in the words of an earlier prophet" as Davies contends. Is it not also possible that a scribe might launch a critique through the mouth of a contemporary prophet given the potential safeguard such prophetic speech might have afforded a subversive scribe?[119]

Consider, for example, the Shaphan family who for three generations supported religious reform and enjoyed places of privilege in the royal administration but who sometimes sided with the prophet Jeremiah rather

---

118. Davies, *In Search of "Ancient Israel"*, 103 (my emphasis). Cf. also his "Is there a Class in this Text?," 39.

119. The Ugaritic Legend of Kirta may illustrate another kind of "front" through which the subversion of royal ideology might have been delivered, namely, via a foreign king. Gary N. Knoppers ("Dissonance and Disaster in the Legend of Kirta," *JAOS* 114 [1994]: 572–82) believes "the Kirta legend exposes the ambiguities in royal ideology and the contrast between ideology and experience, but…does not repudiate human kingship" (p. 582). His discussion of the legend highlights the way in which the story demonstrates the king's unique relationship to the gods while simultaneously highlighting the king's mortality, vulnerability, and frailty, thus supporting and subverting royal ideology. Although Knoppers contends that temple scribes were most likely responsible for producing this text, he does not rule out the possibility that it came from royal scribes. In either case, "focusing attention upon the reign of a non-Ugaritic king enables the author to treat sensitive issues with a degree of freedom and independence not possible otherwise" (p. 574). Moreover, such a focus "partially absolves the authors (if more than one) from the charge that they are criticizing their own royalty" (p. 581). Such cautious activity is clearly of the kind one might expect of (a) subversive scribe(s) whose work would be under some degree of scrutiny.

than the king![120] In the ninth month of the fifth year of King Jehoiakim, in one of the most detailed accounts exposing the division and disagreements existing among Judean royal officials in the late pre-exilic period, Jeremiah's trusted scribe Baruch reads a scroll written at the prophet's dictation several months prior. This scroll is read to "all the people…in the house of the LORD, in the chamber of Gemariah son of Shaphan the secretary (*sōpēr*)" (Jer 36:10). The availability of this room for a reading of the words of Jeremiah via Baruch indicates that Gemariah "was well disposed toward Jeremiah."[121] Moreover, it is Gemariah's son Micaiah who relays these words to a group of officials assembled in the secretary's chamber (36:11–13). In this particular instance, having the descendants of Shaphan in high places made it possible for Jeremiah's message to penetrate the palace walls and be heard by King Jehoiakim who would have been only too glad to be rid of this pesky prophet. Even though the institutionally connected Shaphan scribes seem to not have been directly responsible for the production of this particular document,[122] they certainly endorsed Jeremiah's message to some extent and thus provide us with yet another glimpse of how scribes could use their position and power, if not their pen, to encourage a written critique of the king.[123] Presumably, such scribes were ever ready to write down the words of prophets with whom they shared certain affinities—as long as they didn't have to sign *their* name at the bottom!

### Self-Incriminatory Statements

The final subversive technique we will consider involves quoting a self-incriminating comment not recognized as such by the "speaker." Consider, for example, a person who says, "We've got a great neighborhood.

120. Consider the help Jeremiah receives from Ahikam son of Shaphan (Jer 26:24) and Gedaliah son of Shaphan (Jer 39:14). Note also that Elasah, one of two messengers with whom Jeremiah entrusts a "stay awhile" letter to the exilic community, is a son of Shaphan (Jer 29:3).

121. J. A. Thompson, *The Book of Jeremiah* (NICOT; Grand Rapids: Eerdmans, 1980), 625. That Gemariah had such a room in the temple precincts also bespeaks his privileged position as an influential individual. Cf. the use of "the chamber of the sons of Hanan" in Jer 35:4.

122. Shaphan and those who held the office after him were much more than just average "scribes," and it is unclear how much they would have engaged in such writing.

123. Since there is relatively little prophetic activity in the Solomonic narrative—really only Ahijah in 1 Kgs 11:29–39 since Nathan does not function in a prophetic role in 1 Kgs 1—further discussion of this particular technique will be of minimal significance for our study.

Everybody keeps to themselves and minds their own business!"[124] From the speaker's vantage point, such a statement is positive and complimentary, extolling the virtues of their locale. But imagine the reaction such a comment would elicit if spoken to a group of people who value community, care deeply about helping their neighbors, and actively look for ways to assist one another. From the perspective of these individuals, the speaker would appear hopelessly individualistic and utterly indifferent to the needs of others. In such a setting, the "speaker" has "shot him or herself in the foot" without even realizing it.

A dramatic example of this kind of self-incrimination is found in 2 Sam 4:5–12. Rechab and Baanah, the sons of Rimmon, believe they have done a great thing by killing Ishbaal, the short-lived king of the northern kingdom of Israel. They bring his head to David at Hebron saying, "Here is the head of Ishbaal, son of Saul, your enemy, who sought your life; the LORD has avenged my lord the king this day on Saul and his offspring" (2 Sam 4:8). The sons of Rimmon certainly expected to be rewarded for their deed but instead were summarily executed.[125] Simply allowing people to speak for themselves can be subversive because of what the "truth" of their statements reveals about their true character and morals.

Similarly, simply reporting actions taken or positions held by a particular person—which that individual (and others) may regard positively but which a particular audience(s) might view negatively—can be equally subversive. For instance, describing a president's deep commitment to strengthening the nation's armed forces while emphasizing the enormous amount of money he or she has devoted to this end might seem intended as obvious praise—unless, of course, such facts are aimed at an audience which vigorously opposes militarism! In such a context, "truth-telling," reporting the facts as they are, can be a clever means of subversion.

*Strategic Omissions*
Strategic omissions—instances in which a scribe intentionally deviates from a typical pattern or omits a key element from his composition—may also alert us to the hand of a subversive scribe. The subversive intentionality of such omissions is, however, exceedingly difficult to demonstrate since it basically amounts to an argument from silence. Take for example, Tomoo Ishida's attempt to find subversion in the omission of David's name from an administrative list in 2 Samuel. Upon examination

---

124. I am indebted to Terry L. Brensinger for this item. Someone had made this statement to him.

125. See also 2 Sam 1:1–16.

of the three lists of high officials serving under David/Solomon (2 Sam 8:15–18//1 Chr 18:14–17; 2 Sam 20:23–26; 1 Kgs 4:1), Ishida notes that the king is listed first in each list except the second one (2 Sam 20:23–26).[126] Here Joab tops the list and David appears only at the very end and then only secondarily in reference to Ira, who was "David's priest." Ishida contends that "it cannot be an accident that David as the ruler of the land is omitted from the second list…which is placed immediately after the story of Joab's victorious campaign against Sheba."[127] Instead, he believes "we may assume that by omitting David's name…the second list of David's high officials tells us, though implicitly, that the de facto ruler was then Joab, who ranked at the top of the list."[128] Yet Ishida seems to misconstrue the nature of these lists. In each case, the larger context of these lists clearly portrays the king as being in control, notwithstanding the absence of his name at the beginning of a particular administrative list.

A more promising example might be the omission of any reference to prophetic approval of Solomon's rise to power. Although the court prophet Nathan is involved in the scheme to propel Solomon to the throne, there is no indication that he—or anyone else—functions in the role of "prophet" as Solomon comes to power. If this omission was intended as a critique of Solomon's rise by suggesting it came about without prophetic approval, it subtly subverts the legitimacy of the king. Thus, while strategic omissions certainly could be used as a means of subversion, care must be taken in labeling all such lacunae as intentionally subversive.

*Irony*

In the previous chapter, I briefly discussed irony in relation to Lyle Eslinger's reading of the Deuteronomistic History.[129] Irony is a kind of encrypted speech which says one thing and means another.[130] While the use of patently obvious irony does not qualify as covert subversion,[131]

---

126. Tomoo Ishida, "Solomon's Succession to the Throne of David—A Political Analysis," in *Studies in the Period of David and Solomon and Other Essays* (ed. Tomoo Ishida; Winona Lake, Ind.: Eisenbrauns, 1982), 175–87 (185).

127. Ibid.

128. Ibid.

129. The most comprehensive study of irony in the Hebrew Bible is Edwin M. Good, *Irony in the Old Testament* (Atlanta: Westminster, 1965; repr., Sheffield: Almond Press, 1985).

130. J. C. L. Gibson, *Language and Imagery in the Old Testament* (Peabody, Mass.: Hendrickson, 1998), 60.

131. For example, I would not consider satire, which employs irony in a particular way, *covertly* subversive since the object of attack is usually quite obvious. For

there are instances in which it is difficult to tell whether a word or phrase is intended to be taken at face value, or whether it is meant to be understood ironically. As Abrams describes it, "Irony carries an implicit compliment to the intelligence of the reader, who is invited to associate himself with the author and the knowing minority who are not taken in by the ostensible meaning."[132] In those instances, a potentially ironic reading may be subversive. That such a technique might have been utilized by writers of the Hebrew Bible is noted by David M. Gunn and Danna Nolan Fewell. They recognize "the possibility that a narrator attuned to deploying irony against characters might deploy it against readers."[133] Consider, for example, the artful deployment of the particle *raq* in 1 Kgs 3:3 and 1 Kgs 15:5:

> Solomon loved the LORD, walking in the statutes of his father David; only (*raq*), he sacrificed and offered incense at the high places. (1 Kgs 3:3)

> David did what was right in the sight of the LORD, and did not turn aside from anything that he commanded him all the days of his life, except (*raq*) in the matter of Uriah the Hittite. (1 Kgs 15:5)

At first glance, both references appear to be generally favorable toward Solomon and David. Their record is untarnished with but one exception in each case: Solomon's worship at high places and David's dealings with Uriah. Read in this way, the particular misdeed recounted after the particle *raq* should be understood as a negative exception to their otherwise exemplary behavior. On the other hand, if these clauses are meant to be taken ironically, a rather different connotation emerges.[134] As Gunn and Fewell observe, "An ironic reading of the 'except' clause can turn the narrator's evaluation from laudatory to condemnatory in a stroke."[135] In other words, rather than regarding these evaluations as primarily congratulatory, save for one blemish on an otherwise immaculate record, when viewed suspiciously the apparent praise given these two monarchs is trumped by their troubling failures reported in the each of the "exception" clauses. These examples suggest that irony can be deployed with the utmost efficiency and thereby demonstrates that

an interesting satirical reading of the Ehud story in Judg 3:12–30, see Brettler, *Creation of History*, 79–90, and nn. 71–79 for references to numerous studies of this genre.

132. M. H. Abrams, *A Glossary of Literary Terms* (4th ed.; Montreal: Holt, Rinehart & Winston, 1981), 90, quoted in Eslinger, *Into the Hands*, 32.

133. Gunn and Fewell, *Narrative in the Hebrew Bible*, 55

134. Hays ("Narrative Subtlety," 162) understands *raq* to function ironically in 1 Kgs 3:3.

135. Gunn and Fewell, *Narrative in the Hebrew Bible*, 55.

subversion need not be extensive or elaborate to be effective. Sometimes, just a word will do.

*Ambiguity*
Ambiguity is perhaps one of the most versatile and potentially effective means of delivering a covert critique. Since we have already explored several ways ambiguity could function subversively in the previous chapter, and since we will discuss textual ambiguity more fully in the following section, here I restrict my comments to a single facet of literary ambiguity. One way in which a scribe could conceal a critique in literary form would be by employing an ambiguous or multivalent symbol or tradition. As Habel observes, "A given symbol, such as Abraham, the promised land, or the Sinai covenant may be common to several texts and traditions, but how these symbols are interpreted in each literary complex partly depends on the ideological edge that is being sharpened within a given text."[136] Consider, for example, the Exodus traditions found in various sections of the Hebrew Bible.[137] Sometimes these traditions are used to illustrate God's great care for his people by recalling their deliverance. On other occasions, the Exodus traditions are cited in connection with Israel's rebellion. While Israel's stay in Egypt can be used as a reminder of Yahweh's great deliverance on the people's behalf, it can also be used to recall less pleasant memories of bitter oppression and slavery. This is nicely illustrated by the juxtaposition of Ps 105 and Ps 106. In Ps 105, the Exodus tradition is used to demonstrate God's faithfulness to Israel: "He brought Israel out with silver and gold...Egypt was glad when they departed" (vv. 37–38a). In Ps 106, the same traditions are used to demonstrate Israel's faith*less*ness: "Both we and our ancestors have sinned; we have committed iniquity, have done wickedly. Our ancestors, when they were in Egypt, did not consider your wonderful works; they did not remember the abundance of your steadfast love, but rebelled against the Most High at the Red Sea" (vv. 6–7).

As this example illustrates—and many others could be given—Egypt and the Exodus traditions are rich in ingredients which could be selectively utilized for rather different ends. While the context often reveals which of these alternate emphases is drawn upon, this is not always the case. Where ambiguity remains, the potential for covert subversion exists

---

136. Habel, *The Land is Mine*, 11.
137. What follows could also be said of the wilderness traditions. Cf. Num 11:1–20:29; Pss 78; 95:8–11; 136:16; Jer 2:2–3; Ezek 20:13–36; Hos 2:14–15; 13:5; Amos 2:10.

since the sensitive reader/hearer may recognize (and relish!) the less favorable association.

The foregoing discussion of subversive literary techniques represents just a sampling of the possibilities which scribes had at their disposal. Nevertheless, they should suffice to illustrate some of the means used by individuals who wished to be subversive but needed to be cautious.

### Textual Indeterminacy, Ambiguity, and Intentionality

Before leaving this theoretical discussion of scribal subversion, it is necessary to explore some additional questions we can only begin to address here. For example, when we suspect something in a text to be functioning subversively, can we determine whether this meaning is intentional or inadvertent? Is there a way to be reasonably certain that the subversion we see was actually intended by a subversive scribe? And if so, what criteria might guide us as we look for intentional subversion? These are difficult issues to sort through. They require us to give some attention to matters of textual (in)determinacy and the locus of meaning in the reading process. While an extensive treatment of these topics would take us far beyond the scope of this study, some discussion of these issues is desirable at this point.

Considerable attention has been given to the question of meaning and the reading process in recent years.[138] Where does meaning reside? Is it in the text? Does the reader create it, or is it the product of a dialectic between text and reader? I tend to agree with those who believe texts do have some meaning. I think this idea is important because it keeps one from slipping into wholesale destruction. I do think authors had intentions they wished to communicate when writing. Still, I recognize the difficulty of determining these with any measure of certainty. I also am aware that people sometimes communicate various things of which they are not conscious. Additionally, I realize readers can generate meanings

---

138. For some orientation to this discussion, see Robert C. Culley and Robert B. Robinson (eds.), *Textual Determinacy: Part One* (Semeia 62; Atlanta: Scholars Press, 1993), and Robert B. Robinson and Robert C. Culley, eds., *Textual Determinacy: Part Two* (Semeia 71; Atlanta: Scholars Press, 1995); Kevin J. Vanhoozer, *Is there a Meaning in this Text? The Bible, the Reader, and the Morality of Literary Knowledge* (Grand Rapids: Zondervan, 1998); Steven L. McKenzie and Stephen R. Haynes (eds.), *To Each its Own Meaning: An Introduction to Biblical Criticisms and their Application* (rev. and exp. ed.; Louisville, Ky.: Westminster John Knox, 1999), 183–306; and Charles H. Cosgrove (ed.), *The Meanings We Choose: Hermeneutical Ethics, Indeterminacy and the Conflict of Interpretations* (JSOTSup 411; London: T. & T. Clark, 2004).

from texts that were never intended by their authors. All this complicates our efforts to ascertain authorial intentionality when reading ancient texts. That notwithstanding, it is still reasonable to believe that authors mean to communicate something when they write and that investigating that "something" is a worthy and worthwhile endeavor as one part of the reading process. Thus, I find no compelling *a priori* reason to deny the possibility of intentionally covert scribal subversion in the Hebrew Bible.

Before directly addressing the question of intentionality, however, we must first consider the impact indeterminacy and ambiguity have on our reading of the text.[139] Indeterminacy comes in many shapes and sizes and scholars recognize different kinds of indeterminacy and different causes for the same. Charles Cosgrove defines indeterminacy as "the recurring interpretive situation" which yields "two or more *reasonable* and *competing* interpretations, that is, two or more mutually exclusive interpretations that are plausible/defensible on the basis of a rigorous application of the same methods or...appropriate competing methods."[140] Stuart Lasine, in his article "Indeterminacy and the Bible," establishes "a typology of literary indeterminacy theories" which include ontological, epistemological, and mimetic indeterminacy.[141] Lasine also cites a variety of indeterminacies identified by literary critics which include "indeterminacy caused by the inability of literary texts to appeal to identical life-situations for verification," "indeterminacy produced by the act of overinterpretation," and "indeterminacy which, according to deconstructionists, is generated by all language."[142] Similarly, Cosgrove believes indeterminacies include "ambiguity arising from multiple possibilities for relating part to whole and whole to part, linguistic ambiguity (ambiguity of words and syntax), uncertainties of form and genre...uncertainty arising from apparent contradictions as well as gaps, polyvalence caused by intertextuality (uncertainty about the presence and role of allusions to other texts, cultural symbols, etc.), and so on."[143]

---

139. For a reading of 1 Kgs 3–11 that explores the effects of indeterminacy and intertextuality upon the characterization of Solomon (and Yahweh!), see Stuart Lasine, "The King of Desire: Indeterminacy, Audience, and the Solomon Narrative," in Robinson and Culley, eds., *Textual Determinacy: Part Two*, 85–118. See also, in the same volume, Michael Fox's critique ("The Uses of Indeterminacy," 181–90).

140. Cosgrove, *Meanings We Choose*, 5 (emphasis in original).

141. Stuart Lasine, "Indeterminacy and the Bible: A Review of Literary and Anthropological Theories and their Application to Biblical Texts," *HS* 27 (1986): 48–80 (49–51).

142. Lasine, "Indeterminacy and the Bible," 51. See also his "King of Desire," 87–91, for a classification of various types of indeterminacy in 1 Kgs 3–11.

143. Cosgrove, *Meanings We Choose*, 6.

For the purposes of this study, it is unnecessary technically to differentiate between these terms. Still, a rudimentary distinction may be helpful. I would consider indeterminacy the broader and more general term, describing the "interpretive situation" in which there are "two or more *reasonable* and *competing* interpretations." Literary ambiguity, on the other hand, is one of the leading causes of this interpretive situation.

Although the presence of ambiguity in Hebrew narratives is undeniable, the question of whether this ambiguity can be resolved—and whether meaning can be determined—is disputed. While some believe texts are unstable by nature and open to a wide range of interpretive possibilities, others are confident that textual uncertainties can be minimized or even eliminated by a careful reading. Tremper Longman believes that "while we must reckon with intentional ambiguity, a close reading of the text will allow the reader to close the gap correctly."[144] But is literary ambiguity resolvable? Are textual gaps closeable or do they remain perpetually open for readers to fill? As a way to respond to these questions and to position my reading in this larger conversation, I have chosen to examine the work of two scholars—Meir Sternberg and Peter Miscall—who approach this issue from different perspectives.

In his massive work, *The Poetics of Biblical Narrative*, Meir Sternberg devotes a full chapter to "Gaps, Ambiguity, and the Reading Process." Sternberg defines a gap as "a lack of information about the world—an event, motive, causal link, character trait, plot structure, law of probability—contrived by a temporal displacement."[145] For Sternberg, such gaps can be either temporary or permanent. The missing information needed to close the gap may or may not be supplied later in the narrative. According to Sternberg, any attempt we make to fill the gap and remove the literary ambiguity should be guided by the text. He believes legitimate gap-filling should be dictated "by the texts own norms and directives."[146] To illustrate, consider Sternberg's analysis of 2 Sam 11:1–5, beginning with v. 1:

> At the turn of the year, at the time when kings go forth to battle, David sent Joab and his servants with him and all Israel, and they ravaged the Ammonites and besieged Rabbah, and David stayed in Jerusalem.[147]

144. Tremper Longman III, *Literary Approaches to Biblical Interpretation* (Grand Rapids: Zondervan, 1987), 97.

145. Sternberg, *Poetics of Biblical Narrative*, 235. For a helpful distinction between significant and insignificant omissions, see pp. 236–37 where Sternberg distinguishes between "relevancies ('gaps') and irrelevancies ('blanks'). Cf. Fox, "Uses of Indeterminacy," 175.

146. Sternberg, *Poetics of Biblical Narrative*, 188.

147. Ibid., 193 (Sternberg's translation).

Sternberg emphasizes how various elements in the verse are separated by the conjunctive *waw*, giving the appearance that the author is objectively listing a string of facts. Since no explicit connection is made between these items, this style of presentation protects the author from accusations of intentionally criticizing the king. In reference to the conjunctive *waw* on the final clause of this verse ("and David stayed in Jerusalem") Sternberg writes, "Although the ironic patterning soon turns this 'and' into a 'but,' *this reading does not implicate the 'innocent' narrator.*"

This ostensibly noncondemnatory reporting continues in 2 Sam 11:2 as the narrator recounts David's rooftop stroll. In Sternberg's words, "Again, the narrator 'innocently' relates external events… Yet the reader cannot but see this verse in light of the preceding one and go on to develop the ironic oppositions set up there." Another example of this seemingly straightforward reporting is seen in v. 4 in the juxtaposition of the clauses "and he lay with her, and she was purifying herself from her uncleanness." Initially, this juxtaposition might raise readerly expectations that the writer is attempting to "praise" (or at least exonerate) David since it demonstrates he did not have sexual intercourse with Bathsheba while she was menstruating. But the true significance of this datum becomes apparent in v. 5 when she informs David she is pregnant. Now the reader fills the gap and understands the true significance of this bit of information. Bathsheba's purification establishes David's paternity, though the narrator never says this in so many words. According to Sternberg,

> This gap-filling wholly resolves the collocation of the troublesome phrase with "and he lay with her," and what was previously taken as an objective and impartial recording of external facts now turns into a *covert indictment*. Even more ironic, the very detail that might at first have been interpreted as the sole meritorious feature of David's act ("and he did not transgress the laws of menstrual purity") twists around to condemn him. *Yet once again the indictment is pieced out by the reader, while the "innocent" narrator can deny having had any hand in it.*[148]

Sternberg's repeated emphasis upon the narrator's "innocence" and the possibility that such a narrator could deliver a "covert indictment" particularly intriguing in light of this study's interest in detecting scribal subversion. Clearly, Sternberg believes ancient authors could deliver hidden criticism in the stories they wrote. By omitting causal links and creatively presenting "just the facts," ancient authors had at their disposal the means literarily to critique the king blamelessly.

---

148. Ibid., 198 (my emphasis).

The point for the moment, however, is to note how Sternberg's analysis of 2 Sam 11 illustrates his belief that ancient authors could craft their narratives in such as way that would remove initial ambiguities and allow readers to close temporary gaps. Sternberg refers to this way of writing as "foolproof composition."[149] He believes that even if the author's moral intentions are not clear while reading through the majority of the narrative, they will be so by the end. In the case of the David and Bathsheba story, a "retrospective or last-minute clarification" comes in the explicit narrative condemnation in 2 Sam 11:27b, "But the thing that David had done displeased the LORD."[150] According to Sternberg, "Having presented some drama without any overt commentary, though with sufficient clues distributed along the way to guide the alert, the narrative will often enlighten the naive or superficial toward the end. On the better-late-than-never-principle, it then retrospectively corrects possible variations from the desired attitude by way of univocal utterance, counteract, or disclosure."[151]

Although Sternberg is suggesting that many gaps can be filled and ambiguities resolved, he does not believe this is possible in every instance. For example, Sternberg devotes considerable attention to the question of whether Uriah knew why David recalled him to the capital city and explores the implications of reading this a variety of different ways. In the end he believes the reader cannot make a determination one way or the other. Some gaps are permanent; some ambiguity is irresolvable.

Despite this allowance for permanent gaps, I think Sternberg's notion of "foolproof composition" is overly optimistic and too deterministic. I would question how many narratives can really be conclusively decided (or determined) in the way Sternberg proposes. This certainly does not seem to be the case in regard to the Solomonic narrative as a whole. The plethora of interpretive possibilities put forward regarding this narrative would seem to support this. Moreover, I seriously question the efficacy of this method when explicit moral narratorial evaluations like the one given in 2 Sam 11:27b are lacking.

A less determined (actually undetermined) reading of biblical texts is offered by Peter Miscall in his monograph titled *The Workings of Old Testament Narrative*. Miscall regards many biblical texts as being "undecidable" by which he means that "the reading encounters ambiguity, equivocation, opposed meanings and cannot decide for or establish one

149. Ibid., 48–57, 230–35.
150. Ibid., 54.
151. Ibid., 55.

or the other."[152] He is critical of commentators who force determinate readings from these texts. As Miscall sees it, Hebrew narratives provide both too much and not enough information to do this.[153] For example, in the case of Goliath, his armor and weapons are described with an unusual amount of detail for Hebrew narratives. Yet it is unclear what we, the reader, are to make of this. As Miscall writes, "The description of Goliath introduces an indeterminate aspect into the narrative through its literal and precise details. They are definite; it is their significance for the narrative, the perception of them by a character or reader, that is equivocal."[154] In other words, while we know what the text says, we are uncertain what it means. Is Goliath being portrayed as "a formidable warrior" who is armed to the teeth, or is he "a sitting duck" unable to move freely because he is burdened by so much armor?[155] According to Miscall, this ambiguity is irresolvable.

Miscall's study focuses on two portions of the Hebrew Bible, Gen 12 and 1 Sam 16–22. In both instances, he believes these texts are undecidable in terms of what they tell us about Abraham and David, respectively. In most cases, we cannot ascertain the motives and intentions of these two major figures. This complicates any attempt to evaluate their behavior. For example, Miscall points out that we do not know why Abraham chose to leave Haran and travel to Canaan. We do not know because the author never tells us. Despite the presence of a divine command, the text only says Abraham went *as* the Lord command, not necessarily *because* the Lord commanded. Moreover, even if Abraham went *because* of this divine command, it still remains unclear what his true motivations were. His "obedience" may reflect a deep sense of piety or it might reveal crass opportunism. According to Miscall, the reader cannot determine which of these readings is more plausible.

Similarly, there are numerous episodes from David's life which could reflect positively or negatively on him. This judgment depends on how certain words and deeds are interpreted. For example, just prior to his confrontation with Goliath, David leaves his baggage with the keepers. Is this a responsible or irresponsible act? As Miscall notes, the verb describing David's action (i.e. *nāṭaš*), can mean "to leave" or "to abandon." If the former meaning is taken, then one could regard this as

---

152. Peter D. Miscall, *The Workings of Old Testament Narrative* (Philadelphia: Fortress, 1983), 2.

153. Ibid., 1.

154. Ibid., 61.

155. For a strong critique of Miscall, particularly of his interpretation of the David and Goliath story, see Lasine, "Indeterminacy and the Bible," 51–56.

reflecting favorably upon David by demonstrating "David's concern for property." On the other hand, if the latter connotation of abandoning is inferred, David's actions are less than commendable.[156] As Miscall sees it, there is no way to adjudicate these competing possibilities. The text resists all attempts at closure, and the gaps cannot be filled conclusively. As Miscall puts it, "The readings are frequently, if not always, 'decidedly undecidable' and seem to leave no room for a determinate reading."[157] He believes "David is not being portrayed in a definitive fashion. David is 'good' *and* 'bad.' The text at the same time supports both and does not support a final decision in favor of only one."[158]

I agree with Miscall up to a point. It does seem that David, like Solomon, is portrayed both favorably and unfavorably. Yet even though the text "does not support a final decision in favor of only one" portrayal, the overarching tenor of the narrative does seem to push the reader in one direction more than another. At least on the surface, the text seems generally supportive of David, conveying a portrait of David that is largely positive. To be sure, there are undercurrents just below the surface— some rather forceful—which continually call into question that positive portrayal. Yet even though these undercurrents operative in the background do seem to make a "final decision" impossible, they do not obscure the more positive portrayal which seems to dominate the foreground.

Returning now to the question of ambiguity's resolvability, I would position myself somewhere between Sternberg and Miscall, though closer to Miscall. As noted above, I am not convinced by Sternberg's notion of "foolproof composition" and am skeptical that all readers will get some intended point, moral or otherwise. Similarly, I do not believe texts are as indeterminate as Miscall seems to suggest. Some texts do seem designed to function in certain ways (e.g. as political propaganda supportive of the king) even while other possibilities remain open. If Miscall is saying that it is simply a toss-up, that one meaning is equally as suggestive as another, I would disagree in many instances.

That being said, I still find Miscall's emphasis upon a text's undecidability extremely helpful, particularly if one allows for the possibility that this undecidability is intentional and not merely a product of textual indeterminacy. While there is no question that some literary ambiguity is accidental—or perhaps better, incidental—it seems equally certain that some was intentional. Anyone who has ever written a letter of reference for a less than stellar student or colleague immediately understands this!

---

156. Miscall, *Workings of Old Testament Narrative*, 59.
157. Ibid., 140.
158. Ibid., 2 (emphasis in original).

Sometimes we do not want to be totally transparent or perfectly clear in our writing. Sometimes it would be dangerous or detrimental to do so. In such cases, we may decide to write vaguely or ambiguously. As Walsh observes, "Any language is capable of ambiguous constructions, and any author can inadvertently write ambiguously. But ambiguity can be used to very pointed effect as well."[159] While I am cognizant of the fact that every text has some degree of indeterminacy, this does not negate the possibility of intentional ambiguity. That much should be clear from Meir Sternberg's analysis above. Even though Sternberg believes that the author's agenda eventually becomes transparent, his careful reading of 2 Sam 11 demonstrates that scribes could be intentionally ambiguous if they chose to be.[160]

Of course, there are various reasons why a writer might intentionally choose to be ambiguous.[161] In her study of 2 Sam 11, Gale Yee argues that the ambiguity found there undergirds the moral purpose of the narrative which she regards as the main point of the story. According to Yee,

> Being purposefully ambiguous, he [the author] introduces different and even conflicting narrative possibilities into the story itself and refrains from making a moral judgment until the very end. These possibilities force the readers to confront the situations which he describes and, in doing so, raise moral questions and come to tentative moral judgments about the narrative's characters.[162]

Yee also recognizes that ambiguity may function mimetically. As she observes, "The ambiguity of biblical narrative, the fictive world, reflects the ambiguity of the so-called 'real' world. The readers encounter the same equivocal, ambivalent state of affairs in real life that they do in the realm of story."[163] In other words, the ambiguity found in the text mirrors the ambiguity readers experience and encounter in the world around them.

According to Esther Fuchs, intentional ambiguity may also serve an apologetic function in the text. She believes this is how the ambiguity surrounding Jephthah's sacrifice of his daughter is functioning in Judg 11. She sees it as "a subtle justification of Jephthah's behavior," providing

159. Walsh, *1 Kings*, xvi.

160. Cf. Bodner (*David Observed*, 78) who claims 2 Sam 11 "exemplifies the literary art of *intentional* ambiguity" (my emphasis).

161. For an extensive discussion of the function of ambiguity, see William Empson, *Seven Types of Ambiguity* (2d ed.; New York: New Directions, 1947).

162. Gale Yee, "'Fraught with Background': Literary Ambiguity in II Samuel 11," *Int* 42 (1988): 240–53 (252).

163. Ibid.

"cover" for his horrific act.[164] Leo Purdue offers yet another way literary ambiguity might function in his study of the portrayal of David in the Succession Narrative. He discusses two very different ways of apprehending the character of David, one which views him as a king who "attempts to rule his kingdom with compassion and forgiveness" and the other as one who is "consistently deceitful, treacherous, and ruthless."[165] These readings obviously stand in serious tension, frustrating efforts to construct a monolithic portrait of the king. Yet Purdue believes this ambiguity exists by design, revealing "the complexity of David."[166] According to him, "the narrator's characterization of David is intentionally ambiguous so that two very different interpretations of David may emerge, depending on the reader's own assessment of the motives resting behind the king's actions and speeches."[167]

In this study, I am proposing yet another purpose for intentional ambiguity, namely, scribal subversion. Intentionally irresolvable ambiguity seems to have provided the kind of literary cover a scribe needed to launch a covert critique. Though still risky, writing ambiguously could help shield a scribe from accusations of wrongdoing. Therefore, it should come as no great surprise to find numerous subversive sentiments lurking in ambiguous passages. But to what degree can we determine whether a potentially subversive meaning in a particular word, action, or narrative comment was intended as literary subversion? What criteria can guide us in making such an assessment? And what kind of controls might be developed to keep us from seeing subversion behind every bush and from slipping into wholesale deconstruction? These are not easy questions to answer.

Our efforts are complicated by the fact that the kind of subversion we are interested in detecting depends upon the presence of ambiguity that is ultimately irresolvable. If the ambiguity could be removed, and the scribe's subversive intentions determined beyond a shadow of a doubt, it would hardly qualify as covert subversion. Scribes who concealed their subversion needed to walk a very fine line. They needed to include subversive elements in the text which were discernable without being demonstrable, visible but not verifiable.

---

164. Esther Fuchs, "Marginalization, Ambiguity, Silencing: The Story of Jephthah's Daughter," in Brenner, ed., *A Feminist Companion to Judges*, 116–30 (116).
165. Leo G. Perdue, "'Is there Anyone Left of the House of Saul...?' Ambiguity and the Characterization of David in the Succession Narrative," *JSOT* 30 (1984): 67–84 (80).
166. Ibid., 71.
167. Ibid.

Still, there do seem to be some clues which, if recognized, can alert the careful reader to the presence of potentially subversive elements without sounding the alarm. In what follows, I will identify and describe some of these clues or indicators. In his study of irony, Wayne Booth notes that "in spoken ironies, especially in conversation, we are accustomed to catching a variety of clues that are not in themselves ironic—direct nudges of the elbow and winks of the eye. In written irony that same kind of nudge is often given."[168] I would say much the same prevails in the search for literary subversion. We are looking for those "nudges" and "winks" which invite us to understand the message of the text in ways that complicate reality by revealing alternate meanings that are not only less complimentary, but sometimes downright destructive to the people, positions, and powers they critique. While some of the indicators I identify help us know where to look for subversion, others assist us in determining when it is likely that the subversion we see was intentional. While I have not attempted to be exhaustive or definitive in my selection and discussion of the following items, my hope is that they will provide some guidelines for detecting subversion and determining its potential intentionality.

## Finding Intentional Subversion

### Rhetorical Excess

One place to look for subversive tendencies is in texts that seem to be working very hard, one might even say too hard, to advocate a certain perspective. There is a moment in Shakespeare's *Hamlet* when the queen is asked how she likes the play. She replies, "The lady doth protest too much, methinks." In much the same way, there are occasions when the biblical text seems to be working so hard to make a point that it raises our suspicions. Why, for example, is there such a concerted effort to justify Solomon's execution orders in 1 Kgs 2? At the very least it suggests there were some who needed convincing that such killings were necessary, let alone appropriate. This realization alone is mildly subversive since it subtly indicates not everyone approved of these executions. But might this scribal exertion to exonerate the king signal something far

168. Wayne C. Booth, *A Rhetoric of Irony* (Chicago: University of Chicago Press, 1974), 53. Booth goes on to say that these nudges are sometimes given "to the distress of readers who prefer to work things out on their own," implying that sometimes the author makes it too obvious. The "problem" of this kind of transparency will not be an issue in the present search for intentional covert subversion since by definition it was intended to be hidden.

more sinister? Might it invite the reader to look deeper for signs of subversion in the text? This seems quite possible, especially considering the possibility that the scribe in question might have been sympathetic with those who felt these state-sponsored killings were politically motivated and unjustifiable.

Certain kinds of rhetoric, especially that which appears "over the top," may invite closer inspection. J. W. Wesselius makes this point when discussing what he refers to as "over-stress." He defines over-stress as "something which is evidently true…stressed in the course of the narrative much more than necessary."[169] Wesselius believes over-stress was intended to get a reader's attention for the purpose of causing him or her to consider certain aspects of the narrative which might not be apparent on the surface. According to Wesselius, "The narrator seems to use this as a device, *not so much to raise doubt about what is described*, but as an indicator that what is told is but part of the truth and that other aspects of the events can easily be detected."[170] Here is where I differ. It seems to me this technique sometimes was used "to raise doubt about what is described." Thus, while Wesselius does not think that the over-stress in 2 Sam 4 and 21 was intended "to raise doubt about David's innocence," that may be precisely the point! When we detect over-stress, this rhetorical excessive should raise our suspicions that scribal sub-version may be close at hand. To illustrate, consider the narrator's words in 2 Sam 3:36–37, a text that was considered briefly in the previous chapter:

> All the people took notice of it, and it pleased them; just as everything the king did pleased all the people. So all the people and all Israel understood that day that the king had no part in the killing of Abner son of Ner.

This passage follows Joab's assassination of Abner and David's very ostentatious and very public grief. While the text certainly seems to reflect positively on David, excusing him from wrongdoing in the case of Abner, all is not as clear-cut as it seems. Citing Brueggemann's reference to "the careful and seemingly exaggerated rhetoric of 2 Samuel 3,"[171] Bodner believes "one may indeed deduce that the subtext of the line is

---

169. J. W. Wesselius, "Joab's Death and the Central Theme of the Succession Narrative (2 Samuel IX–1 Kings II)," *VT* 40 (1990): 336–51 (339–40). Wesselius finds examples of this technique in 2 Sam 13–14; 1 Kgs 1:32–49; 2 Sam 4, 21; and 1 Kgs 2.

170. Ibid., 339 (my emphasis).

171. Walter A. Brueggemann, *1 & 2 Kings* (Smyth & Helwys Bible Commentary; Macon, Ga.: Smyth & Helwys, 2000), 35.

that *there is an air of doubt* that envelopes David in this matter."[172]
Bodner also cites Hugh Pyper who asks,

> Is this the noble-hearted king acknowledging the death of a worthy adversary and a potential ally? A more suspicious reading might wonder how far all this is convenient to the king, or to the image of the king. One might also see *a veiled criticism* in the very explicitness of the account as it appears here in 2 Samuel. The wide-eyed acceptance of the king's innocence goes beyond what might be expected, *raising the doubts that superfluous assurances always raise.*[173]

If Pyper is right, then we ought to be particularly attentive to the presence of "exaggerated rhetoric" and "superfluous assurances" when we encounter them in the text. They may be scribal signals to the discerning reader that more is happening than meets the eye. As we will discover, political propaganda—a literary technique known for rhetorical excess—seems to have been one very effective way to disguise scribal subversion.

*The Presence of Multiple Instances of Evaluative Ambiguity*
Another feature of Hebrew narrative which seems especially suggestive for locating intentional subversion is the presence of what I refer to as evaluative ambiguity. When a text can be understood as containing both favorable *and* unfavorable evaluations of an individual such as a king, and there is no way to adjudicate between competing interpretations, our suspicions are raised. When numerous examples of this kind of ambiguity emerge around a central figure in the narrative (e.g. David or Solomon), it is quite possible we are dealing with some form of intentional subversion. While one or two ambiguous texts might be attributed to the surplus of meanings any text generates, a larger number of them all centered on a particular individual or institution gives us cause to see more than coincidence at work.[174]

---

172. Bodner, *David Observed*, 62.
173. Hugh S. Pyper, "Reading David's Mind: Inference, Emotion and the Limits of Language," in *Sense and Sensitivity: Essays on Reading the Bible in Memory of Robert Carroll* (ed. Alastair G. Hunter and Phillip R. Davies; JSOTSup 348; Sheffield: Sheffield Academic Press, 2002), 73–86 (78, my emphasis), cited in Bodner, *David Observed*, 63.
174. Cf. Amit's (*Hidden Polemics*, 95–96) insistence that there be multiple signs. She writes, "The discovery of one sign alone does not constitute sufficient evidence for the existence of a hidden polemic, because it may be interpreted as accidental… [T]he uncovering of a hidden polemic relies upon accumulative evidence—in this case, a series of signs that converge at one point: the hidden subject of the polemic" (p. 96).

If there is some degree of consistency in the nature of the negative undertones, this further heightens our expectations that intentional subversion is operative. As we will see when examining Solomon's three killings in 1 Kgs 2:13–46, each one appears to be an effort to defend Solomon's bloody actions. Yet each of them is predicated on dubious justifications. In each case it seems that Solomon's execution orders have more to do with eliminating political rivals than with being a conduit of divine judgment/justice. When a pattern like this develops, it seems likely that intentional subversion is at work.

### The Unchallenged Inclusion of Corrosive Elements

Scribes sometimes included elements in their accounts which were potentially corrosive and which appear to undermine the dominant message of the text. Though these elements might be rather brief and sometimes seem tangential or incidental, they work at cross-purposes with other aspects of the story. Yet very often, no effort seems to have been made to neutralize their deleterious effects. Instead, they are simply allowed to stand as they are, quietly but effectively eroding the dominant discourse of the narrative. When this happens, it is highly suggestive of intentional scribal subversion.

To give just one example that will be treated later in more detail, consider Adonijah's claim in 1 Kgs 2:15. In presenting his request to Bathsheba, Adonijah makes this bold claim: "You know that the kingdom was mine, and that all Israel expected me to reign." Though he acknowledges the kingdom became Solomon's according to Yahweh's design, the claim that all Israel expected Adonijah to reign is never disputed. Incorporating that element into the story destabilizes the passage and implicitly raises uncomfortable questions about Solomon's right to rule. If the kingdom was Adonijah's and all Israel expected him to reign, why is Solomon sitting on the throne? Corrosive elements like Adonijah's unchallenged assertion, quietly included in the text, are suggestive of intentional scribal subversion.

### The Presentation of Potentially Problematic Conduct Criticized Elsewhere in the Hebrew Bible[175]

In some places, scribes depict people engaging in activities which would have been regarded as unacceptable in some—though not all—segments of Israelite society. We know these activities would have been unacceptable because there are other biblical texts and traditions which *overtly*

---

175. See Amit's (*Hidden Polemic*, 96) second criteria: "The evidence of other biblical materials regarding the existence of a polemic on the same subject."

condemn them. Amit believes that identifying a hidden polemic requires the interpreter "to find support for this claim in other biblical passages… that will indicate in an overt and/or indirect way that the subject in question in fact served as a polemic issue among other biblical authors at one point or another."[176] Thus it seems that the inclusion of potentially problematic conduct without explicit critique may serve as yet another indicator of intentional scribal subversion.

One can find numerous examples of potentially problematic conduct in the Solomonic narrative, such as Solomon's marriage to an Egyptian princess (3:1), his practice of forced labor among the Israelites (5:27 [Eng. 5:13]), and his relinquishment of Israelite territory (9:10–14). Events like these would have been deeply disturbing for many readers, and would have raised more than a few eyebrows. Elsewhere in the Hebrew Bible, foreign marriages, slave labor, and the cession of Israelite land are viewed negatively, indicating that at least some people found such practices troubling. Solomon's reported involvement in these questionable activities certainly would have been controversial. And while there are positive ways of evaluating Solomon's conduct in each of these instances, pursing a favorable reading does not neutralize the subversive potential of these reports. Detecting potentially problematic conduct not explicitly criticized in one passage but condemned in another provides a further indicator that scribal subversion is operative.

*The Lack of More Compelling Explanations for Mutually Contradictory Readings*
In his book *A Rhetoric of Irony*, Booth includes a chapter titled "Is it Ironic?" In this chapter, Booth develops several criteria for identifying irony. Specifically, he identifies five "clues" he believes are helpful in determining whether something was meant to be ironic. These are (1) straightforward warnings in the author's own voice, (2) known error proclaimed, (3) conflicts of facts within the work, (4) clashes of style, and (5) conflicts of belief.[177] Just prior to his discussion of these Booth writes,

> Any one of the clues I turn to now can be stated in the form of an inference about an implied author's intentions: "If the author did not intend irony, it would be odd, or outlandish, or inept, or stupid of him to do things in this way." Every clue thus depends for its validity on norms (generally unspoken) which the reader embraces and which he infers, rightly or wrongly, that his author intends.[178]

176. Ibid., 94. Similarly, this is *the* defining criterion Hays ("Narrative Subtlety") uses for detecting covert criticism of Solomon in 1 Kgs 1–11.
177. Booth, *Rhetoric of Irony*, 53–76.
178. Ibid., 52–53.

While Booth's statement is too strong to allow us simply to swap "covert subversion" for "irony," it is suggestive for determining whether a text was meant to be intentionally subversive. For example, reading a text which seems largely supportive of Solomon but which also undermines him in subtle ways raises serious questions about the author's intentions. In these instances, it would seem "odd, or outlandish, or inept, or stupid" to craft the account in this way if there was no desire to be subversive. It is clear that scribes could eliminate or at least minimize ambiguities if they so desired (e.g. no scholar would argue the author of 1 Kgs 11 intended that material to reflect positively on Solomon!). Therefore, when ambiguities remain which could have been easily eliminated, it is reasonable to assume they may have been placed there intentionally. When it is impossible to adjudicate between contradictory interpretive possibilities, we have good reason to consider the possibility that it was intended to be irresolvably ambiguous and potentially subversive.

*Scholarly Suspicion that Intentional Subversion is Present*
Finally, I mention one additional indicator which stands outside the text but which, when taken in conjunction with other evidence, may also support regarding a particular text as being intentionally subversive. If a number of biblical scholars agree that a particular item is intentionally— or at least potentially—subversive, this encourages us to consider reading it in the same way. On the contrary, if no scholars regard the item in question as being subversive, this should give us pause. Here I am borrowing Amit's fourth criteria for finding hidden polemics.[179] According to Amit, "It is…desirable that the commentator find support for the hidden subject of the polemic within the exegetical tradition."[180] Identifying something in the text as being subversive, let alone *intentionally* subversive, is certainly bolstered by other scholars who have apprehended the text in the same way. If the subversion we seek is largely concealed but not totally obscured, it would seem that at least some scholars would have recognized this over the years. Yet as Amit notes, "If the polemic is so well concealed that no commentator throughout the generations has so much as suspected its existence, perhaps it doesn't really exist."[181] While this does not rule out the possibility of finding subversion none have seen before, it does serve as a control of sorts.

---

179. Amit's (*Hidden Polemics*, 97) fourth criteria: "Reference to the hidden subject of the polemic in the exegetical tradition concerning the text in question."
180. Ibid., 96.
181. Ibid.

Several indicators which are suggestive of the presence of intentional scribal subversion have now been identified. They provide some basis for understanding where and how I will detect scribal subversion which seems to have been intentionally deployed. As we will see, on numerous occasions the Solomonic narrative does contain elements which seem to invite a subversive reading. In fact—and here I am anticipating some of my conclusions—given the frequency of such elements in the Solomonic narrative, a cumulative case can be made to support the notion of intentional scribal subversion at various points in the narrative.

That being said, I would reiterate that these are merely indicators, not guarantors of intentional subversive activity. Ascertaining scribal intentions in ancient texts with any degree of certainty is difficult and conclusions about these matters must always be held tentatively. Moreover, even though I am particularly interested in determining the extent to which we can detect willful covert scribal activity in the Solomonic narrative, I am *not* suggesting that every potentially subversive element was deliberately placed there. It is quite possible that certain aspects of a text might inspire subversive readings even if that was not the author's intent. The polyvalent nature of language and the indeterminate nature of literary texts allow for a certain openness when making meaning of biblical narratives. Thus, readers may find certain elements to be subversive even if they were not intentionally placed there for that purpose by the writer. Still, once present in the text, these elements do possess corrosive power for those with eyes to see. As John Goldingay observes, "Sometimes authors do not make themselves clear. This may happen either by accident or on purpose; whichever is the case, ambiguity is then a fact to be acknowledged and made the most of. It can be creatively provocative."[182] Even if we cannot fully decide whether certain potentially subversive elements in the Solomonic narrative were placed there intentionally, it is still of interest to consider how they might have been understood subversively by various readers.

## Conclusion

This chapter has been devoted to investigating scribes and scribal techniques from a variety of perspectives. It began by noting that scribes thought very highly of themselves and their profession. As part of a small minority of individuals in their society who could properly be called "literate," they possessed the necessary skill to produce written documents

---

182. John Goldingay, *Models for Interpretation of Scripture* (Grand Rapids: Eerdmans, 1995), 39.

of various kinds. This gave them unique access to, and brought them into direct contact with, the major power brokers of their society. Although very little is known about the kind of training that enabled such individuals in ancient Israel to gain such significant posts, the specialized skill of professional writers was probably passed on formally, presumably in the form of scribal schools.

In the second section of this chapter, an attempt was made to distinguish between three pairs of scribes. I suggested that all scribes could be classified as either being tethered (institutionally attached) or untethered (institutionally independent). From there the focus quickly narrowed to further ways of discussing various aspects of institutionally attached, or tethered, scribes. It was noted that these scribes could further be classified according to their institutional attachment (palace or temple) or their allegiance *vis-à-vis* the institution (submissive or subversive). Special attention was given to this final pair since the distinction is particularly suggestive for the present study.

By utilizing Weber's concept of the ideal type, I then attempted to sketch a portrait of these submissive and subversive scribes. While individual scribes could and certainly did fluctuate between these categories —sometimes writing for and other times writing against their patrons and/or various facets of the dominant ideology—we attempted to sketch some general typologies of these two different "types" of scribes. Accordingly, submissive scribes were described as loyalists, writing in favor of the royal establishment and their supporters. Such individuals were responsible for producing religious and political propaganda in addition to a variety of other texts. Subversive scribes, on the other hand, were scribes who sought to undermine the ruling elite by critiquing the royal establishment. Although it was noted that such scribes could work overtly and covertly, primary attention was directed toward exploring the methods used by those scribes who opted carefully to conceal their covert critique. In this regard, I noted a variety of scribal techniques which could be deployed for this purpose, techniques which will again occupy our attention when investigating a variety of possible subversive elements in the Solomonic narrative.

The chapter concluded by giving some attention to the question of scribal intentionality and the degree to which we can be reasonably confident that the subversion we see was deliberately deployed. After considering both Sternberg's and Miscall's treatment of ambiguity, I concluded that some literary ambiguity does seem intentional and ultimately irresolvable. Further, I rejected the notion that texts are wholly indeterminate, believing it is still possible to detect a certain emphasis (meaning) on the surface of the text even if this is destabilized by other possible readings lurking just beneath the surface.

Finally, several indicators for detecting intentional scribal subversion were proposed. Recognizing the difficulties of deciding whether a scribe intended to be subversive in a particular instance or in a particular way, some suggestions were offered about where to look and when to suspect this subversion was purposeful and not just the result of textual indeterminacy. In the pages that follow, I will experiment with these ideas by applying them to 1 Kgs 1–11 in an attempt to discern evidence of subversion in the Solomonic narrative.

PART II


AN INVESTIGATION OF SCRIBAL SUBVERSION
IN 1 KINGS 1–11

Chapter 3

## PROLEGOMENA TO READING 1 KINGS 1–11

*It is also a delight to read the* Prolegomena.

—Douglas A. Knight[1]

The material in 1 Kgs 1–2 provides some of the clearest examples of propaganda and subversion in the entire Solomonic narrative and will be explored at some length in the following chapter. This will be followed by a discussion of selected passages in 1 Kgs 3–11 which can be regarded as being subversive in one way or another. But before we are ready to engage in those tasks, several preliminary matters require our attention. First, it is necessary to discuss the manuscript evidence for 1 Kgs 1–11 and the role textual criticism will play in this study. Second, brief attention will be given to the question of the appropriateness of speaking about a Deuteronomistic History (DtrH) and consequently, of referring to the activity of the Deuteronomist (Dtr). Third, questions will be raised about the propriety of the debate over whether this narrative was originally pro- or anti-Solomonic clearing the way for an alternative approach broad enough to embrace both favorable *and* unfavorable evaluations of the king. Fourth, I will offer a brief assessment of the Succession Narrative, particularly focusing on the relationship between portions of 2 Samuel and 1–2 Kings. Finally, some preliminary comments about the presence of the Dtr in 1 Kgs 1–2 will be given. It is asked that the reader be patient at this point, given the promise that future chapters will move more quickly and directly to an analysis of the biblical text itself.

### Textual Criticism

From a text-critical point of view, the most important witnesses to 1 Kings include the Masoretic text (MT), Codex Vaticanus ($G^B$), and the

1. Douglas A. Knight, forward to *Prolegomena to the History of Israel*, by Julius Wellhausen (Atlanta: Scholars Press, 1994), xvi. This epigraph is used with hopes that the same might be said of this present prolegomenon, albeit far shorter and much humbler.

Lucianic recension ($G^L$).[2] The standard MT, based upon the Codex Lenin-gradensis, is dated to 1009 CE, while Codex Vaticanus, which boasts of being the oldest complete manuscript of 1 Kings in Greek, dates to the fourth century CE. The value of $G^B$ as a witness to a textual tradition independent of the MT is compromised in those sections customarily referred to as the *Kaige* revision or recension. Henry St. J. Thackeray was the first to recognize the presence of different hands at work in the translation of Samuel–Kings in $G^B$.[3] He argued that an earlier translator, working from a Hebrew *Vorlage* of Egyptian provenance, produced the Greek translation of 1 Sam 1:1–2 Sam 11:1 and 1 Kgs 2:12–21:43. The intervening materials, 2 Sam 11:2–1 Kgs 2:11, along with 1 Kgs 22 and almost all of 2 Kings was thought to be translated by a different individual with a preference for preserving Hebrew idioms. This material, part of the *Kaige* revision, appears to have been corrected towards a pre- or proto-MT and therefore is less helpful as an independent textual witness. It is the non-*Kaige* portions of the Lucianic recension which are especially beneficial since they appear to have been unaffected by the Babylonian textual tradition and may therefore preserve readings which are closer to the Old Greek (OG).[4] And while the Lucianic revision is characterized by simplification, smoother grammatical and stylistic readings, and expansionistic glosses,[5] its apparent independence from the proto-Masoretic tradition makes it especially valuable.[6]

2.   For a general discussion and evaluation of available resources for a textual investigation of 1 Kings, see conveniently the standard commentaries: Simon J. DeVries, *1 Kings* (WBC 12; Waco, Tex.: Word, 1985), lii–lix; Gray, *I & II Kings*, 43–55; Jones, *1 and 2 Kings*, 2–9; James A. Montgomery and Henry Synder Gehman, *A Critical and Exegetical Commentary on the Books of Kings* (ICC; Edinburgh: T. & T. Clark, 1951), 8–24. More specialized studies include James D. Shenkel, *Chronology and Recensional Development in the Greek Text of Kings* (HSM 1; Cambridge, Mass.: Harvard University Press, 1968), and Julio Trebolle, "The Text-Critical Use of the Septuagint in the Books of Kings," in *VII Congress of the International Organization for Septuagint and Cognate Studies, Leuven 1989* (ed. Claude E. Cox; SBLSCS 31; Atlanta: Scholars Press, 1989), 285–99.

3.   Henry St. J. Thackeray, "The Greek Translators of the Four Books of Kings," *JTS* 8 (1907): 262–78; idem, *The Septuagint and Jewish Worship* (2d ed.; London: Oxford University Press, 1923).

4.   Bernard A. Taylor, *The Lucianic Manuscripts of I Reigns*. Vol. 2, *Analysis* (HSM 51; Atlanta: Scholars Press, 1993), 127–28, however, disputes the claim that the Lucianic text should be regarded as the OG.

5.   Gray, *I & II Kings*, 49.

6.   To these important manuscripts we could also add Chronicles, both the MT and Paralipomenon, though a discussion of the Solomonic material in 2 Chr 1–9 lies outside the scope of the present study.

Unfortunately, the Dead Sea Scrolls have yielded extremely limited material from 1 Kings and so contribute little to our investigation.[7] From the three identifiable manuscripts found in caves 4, 5, and 6, only fragmentary portions of 1 Kgs 1, 3, 7, 8, 12, 22, and 2 Kgs 5–8 remain. Although the evidence is slender, these materials do seem to confirm the notion that Kings, like Samuel, existed in *various* Hebrew forms in antiquity. That having been said, I would hasten to add that these fragments are largely in agreement with the proto-MT, demonstrating a marked preference for the Babylonian text type even though standardization was some time distant (the end of the first century CE). It has also been suggested that these fragments may lend modest support to the notion that the text behind Chronicles was not the MT but a longer, more expansive Hebrew *Vorlage*.[8]

Finally, we should call attention to the so-called "miscellanies" found at 3 Reigns 2:35a–o and 2:46a–l. These additions have been the object of intense scrutiny[9] and raise a variety of intriguing questions regarding their origin, unity, and purpose. Do they bear witness to a different *Vorlage* from the MT and might they contain more authentic readings? Have they been intentionally arranged around a common theme, are they simple anthologies, or is there no easily discernable explanation for their organization? Did these additions once stand at the end of Samuel or the beginning of Kings or do they reflect much later Greek exegesis?[10] It is not our intention to enter into that broader discussion here. Instead, for the purposes of this study, only very limited attention will be given to the miscellanies insofar as they relate to our interest in exploring propaganda and subversion.[11]

The scope and constraints of this present study (not to mention the author's linguistic limitations!), dictate the way in which textual criticism will factor into the following investigation. Though fully aware that the Greek versions can and sometimes do preserve superior readings to the MT, the MT will serve as the standard text for this study. Textual variants

7. For a brief discussion and English translation of the extant material, see Martin Abegg, Jr., Peter Flint, and Eugene Ulrich, *The Dead Sea Scrolls Bible: The Oldest Known Bible Translated for the First Time into English* (San Francisco: HarperCollins, 1999), 260–64.

8. So ibid., 260, 262.

9. See, e.g., D. W. Gooding, *Relics of Ancient Exegesis: A Study of the Miscellanies in 3 Reigns 2* (SOTSMS 4; Cambridge: Cambridge University Press, 1976); Emanuel Tov, "The LXX Additions (Miscellanies) in 1 Kings 2 (3 Reigns 2)," *Text* 11 (1984): 89–118.

10. These questions are all treated by Tov, "The LXX Additions."

11. See my discussion of 1 Kgs 3:1–3 in Chapter 5.

that are deemed important within certain key passages under investigation will be noted, especially when they might substantially alter the interpretation of a particular verse or passage.

## The Deuteronomist and the Deuteronomistic History

An earlier generation of scholars pursued with great enthusiasm the task of foraging through Deuteronomy–Kings in an attempt to distinguish original source material from the Dtr's redactional activity. Though some difference of opinion existed regarding the provenance of this or that particular verse, there was widespread consensus that the tools of critical scholarship could be used clearly to identify Dtr interference in the Deuteronomy–Kings complex. John Gray's confident assertion captures this *Zeitgeist*: "Deuteronomic comment and interpretation is added, but in such a way as to leave little doubt as to what is source and what is editorial comment."[12] Times have changed. Today there are many widely differing assessments of what is original source material and what should be regarded as secondary. This is due, in part, to the increasingly complex theories of Dtr redaction which have surfaced in the past thirty years. Questions about the limits, unity, and authorship of the Dtr have also contributed to the erosion of confidence in determining exactly what should or should not be assigned to the Dtr.[13]

In recent years, the very appropriateness of speaking of a DtrH has been called into question.[14] Some believe new models are needed for a proper understanding of this material, models which sometimes greatly reduce the presence of the Dtr if not doing away with this individual altogether.[15] The most serious challenges to the very notion of a Dtr, and to more traditional redactional-critical readings of Deuteronomy–Kings, have come from those who emphasize a strictly literary approach to the biblical text. For these individuals, features such as duplications and

---

12. Gray, *I & II Kings*, 15.

13. A full discussion of these issues lies outside the scope of this study. For some orientation, see the convenient collection of essays in Gary N. Knoppers and J. Gordon McConville, eds., *Reconsidering Israel and Judah: Recent Studies on the Deuteronomistic History* (Winona Lake, Ind.: Eisenbrauns, 2000).

14. For "a moderate defense" of the DtrH and an excellent review of the issues involved, see Knoppers, "Is there a Future for the Deuteronomistic History?," 119–34.

15. There have, for example, been efforts to read Genesis–Kings as a single connected story of Israel's origins composed largely in the Persian period. While this seems extreme, it represents a challenge to those—like myself—who continue to find the language of a DtrH and a Dtr appropriate.

disjunctions that were once believed to mark redactional activity are regarded as the tools of narrative art, intentionally deployed and ultimately indispensable when crafting a narrative. Literary critics pay careful attention to a variety of nuances, innuendos, and ambiguities when reading a text since these may be regarded as part of the narrative strategy. Jerome T. Walsh's commentary on 1 Kings in the Berit Olam series epitomizes this approach. Not surprisingly, questions about the Dtr or the DtrH are totally absent from his discussion in favor of a more "integrated reading" of the text as story.[16]

My reading of 1 Kings attempts to be sociologically sensitive while combining insights from traditional historical criticism with newer literary modes of reading.[17] It might be objected that this is impossible, or at least imprudent, given the apparent incompatibility of these approaches to the biblical text. But I do not think this must be the case. As I will argue, an appreciation of the sociological impulses behind the production and consumption of the Solomonic narrative not only allows room for both approaches to the text,[18] it also helps to explain the pervasive ambiguity which lingers over the character of Solomon.

## *Pro- or Anti-Solomonic: A False Dichotomy?*

Since neither source nor redaction criticism has traditionally had much appreciation for the literary artistry of ambiguity, narrative tension, or differing points of view—such features were routinely seized as evidence of multiple authorship—contradictory character assessments and conflicting evaluations of events became the raw material which allowed the text to be divided up into its constituent pieces. Such efforts have had a tremendous impact upon the study of materials in Samuel–Kings and

---

16. To my knowledge, except for an explanatory footnote on p. 37, Walsh does not even mention the Dtr in his section on 1 Kgs 1–11.

17. For example, while appreciating a scribe's ability to utilize literary tools such as repetition, reticence, and ambiguity to craft a narrative, I am also interested in exploring how the presence of secondary material affects my basic thesis and am not willing to ignore the contributions of traditional historical criticism.

18. I strongly favor the methodological approach programmatically set forth in Charles Conroy, "A Literary Analysis of 1 Kings I 41–53, with Methodological Reflections," in *Congress Volume: Salamanca, 1983* (VTSup 36; ed. J. A. Emerton; Leiden: Brill, 1985), 54–66. Rather than opting for either a historical or a literary approach, Conroy believes these two disciplines can and should inform one another. In his words, "It is not a question, then, of 'literary versus historical' in the sense of an either/or antagonism, but rather of working towards a responsible integration of the two areas of scholarly endeavour" (p. 55). With that I heartily concur.

earnest attempts have been made to determine whether the stories about Solomon's rise to power reflect positively or negatively on the "wise" king. As Simon J. DeVries puts it,

> There have been all sorts of pro and con arguments whether the throne-succession narrator actually wrote his history to legitimize Solomon in the place of his older brother, or wrote it disparagingly, to show how ruthless Solomon and his party had been in seizing what properly belonged to another.[19]

Yet must we choose? Must the original narrative have been *either* pro- *or* anti-Solomonic? Is it possible that traditional historical-critical research has imposed an unnecessary and possibly false dichotomy here? Rather than insisting that 1 Kgs 1–2, for example, be either for or against Solomon, might it not be *both* favorable *and* unfavorable to the king at the same time? I will argue that this is not only possible but highly probable, given the sociological context out of which this and similar texts emerged. The presence and activity of subversive scribes actually causes us to expect the production of highly ambiguous texts open to multiple readings *simultaneously*.

Many scholars contend that these chapters originally functioned as political propaganda designed to legitimate Solomon's right to rule.[20] As such, 1 Kgs 1–2 justified Solomon's kingship in two ways. First, it attempted to explain the reason for his unexpected rise to power. Second, it provided a defense for the concomitant acts of brutality which took place within the first few years of his reign. Yet even as the narrative defends Solomon, it implicitly raises troubling questions about the young king's rise to power, questions which give us pause. Might these unsettling innuendos suggest a subversive scribe at work here? Or was this simply a case in which a submissive scribe did his best to defend the

19. DeVries, *1 Kings*, 11.
20. See, for example, Whybray, *Succession Narrative*, 50–55, who is critiqued by James L. Crenshaw, "Method in Determining Wisdom Influence Upon 'Historical' Literature" *JBL* 88 (1969): 129–42 (137–40, esp. 138). Whybray is followed by Jones, *1 and 2 Kings*, 55–56; cf. A. A. Anderson, *2 Samuel* (WBC 11; Dallas: Word, 1989), xxxiv, who prefers describing this material as an "apology." Likewise, P. Kyle McCarter, Jr. ("Plots, True or False: The Succession Narrative as Court Apologetic," *Int* 35 [1981]: 355–67) speaks of 1 Kgs 1–2 as "court apologetic," though he does not distinguish this from political propaganda. For an alternate view, see Gunn, *Story of King David*, who proposes that the narrative functions as "serious entertainment" (pp. 61–62) rather than political propaganda (pp. 21–26). Cf. James S. Ackerman, "Knowing Good and Evil: A Literary Analysis of the Court History in 2 Samuel 9–20 and 1 Kings 1–2," *JBL* 109 (1990): 41–60 (59).

king, addressing delicate and potentially damaging issues which were well known to his audience and therefore unavoidable? Answers to these kinds of questions await our investigation of 1 Kgs 1–2, an investigation that will give attention to elements of both propaganda *and* subversion within 1 Kgs 1–2.

### The Succession Narrative

Also important to our study is the relationship between 1 Kgs 1–2 and 2 Samuel. Since Leonhard Rost's 1926 publication, *Die Überlieferung von der Thronnachfolge Davids*, many scholars have regarded 2 Sam 9–20 and 1 Kgs 1–2 as an independent document customarily referred to as the Succession Narrative. Among other things, Rost argued that 2 Sam 9–20 and 1 Kgs 1–2 constituted a unified composition written by someone close to the royal court early in Solomon's reign. Its purpose was to justify the king's seizure of power, thus defending his right to rule. Though Rost was not the first scholar to notice certain affinities between the second half of Samuel and the first two chapters of Kings, by systematically investigating these similarities he was able to mount an impressive and persuasive argument resulting in the widespread acceptance of his thesis. Since the publication of his programmatic essay there has been a constant stream of studies which have adopted, expanded, or otherwise clarified his conclusions.[21]

Yet despite the persistent popularity of Rost's proposal, there is considerable disagreement among scholars today about the limits, unity, purpose, dating,[22] and authorship[23] of the Succession Narrative. A few

---

21. For select examples, see Whybray, *Succession Narrative*, 1968; T. C. G. Thornton, "Solomonic Apologetic in Samuel and Kings," *Church Quarterly Review* 169 (1968): 159–66; Mettinger, *King and Messiah*, 27–32; Ishida, "Solomon's Succession," 175–87; Albert de Pury and Thomas Römer (eds.), *Die sogenannte Thronfolgegeschichte Davids: Neue Einsichten und Anfragen* (OBO 176; Freiburg: Universitätsverlag; Göttingen: Vandenhoeck & Ruprecht, 2000). For a structuralist approach highly critical of the "narrowly political reading" advanced by Rost and followed by others, see Burke O. Long, "A Darkness between Brothers: Solomon and Adonijah," *JSOT* 19 (1981): 79–94.

22. For a recent discussion of this issue, see John Barton, "Dating the 'Succession Narrative,'" in *In Search of Pre-exilic Israel: Proceedings of the Oxford Old Testament Seminar* (ed. John Day; JSOTSup 406; London: T. & T. Clark, 2004), 95–106. Barton favors a date some time in the eighth or seventh century.

23. Attempts to identify a specific author amount to pure conjecture. See, for example, Gray, *I & II Kings*, 24–25, who believes Nathan wrote this to justify his role in helping Solomon gain the throne, and Ishida, "Solomon's Succession," 187, who favors one of Nathan's followers.

have completely abandoned the very notion of such a narrative.[24] Since the connection (or disconnection) of 1 Kgs 1–2 with the Samuel materials has a direct bearing upon how we understand the purpose of the initial chapters in the Solomonic narrative, it behooves us to give some attention to these issues.

Regarding the limits or boundaries of the Succession Narrative, numerous studies have sought to clarify the initial efforts of Rost. Indeed, as Rost himself was aware, there are some formidable difficulties involved with positing 2 Sam 9 as the starting point of the Succession Narrative. It is not surprising, then, that various proposals have been put forth to establish an earlier beginning for the narrative in the books of Samuel.[25] These proposals have appeared in bewildering variety. Since establishing the most appropriate starting point of the Succession Narrative does not affect the substance of this study, it is unnecessary to discuss the relative merits of the proposals here. Suffice it to say there is no consensus regarding the narrative's *terminus a quo*. Less controversial has been establishing the ending of the narrative. Attempts to shorten the ending, including Tryggve N. D. Mettinger's proposal that the original narrative came to a close in 1 Kgs 2:12 (minus 1 Kgs 1:41–2:4, 10–11), have not been well received.[26] The standard view that 1 Kgs 2:46 marks the conclusion of the Succession Narrative is still widely accepted.[27]

Discussions of the interrelated issues of the unity, composition, and purpose of the Succession Narrative have been especially complex and contentious. Since Rost's study, many have wondered whether the Succession Narrative can rightly be regarded as an independent and unified composition with a single purpose. As early as the 1960s, scholars were asking questions about the fundamental unity of the Succession Narrative. Blenkinsopp, for example, wondered whether it might not be better to "distinguish two distinct if connected themes: the legitimisation of

---

24. R. A. Carlson, *David, the Chosen King: A Traditio-Historical Approach to the Second Book of Samuel* (Uppsala: Almquist & Wiksell, 1964). Carlson has not, however, attracted many followers.

25. Sometimes as early as 2 Sam 1:1! See, e.g., Anderson, *2 Samuel*, xxxi.

26. Mettinger, *King and Messiah*, 27–32. For a brief but incisive critique, see Long, "Darkness between Brothers," 80.

27. Though compare Robert P. Gordon's ("A House Divided: Wisdom in Old Testament Narrative Traditions," in Day, Gordon, and Williamson, eds., *Wisdom in Ancient Israel*, 94–105 [104–5]) strong opposition to "the hermetic sealing off of ch. ii from ch. iii" (p. 104). Additionally, the miscellanies in 3 Reigns 2 would also suggest a greater relationship between 1 Kgs 2 and what follows than is usually assumed, as noted by Knoppers, *Two Nations*, 62.

David's own claim, and the struggle for succession."[28] Building upon this notion, James W. Flanagan attempted to distinguish two separate stages in the formation of the Succession Narrative.[29] He argued that the first stage consisted of a literary unit which he described as a Court History (2 Sam 8:16–20:26) intended to legitimate David's rule over *all* Israel. Flanagan based his proposal on certain literary differences between 2 Sam 9–20 and 1 Kgs 1–2 as well as on the "literary balance" evident in 2 Sam 9–20 once the Solomonic material (2 Sam 11–12 and 1 Kgs 1–2) was set aside. Flanagan's second phase identified a later redactor who added the Solomonic sections, giving the overall narrative a succession flavor.

Similarly, P. Kyle McCarter, Jr. argues that 1 Kgs 1–2 was written at a different time by a different hand than the Samuel materials.[30] But unlike Flanagan, he is not content to speak of a single "court history" lying behind the Succession Narrative. Instead, he believes a series of independent documents with various themes and functions (though primarily concerned with David not Solomon) were utilized by the author of 1 Kgs 1–2. Since there is virtually no reference to Solomon or to the urgent matter of succession in 2 Samuel, McCarter believes 1 Kgs 1–2 was "composed *in reference to* materials in Second Samuel, which must have already existed when 1 Kings 1–2 were written."[31] McCarter's construal seems fundamentally convincing and serves as the basis for the present study.[32]

More radical attempts to view 1 Kgs 1–2 as an originally independent unit have met with little success, as have efforts to regard these chapters as originally part of the larger Solomonic narrative rather than part of the Samuel materials.[33] Nevertheless, it can no longer simply be taken for

---

28. Joseph Blenkinsopp, "Theme and Motif in the Succession History (2 Sam. XI 2ff) and the Yahwist Corpus," in *Volume du Congrès: Genève, 1965* (VTSup 15; Leiden: Brill, 1966), 44–57 (47).

29. J. W. Flanagan, "Court History or Succession Document? A Study of 2 Samuel 9–20 and 1 Kings 1–2," *JBL* 91 (1972): 172–81 (172–73 et passim). His view is rejected by Jones (*1 and 2 Kings*, 49) on thematic and stylistic grounds.

30. McCarter, "Plots True or False," 355–67.

31. Ibid., 361–62 (emphasis in original). McCarter is followed by C. L. Seow, "1 Kings 1:1–11:43: The Reign of Solomon," *NIB* 3:13–97 (13).

32. Cf. Kang, *Persuasive Portrayal of Solomon*, 101–39. Kang rejects the notion that 1 Kgs 1–2 is the end of the Succession Narrative and argues at length that 1 Kgs 1–11 is "a rhetorical unit" in its own right. In contrast to McCarter, Kang regards 1 Kgs 1–2 (and the entire Solomonic narrative) as an exilic composition (pp. 265–95).

33. See the attempt of Sigmund Mowinckel, "Israelite Historiography," *ASTI* 2 (1963): 4–26 (11–13).

granted that the Succession Narrative is an independent, unified composition written in the tenth century in defense of Solomon. The picture is surely much more complex.[34] Happily, in spite of the cloud of uncertainty which hangs over many aspects of the Succession Narrative, there seems to be general agreement about the nature and function of 1 Kgs 1–2. Whatever its relation to the Samuel material, most scholars acknowledge that 1 Kgs 1–2 was written in defense of Solomon. This has not always been the case. In the late 1960s and early 1970s several European scholars attempted to demonstrate that the Succession Narrative was originally anti-Solomonic. Leading the way was Lienhard Delekat, who emphasized the unflattering and critical reports about David and Solomon in the Succession Narrative.[35] Particularly, Delekat had in mind the Bathsheba narrative, Absalom's rebellion, and Solomon's accession to the throne.[36] According to Delekat, none of these incidents would have been included by a pro-monarchic writer, thus suggesting an author hostile to the Davidic monarchy. Delekat was followed by Ernst Würthwein, Timo Veijola, and F. Langlamet, who agreed that the text was originally anti-Solomonic but later underwent a pro-Solomonic redaction.[37] Yet this view has not attracted widespread support. Such efforts to regard the text as originally anti-Davidic/Solomonic on the basis of "negative" elements in the text have rightly been criticized by both McCarter and Ishida.[38] McCarter's critique is especially insightful and worth quoting at length. Speaking in reference to the aforementioned European scholars, he writes:

34. Peter R. Ackroyd, "The Succession Narrative (So-Called)," *Int* 35 (1981): 383–96, raises several critical issues which cast doubt upon the conventional boundaries of the Succession Narrative, challenge its supposedly unified theme, and warrant further investigation. His call for a broader, "less rigid reading" seems appropriate.

35. Lienhard Delekat, "Tendenz und Theologie der David-Salomo-Erzählung," in *Das ferne und nahe Wort* (ed. F. Maass; BZAW 105; Berlin: Topelmann, 1967), 22–36.

36. Ibid., 27.

37. Ernst Würthwein, *Die Erzählung von der Thronfolge Davids—theologische oder politische Geschichtsschreibung?* (Theologische Studien 115; Zürich: Theologischer Verlag, 1974); Timo Veijola, *Die Ewige Dynastie: David und die Entstehung seiner Dynastie nach der deuteronomistischen Darstellung* (Annales Academiae Scientiarum Fennicae B193; Helsinki: Suomalainen Tiedeakatemia, 1975); and F. Langlamet, "Pour ou contre Salomon? La rédaction prosalomonienne de I Rois, I–II," *RB* 83 (1976): 321–79, 481–529. I am indebted to McCarter, "Plots, True or False," 360 n. 12, for alerting me to these positions.

38. McCarter, "Plots, True or False," 359–61; Ishida, "Solomon's Succession," 186.

Much of the evidence they cite vanishes when the narrative is read as apologetic. Apologetic writing presents unfavorable circumstances forthrightly in order to cast a favorable light on them by a variety of means. By its very nature, then, it holds conflicting ideas in literary tension. The elimination of the literary blandishments of the author by appeal to higher critical or other considerations, therefore, will inevitably produce a recital of unfavorable circumstances, but it will also distort the writer's intended product beyond recovery. It is a mistake to rely heavily on the criterion of narrative tension for identifying redactional material in these stories, when such tension is the very essence of the writer's technique.[39]

Surely McCarter is right. Submissive scribes, commissioned to produce political propaganda, often faced the formidable task of putting the best possible face on unpleasant events. Such literary efforts attempting to neutralize highly questionable or patently unlawful royal behavior undoubtedly resulted in significant narrative "tension." This fact alone should caution us against demanding the hand of an anti-establishment (subversive) scribe whenever we encounter materials which may, at first glance, appear damaging to the king. Instead, it is reasonable to assume that such inclusions were made simply because the incident in question was too well-known to be swept under the rug. Its notoriety demanded a response lest the king succumb to charges of injustice, illegitimacy, or worse! By carefully presenting the facts in a way most favorable to the king, the submissive scribe(s) who produced the "official report" sought to exonerate him from all charges of wrongdoing or foul play. The next chapter will attempt to demonstrate how this was accomplished for King Solomon by the writer of 1 Kgs 1–2.

Though establishing a specific date for the composition of 1 Kgs 1–2 is elusive, it seems reasonable to assign at least the genesis of this text to the first half of Solomon's reign when the need for self-justification and legitimation were particularly acute.[40] Of course, such a dating assumes the existence of the historical, tenth-century Solomon. While few would have seriously challenged such a notion thirty years ago, several "minimalists" today—highly skeptical that the biblical texts even remotely reflect the historical situation in ancient Palestine—have raised substantial doubts about the existence of such noteworthy figures as David and Solomon.[41] While such conclusions are surely exaggerated, it is not

39. McCarter, "Plots, True or False," 360 n. 12.
40. Cf. Ishida, "Solomon's Succession," 187.
41. The best up-to-date survey of the current debate with generous bibliographic notation is Gary N. Knoppers, "The Vanishing Solomon: The Disappearance of the United Monarchy from Recent Histories of Ancient Israel," *JBL* 116 (1997): 19–44. See also William G. Dever, *What Did the Biblical Writers Know & When Did they*

my intention to enter into that debate here except to say that accepting Solomon (and David) as (a) historical figure(s) who exercised considerable control over significant portions of ancient Israel in the tenth century BCE is a different matter from determining how much or how little historically reliable information about Solomon can be extracted from 1 Kings.

Ishida is one of several scholars who accepts the general historicity of the Succession Narrative and the events it reports.[42] This assumption is especially crucial to him given his repeated appeals that the Succession Narrative be read as Solomonic apologetic. Through a variety of publications he has attempted to demonstrate that 1 Kgs 1–2 is "an apologetic composition from the early days of Solomon, aiming at legitimizing not only his irregular succession but also his execution of his brother, high officials of the old regime and a leader of the Saulides."[43] While I would agree with Ishida's sentiments that 1 Kgs 1–2 be read as Solomonic apologetic (though I will argue not *only* as that), I am less comfortable with his suggestion that the Succession Narrative was written in "defense of Solomon against the old regime of David."[44] As will be argued in the following chapter, the situation appears to be rather more complex. The contest appears to have been ideologically charged, pitting supporters of the old Israelite features of the kingship of David against those who advocated a new state system already, at least to some extent, initiated by David.

Because the Succession Narrative shares a number of common features with certain ancient Near Eastern parallels which function similarly, Ishida believes it ought to be included in the same genre, a genre he has proposed calling, "Royal Historical Writings of an Apologetic Nature in the Ancient Near East."[45] Other documents which Ishida would place in this category include the Telepinu Proclamation, the Apology of Hattu-

*Know It? What Archaeology Can Tell Us about the Reality of Ancient Israel* (Grand Rapids: Eerdmans, 2001), 97–157, for an assessment of the relevant archaeological data.

42. In this regard, see Tomoo Ishida, "Adonijah the Son of Haggith and his Supporters: An Inquiry into Problems about History and Historiography," in *The Future of Biblical Studies: The Hebrew Scriptures* (ed. Richard E. Friedman and H. G. M. Williamson; Decatur, Ga.: Scholars Press, 1987), 165–87 (165–71).

43. Tomoo Ishida, "Solomon Who is Greater than David: Solomon's Succession in 1 Kings I–II in the Light of the Inscription of Kilamuwa, King of y'dy-Šam'al," in Emerton, ed., *Congress Volume: Salamanca, 1983*, 145–53 (145).

44. Ibid. This argument is made at length in Ishida, "Solomon's Succession," 175–87.

45. Ishida, "Adonijah the Son of Haggith," 168.

sili III, the Neo-Assyrian apologies of Shamshi-Adad V, Esarhaddon and Ashurbanipal, and the inscription of Kilamuwa.[46] He highlights several elements which these narratives have in common, namely, an emphasis upon the reigning king's (1) royal lineage, (2) his rival's unworthiness, (3) his rival's rebellious attempt to gain the throne, (4) counter-attack and victory, (5) magnanimity toward or elimination of his enemies, and (6) establishment of justice.[47] We will explore several of these items more thoroughly in the following chapter.

### The Deuteronomist in 1 Kings 1–2

The final preliminary matter requiring our attention concerns the presence of the Dtr in 1 Kgs 1–2. Historically scholars have found little evidence of Dtr editing in this portion of the Solomonic narrative. Rost, for example, attributed less than four verses out of a total of ninety-nine to the Dtr, finding no evidence of the Dtr in ch. 1 and only minimal interference in ch. 2 (vv. 2–4, 27b).[48] While some scholars have followed Rost by insisting that there is no evidence of the Dtr in 1 Kgs 1,[49] most allow for some secondary material. A moderate assessment is offered by Gwylim H. Jones who argues that vv. 35b–37 and 46–48 are secondary and that some light reworking of v. 30 is evident.[50]

The situation in ch. 2 is considerably more complicated. Many have argued for extensive Dtr editing in the so-called "Testament of David" (2:1–9) and the following annalistic notation (2:10–12). Gray, for example, believes 2:1–4 and 10–12 is "certainly secondary" and regards nly secondary" and regards vv. 5–9 as suspect, though allows that they may have come from the original source. At least one or more verses in each of the four episodes which follow have also been attributed to the Dtr: Adonijah (v. 24), Abiathar (v. 27), Joab (vv. 31b–33), and Shimei (vv. 44–45).[51] On the whole, most scholars regard the majority of chs 1–2

46. Ibid., 168–69. Ishida's more detailed studies of the Kilamuwa inscription and the Esarhaddon's Apology can be found in his "Solomon Who is Greater than David," 145–53, and "The Succession Narrative and Esarhaddon's Apology: A Comparison," in *Ah, Assyria: Studies in Assyrian History and Ancient Near Eastern Historiography Presented to Hayim Tadmor* (ed. Mordecai Cogan and Israel Eph'al; ScrHier 33; Jerusalem: Magnes, 1991), 166–73.
47. Ishida, "Adonijah the Son of Haggith," 169.
48. Rost, *Succession to the Throne*, 87.
49. So DeVries, *1 Kings*, 9.
50. Jones, *1 and 2 Kings*, 51.
51. For a very careful—though in my opinion somewhat exaggerated—analysis of the Dtr expansion in 1 Kgs 2, see Jeffrey S. Rogers, "Narrative Stock and

as intact material which experienced relatively light editing, even if more extensive than Rost's earlier thesis would allow. While my investigation of 1 Kgs 1–2 will primarily be focusing on those elements in the non-Dtr sections of the narrative which date to the reign of Solomon, there will also be some discussion of these supposed Dtr expansions and their effect upon our reading of the narrative.

Deuteronomistic Elaboration in 1 Kings 2," *CBQ* 50 (1988): 398–413, who assigns 2:3–4, 11–12 (?), 22b, 24, 26–27, 31b–33, 35, 44–45 to the Dtr. Cf. Knoppers, *Two Nations*, 64.

Chapter 4

PROPAGANDA AND SUBVERSION IN SOLOMON'S
RISE TO POWER: 1 KINGS 1–2

*It is necessary for a prince wishing to hold his own to know how
to do wrong, and to make use of it or not according to necessity.*

—Machiavelli[1]

*But as knowledge of the facts may lead a person to dangerous
thoughts, the facts must be presented so as to direct the mind
into the proper channels.*
—the prophet "Nathan"[2]

*The telling of a story, the writing of a text, is often an attempt
to control—to influence an attitude, to reinforce a world-view,
to reconfigure (and thus render acceptable or understandable)
a critical experience.*

—David Gunn and Danna Fewell[3]

The book of 1 Kings begins with a brief spotlight on David who appears
as an aging and sexually impotent monarch. "Old and advanced in
years," it is only a matter of time before David will die and a new king
will take his place. But who? As David's fourth and oldest surviving son,
it seems that Adonijah believed he would succeed his father. Apparently
many others thought likewise since he found significant support among
some fairly notable persons including Abiathar, the Israelite high priest,
Joab, the commander of the national army, all the king's sons (except
Solomon),[4] and the leaders of the army.[5] Still, not everyone sided with

1. Nicolò Machiavelli, *The Prince* (trans. W. K. Marriott; ed. Robert Maynard
Hutchens; Chicago: William Benton, 1952), Chapter 15.
2. Stefan Heym, *The King David Report* (New York: G. P. Putnam's Sons,
1973), 82.
3. Gunn and Fewell, *Narrative in the Hebrew Bible*, 157.
4. 1 Kgs 1:9–10, 19, 25–26.
5. This final group, *śāre haṣṣābāʾ*, is according to Nathan's report in the MT and
G$^B$ at 1 Kgs 1:25. The NRSV follows G$^L$ which reads τον αρχιστρατηγον ιωαβ.

Adonijah. Conspicuously absent from his regal revelry by the rock at En-rogel were Zadok the (Jebusite?) priest, Benaiah the commander of David's non-Israelite mercenaries, Nathan the prophet, and David's personal guard (1:8).[6] Specific attention is drawn to the fact (?) that Adonijah reportedly did not invite Nathan, Benaiah, David's personal guard, or Solomon to the festivities (1:10).

This alignment suggests that the struggle for the throne was more than just a battle between brothers. Iain W. Provan believes "the conflict in ch. 1 to be largely conflict between old, Judah-based comrades of David from the Hebron days, and newer, Jerusalem-based associates."[7] This implies that the struggle between the supporters of Adonijah and the supporters of Solomon mirrors an ideological dispute over traditional Israelite values and the nature of kingship itself.[8] Joab and Abiathar, two of Adonijah's key supporters, were long-time associates of David from his earliest days.[9] They were the old guard who represented the values and beliefs of traditional Israel.[10] Solomon's supporters, on the other hand, may be regarded as avant-garde royalists whose innovative political

6. Shimei and Rei are apparently also among Solomon's supporters, though nothing further is known about these individuals, unless this Shimei was the son of Gera, the same individual who insulted David (2 Sam 16:5–13) and was later killed by Solomon (1 Kgs 2:8–9, 39–46). While Iain W. Provan (*1 and 2 Kings* [NIBCOT; Peabody, Mass.: Hendrickson, 1995], 28) favors such an identification, this position is the minority view and does not seem to fit the context. In 1 Kgs 2, Solomon is eliminating those who have opposed him. Why in this one isolated case would he kill one of his own supporters? It seems better to regard the Shimei who does not side with Adonijah (1 Kgs 1:8) and Shimei son of Gera as two separate individuals. For a discussion of alternative readings of *šimʿî* and *rēʿî* by those who regard the text as corrupt, see C. F. Burney, *The Book of Judges with Introduction and Notes and Notes on the Hebrew Text of the Books of Kings with an Introduction and Appendix* (New York: Ktav, 1970), 4–5; repr. of *Notes on the Hebrew Text of the Books of Kings with an Introduction and Appendix* (n.p., 1903); Montgomery and Gehman, *Kings*, 84; and most recently, Cogan, *I Kings*, 158, who refers the reader to Noth "for a survey of suggested emendations and his hesitant retention of MT." See Martin Noth, *Könige* (BKAT 9/1; Neukirchen–Vluyn: Neukirchener, 1968), 16–17.

7. Iain W. Provan, "Why Barzillai of Gilead (1 Kings 2:7)? Narrative Art and the Hermeneutics of Suspicion in 1 Kings 1–2," *TynBul* 46 (1995): 103–16 (114 n. 10).

8. Cf. Walsh, *1 Kings*, 8.

9. Abiathar: 1 Sam 22:20–23; Joab: 2 Sam 2:12–17; cf. 1 Sam 26:6.

10. Notice, for example, when both Adonijah and Joab fear for their life they flee to the *ʾōhel yhwh* (1 Kgs 1:50; 2:28), appealing to old Israelite tradition. Benaiah, on the other hand, apparently has no special attachment to such tradition and exhibits no compunction about killing Joab within these sacred precincts (1 Kgs 2:34), a murderous act comparable to Doeg the Edomite's gruesome slaying of the priests at Nob (1 Sam 22:18).

agenda would necessitate some dissociation from Israel's past.[11] Notice, for example, that two of Solomon's key supporters, Nathan and Zadok (who is of uncertain ancestry[12]), are only associated with David *after* he moves his capital to Jerusalem.[13] Presumably, they and their like-minded compatriots held different ideas about the role and nature of the monarchy which would be developed in distinctly new ways under Solomon. This fundamental tension between the old and the new—a tension which would have been quite familiar to the original readers/hearers of this narrative—may provide significant insight into the motivation for the succession struggle described in 1 Kgs 1 even though it is not particularly emphasized by the text.

Whatever the particular reasons lying behind this conflict, as the text portrays it, it is Adonijah's reportedly pre-emptive actions which precipitate the combined and carefully choreographed efforts of Bathsheba and Nathan who successfully persuade the aging king to appoint Solomon as his successor. Although the news of Solomon's anointing and installation causes Adonijah and his supporters to scatter, they are still perceived as a threat (cf. 1 Kgs 2:13, 22), a threat which is eliminated by the time we reach the end of 1 Kgs 2.

In a series of four episodes which leaves three men dead and one in "exile," Solomon consolidates his power. First, Adonijah is murdered for the risky request he reportedly made. Abiathar is then sent into Anathothian exile and replaced by Zadok. Joab is the next to go and suffers an altar-side execution at the hands of Benaiah, his replacement. And finally, three years later, Shimei is executed for making an inoffensive but forbidden journey. In short, the kingdom is firmly established in Solomon's hand (2:46). While these reports can be understood as pro-Solomonic propaganda, there are, nevertheless, some disturbing undercurrents that cast suspicion upon the motives and actions of Solomon. As Noth observed many years ago, "Der Inhalt dieser Abschnitten spricht kaum zu seinen Gunsten."[14] It is this disadvantageous discourse that will be of particular interest when we examine the final four episodes of 1 Kgs 2.

---

11. Brueggemann (*1 & 2 Kings*, 12) describes the struggle as being between "theological conservatives who take more seriously the old covenantal traditions" and "those who want to see royal policies of a more 'developmental' kind."

12. For a discussion of Zadok's ancestry, see Cross, *Canaanite Myth and Hebrew Epic*, 207–15, who argues against the "Jebusite hypothesis" and favors viewing Zadok as an Aaronid from Hebron.

13. Nathan first appears in the narrative at 2 Sam 7:2, Zadok at 2 Sam 8:17.

14. Noth, *Könige*, 39: "The content of these sections [of ch. 2] hardly speak to his advantage" (translation mine). I am indebted to DeVries (*1 Kings*, 43) for alerting me to Noth's assessment that 1 Kgs 1–2 is unfavorable toward Solomon.

## An Outline of What is Reported in 1 Kings 1–2[15]

1:1–4      AN IMPOTENT KING
1:5–53     A STRUGGLE FOR THE THRONE

       1:5–10       Adonijah's self-appointed kingship
       1:11–14     Nathan's calculated proposal
       1:15–40     David's induced appointment
       1:41–49     Jonathan's alarming report
       1:50–53     Solomon's initial restraint

2:1–12     DAVID'S LIFE WANES

       2:1–9        David's final instructions
       2:10–12     David's death and burial

2:13–46 SOLOMON'S POWER GROWS

       2:13–25     Adonijah's deadly desire
       2:26–27     Abiathar's exile to Anathoth
       2:28–35     Joab's altar-side execution
       2:36–46     Shimei's forbidden journey

## Propaganda and Subversion in 1 Kings 1[16]

In Rost's original proposal, he argued that the author of the Succession Narrative set out to answer the question, "Who will sit on David's throne?" This was later challenged by T. C. G. Thornton who felt the underlying question was not simply, "'Who will succeed David to the throne?', but rather 'Why was it Solomon who succeeded David to the throne?'"[17] Given the fact that Solomon was not David's oldest surviving son, such a question was to be expected. In fact, if the Chronicler's account is trustworthy, Solomon could not even claim to be the first born son of Bathsheba, having been preceded by three other baby boys (1 Chr 3:5). As, according to 1 Chronicles, Bathsheba's fourth[18] and David's

---

15.   Given the rather tendentious nature of these chapters, there is good reason to question the characterization of the main players. Additionally, in some cases it is debatable whether the events reported ever took place at all. The following discussion attempts to account for this uncertain portrayal of characters and events by nuancing certain features of the narrative by prefacing them with words and phrases which raise questions about the reliability of the story at hand.

16.   My procedure for 1 Kgs 1–2 will be to examine each chapter separately, realizing that while they are undoubtedly related, each exhibits an essential unity. This point is forcefully argued by Long, "Darkness between Brothers," passim, in regard to 1 Kgs 1.

17.   Thornton, "Solomonic Apologetic," 160.

18.   If this datum is reliable, it would suggest that Solomon was considerably younger than Adonijah. For alternate understanding of Solomon's birth position,

tenth (!) son,[19] it is not difficult to imagine that there were suspicions surrounding Solomon's legitimacy as successor even if we assume that many of Solomon's presumed older brothers did not survive childhood.

In many ways, 1 Kgs 1 robustly responds to these challenges as it rises in defense of King Solomon. For example, Adonijah's pro-active efforts to become king are painted in stark contrast to Solomon's total passivity throughout the entire affair. According to the narrative account, Solomon is simply the fortunate recipient of the crown due to the efforts of others. As I will argue below, this emphasis on Solomon's involuntary participation was intended to neutralize charges of usurpation and illegitimacy. Additionally, the text appears to be at great pains to demonstrate that Solomon was both selected by David *and* elected by God. Both features are common marks of political propaganda and would have further justified Solomon's right to rule.[20]

The following analysis of 1 Kgs 1 will explore a variety of elements in this chapter which demonstrate its propagandistic functions. We will also be interested in noting several ambiguous features which raise questions about whether Solomon's accession was entirely in order. To take one example, we will need to explore the question of whether David actually made a divine oath to Bathsheba promising Solomon to be his successor. If the text leaves open the possibility that Nathan and Bathsheba simply concocted the whole story, taking advantage of David's failing health in order to get their man on the throne, it would appear to subvert rather than support Solomon by raising questions about his legitimacy.

*Adonijah's Ambitions and Solomon's Passivity*
As noted above, the narrative opens with a brief vignette of King David's advanced age (1:1–4), implicitly raising the question of who will succeed him after his death. The answer is not long in coming, as the story

see Timo Veijola, "Salomo—der erstgeborgene Bathsebas," in *Studies in the Historical Books of the Old Testament* (ed. J. A. Emerton; VTSup 30; Leiden: Brill, 1979), 230–50.

19. The order, according to 2 Sam 3:2–5 (Hebron) and 5:14–16 (Jerusalem) is as follows: (1) Amnon, (2) Chileab, (3) Absalom, (4) Adonijah, (5) Shephatiah, (6) Ithream, (7) Shammua, (8) Shobab, (9) Nathan, (10) Solomon, (11) Ibhar, (12) Elishua, (13) Nepheg, (14) Japhia, (15) Elishama, (16) Eliada, and (17) Eliphelet. The Chronicler (1 Chr 3:1–9) preserves a slightly different list, with two duplicate names (Elishama and Eliphelet) and two different names (Daniel in place of Chileab and Nogah in place of Elishua) resulting in a total of nineteen rather than seventeen.

20. Cf. Ishida ("Adonijah son of Haggith," 170) who cites three common features in ancient Near Eastern attempts to justify kings: "royal lineage," "divine election," and "his competency to rule."

immediately shifts to some extraordinary events taking place just outside the palace where Adonijah is making a bid for the throne (1:5–10).

From all external indicators, Adonijah seemed a logical choice to succeed David. This *appears* to be the intent of the parenthetical statement in v. 6, though momentarily we will consider other possibilities. Adonijah, we are told, never had reason to suspect David's displeasure with him.[21] This is probably meant to suggest that David had been rather indulgent with his son, giving no prior indications that he would be disqualified from kingly consideration when the appropriate time came. It would appear, therefore, that David's lenient attitude toward Adonijah amounted to tacit approval that he would be the next king, a claim never disputed in the text and thus one which seems mildly subversive of Solomon's legitimacy. We are also informed that Adonijah was "handsome," a characteristic he shared in common with Absalom and David. In other words, he had the kind of personal appearance associated with kingship in the Davidic period.[22] And finally, it is noted that he was "born next after Absalom." As David's oldest surviving son (presumably Chileab/Daniel was dead), Adonijah would have been the most likely candidate[23] to succeed David based on the principle of primogeniture.[24] While Adonijah's privileged position did not automatically guarantee his accession, it surely provided him with a reasonable basis for his actions. As Gary N. Knoppers observes, "Adonijah had clearly reckoned that primogeniture counted for something."[25] Apparently, he was not the only

21. Cf. the similar comment regarding David's oldest son Amnon in 2 Sam 13:21b, which is supported by 4QSam[a] and the LXX, though omitted in the MT (by *homoioteleuton*): "but he [David] would not punish his son Amnon, because he loved him, for he was his firstborn."

22. Adonijah is described as being *ṭōb tōʾar* (*mĕʾōd*). With the possible exception of an unnamed Egyptian in 2 Sam 23:21—though the text may be corrupt here—the only other men in the DtrH noted for their attractive appearance are royal (or potentially royal) figures: Saul (*wĕʾên ʾîš mibbĕnê yiśrāʾēl ṭōb mimennû*, 1 Sam 9:2); Eliab (implicitly, 1 Sam 16:6); David (*ʾîš tōʾar*, 1 Sam 16:18; cf. 17:42); Absalom (*lōʾ hayâ ʾîš yāpê bĕkol yiśrāʾēl lĕhallēl mĕʾōd*, 2 Sam 14:25). Cf. Abigail who is described as being *yĕpat tōʾar* (1 Sam 25:3). In the DtrH, however, impressive physical appearance alone is not the determinative criteria of kingship since Yahweh "looks on the heart" (1 Sam 16:7).

23. Certainly more likely than Solomon who was Adonijah's *younger* brother (1 Kgs 2:22).

24. For a recent defense of the practice of primogeniture in ancient Israel against the efforts of F. E. Greenspahn who argues to the contrary, see Gary N. Knoppers, "The Preferential Status of the Eldest Son Revoked?," in *Rethinking the Foundations: Historiography in the Ancient World and in the Bible* (ed. Steven L. McKenzie and Thomas Römer; Berlin: de Gruyter, 2000), 115–26.

25. Ibid., 120.

one. In a revealing statement, Adonijah tells Bathsheba: "You know that the kingdom was mine, and that *all Israel expected me to reign*" (2:15a). And while the claim of pan-Israelite expectation is certainly a bit exaggerated, as 1 Kgs 1:8, 39–40 make clear, it seems many people—perhaps most—had actually looked to Adonijah to be their next king. According to David Marcus, "there is no clear indication that Adoniyah had revolted at all. As the heir apparent, and with David so close to death, there would have been no need to do so."[26]

Whatever legitimate claims of succession Adonijah may have had, the text has all but obscured them by painting his bid for the throne as an act of personal self-aggrandizement. Notice the way in which the text portrays an ambitious and very pro-active quest for the kingship in vv. 5–10:

1. He exalted himself (*mitnassê*[27]) by proclaiming himself king (v. 5)
2. He prepared chariots and horsemen to run before him (v. 5)
3. He conferred with[28] Joab and Abiathar (v. 7)
4. He sacrificed sheep, oxen, and fatted cattle (v. 9)
5. He invited (*qārā*) his brothers and royal Judahite officials to the sacrifice (v. 9).

The questionable side of Adonijah's aspirations are also indicated by his reportedly restrictive guest list. Although the reader is initially informed that Adonijah invited all his brothers and all the royal officials, this is quickly qualified. Several key invitations were apparently never made. Nathan, Benaiah, David's mercenaries, and Solomon (!) are all said to be excluded (*lô qārā*) by Adonijah and take no part in his festivities. This implies "that Adonijah's invitations are extended on a partisan basis,"[29] imputing sinister, or at least "calculated," motives to Adonijah, thereby leaving his actions open to suspicion.[30]

The rather unflattering portrait of Adonijah which emerges here also challenges my previous assertion that the narrative aside in v. 6 reflects

26. David Marcus, "David the Deceiver and David the Dupe," *Proof* 6 (1986): 163–71 (167).

27. The use of the Hithpael is suggestive here, especially given the factitive nature of its reflexive force. On this, see Bruce K. Waltke and M. O'Connor, *An Introduction to Biblical Hebrew Syntax* (Winona Lake, Ind.: Eisenbrauns, 1990), §26.2b–c. From the writer's perspective, Adonijah's bid for kingship may be just that, *Adonijah's* bid! We might say that Adonijah "makes himself exalted." Note also the use of the emphatic first person pronoun *ănî*.

28. Literally, "his words were with." This seems to imply that Adonijah eagerly sought the support of key Judahite officials.

29. Walsh, *1 Kings*, 9.

30. Of course, the same accusation could be leveled against Solomon as well!

positively upon the hopeful king.[31] Rather than suggesting that Adonijah had David's tacit approval, a less favorable reading might suggest that Adonijah enjoyed a great measure of parental indulgence and was accustomed to doing and getting whatever he wanted. Similarly, Adonijah might have simply presumed, on the basis of his birth position (and perhaps his good looks), that he would enjoy popular support as king.[32] Additionally, the reference to being "next after Absalom" may be particularly foreboding if intended to associate Adonijah's bid for the throne with Absalom's. Given the many implicit parallels between the actions of Adonijah and Absalom,[33] by highlighting this unhappy association, "Adonijah is skillfully tarred with Absalom's brush."[34] Moreover, an emphasis upon Adonijah's position as the *eldest* son casts a shadow over the presumed heir apparent. As McCarter observes,

> Adonijah, already inculpated by association with the conduct of Absalom, is brought under further suspicion as successor to the position of eldest son. The status of eldest son of David—once held by Amnon, then Absalom, and now Adonijah—looks almost like a curse, condemning a young man to a life of prodigal unreliability, selfishness, and even villainy. How much better, we are invited to conclude, that a king's son of lower rank, free throughout his childhood from the spoiling privileges of first position, should ascend the throne as the considered choice of his father![35]

Adonijah is further villainized through the speeches of Nathan and Bathsheba[36] who portray his enthronement as a *fait accompli* (1:13, 18, 25). When Nathan first approaches Bathsheba he asks whether she is aware of the fact that Adonijah has become king (*mālak*). Bathsheba, in turn, repeats this charge in the presence of David (v. 18). And when

31. See Ishida, "Adonijah the Son of Haggith," 171–74, who regards vv. 5–6 as totally unfavorable to Adonijah given the parallels drawn in these verses—implicitly and explicitly—between this aspiring king and the rebellious Absalom. See below for discussion.

32. As Walsh (*1 Kings*, 7) sees it, "Adonijah…is not only presumptuous; he is also spoiled and vain, counting on his father's indulgence and his own beauty to gain him the throne."

33. The parallels include (1) gathering chariots and horsemen (v. 5; 2 Sam 15:1), (2) being physically attractive (v. 6; 2 Sam 14:25), (3) celebrating a feast and offering sacrifices (v. 9; 2 Sam 15:11–12), and (4) being sent home by the reigning king (v. 53; 2 Sam 14:24).

34. Richard D. Nelson, *First and Second Kings* (IBC; Louisville, Ky.: John Knox, 1987), 19.

35. McCarter, "Plots, True or False," 366.

36. Their carefully synchronized efforts (1 Kgs 1:14), raise certain suspicions about the propriety of their actions. Provan (*1 and 2 Kings*, 26) believes this pair was hoping "to avoid the impression of collusion."

Nathan enters, he even goes to the extent of telling David that people are saying, "Long live King Adonijah."[37]

These claims are cleverly "supported" by various means. First, both Nathan and Bathsheba capitalize on Adonijah's alleged exclusionary activities noted above, particularly his failure to invite "your servant Solomon" (1:19, 26).[38] This is especially onerous given the fact he had otherwise invited *all* the king's sons![39] Presented in this way, the clear implication is that such an omission—if real—was both intentional and devious.[40] Second, the threefold reporting of Adonijah's sacrificing in 1 Kgs 1 does not bode well for the aspiring king. The initial report says nothing about how many animals were offered, simply informing the reader that "Adonijah sacrificed sheep, oxen, and fatted cattle" (1:9). In and of itself, such an act was not unusual or necessarily seditious.[41] As Provan remarks, "There is really nothing in 1:9–10 to suggest that Adonijah's meal is the coronation banquet it appears to have become in vv. 13, 18–19, 24–25."[42] Notice that when Bathsheba and Nathan report this activity to the aged King David (vv. 19, 25), they both comment on the massive quantity of Adonijah's sacrifices by adding one small word: *lārōb*. They accuse Adonijah of sacrificing animals "in abundance." Since their speeches seem to be an artful attempt to portray Adonijah as having already assumed the kingship, this small addition takes on great significance. This is particularly true in light of the fact that despite David's apparent agedness, he is, nevertheless, still the king. The implication is that Adonijah's actions pose a threat not only to Solomon, but to David himself! Finally, the treacherous nature of Adonijah's actions

37. Interestingly, this is the only reference in the entire narrative to "King Adonijah." Elsewhere he is simply referred to as Adonijah, or Adonijah son of Haggith (1:5, 11; 2:13).

38. Solomon's exclusion from the feast is never explained in the narrative. Although Bathsheba and Nathan insinuate that Adonijah's intentions were evil, it may be that Solomon was not invited simply because he was thought to be of such little consequence (cf. Provan, *1 Kings*, 25). If so, this is reminiscent of David's initial exclusion when Samuel invited Jesse and his sons to the sacrifice he was making (1 Sam 16:1–13). David was absented from the festivities simply because he was the youngest and least likely candidate, not as the result of any devious exclusionary designs.

39. Mentioned by both Bathsheba (v. 19) and Nathan (v. 25).

40. Secondarily, it also has the neat effect of removing Solomon from complicity in Adonijah's activities (cf. Seow, *1 Kings*, 19).

41. Contra C. L. Seow, "The Syro-Palestinian Context of Solomon's Dream," *HTR* 77 (1984): 141–52 (145), who contends that Adonijah's actions were tantamount to claiming the throne.

42. Provan, *1 Kings*, 28.

are accentuated by emphasizing that they have reportedly taken place without David's knowledge (1:11, 18). In this way, Adonijah is portrayed as scheming and untrustworthy.

Still, there is enough ambiguity in the text to raise questions about Adonijah's precise intentions. For instance, while Adonijah expresses a desire to become king (1:5), there is no clear indication that he actually becomes king. Likewise, his festivities need not be construed as an "unauthorized coronation" but may have simply been one of several necessary steps for support gathering on his way to kingship.[43] Finally, given the inherent difficulty of determining Adonijah's true intentions, the words of Bathsheba and Nathan—neither of whom are disinterested parties—are immediately suspect.

That notwithstanding, I submit that the foregoing analysis reveals a rather extensive effort to paint Adonijah in the darkest hues. In many ways, this negative characterization is strongly reminiscent of the malicious Kashtiliash as depicted in the Tukulti-Ninurta Epic[44] where such a caricature is used with strong propagandistic effect. Within the world of this text, Tukulti-Ninurta can do no wrong while Kashtiliash, the ill-fated Kassite king ruling in Babylon, can do no right. Early in the Epic, Kashtiliash is decried as "the transgressor of an oath" (line 34; cf. lines 53, 72, 75). Later he is called "the wicked, the obstinate, the heedless" (line 109; cf. line 136). In fact, the Epic repeatedly "contrasts the treaty treachery of Kaštiliaš with the treaty loyalty of Tukulti-Ninurta. Indeed, Kaštiliaš can hardly be mentioned without being denounced for his treachery, nor Tukulti-Ninurta without being praised for his loyalty."[45] The text even includes a self-incriminating soliloquy "spoken by" Kashtiliash (lines 166–97). The words of the Kassite king read like a guilty plea submitted to a judge: "Many are my wrong-doings before Shamash," confesses Kashtiliash, "great are my misdeeds" (line 178).

Even though Adonijah speaks no self-incriminating soliloquy as does Kashtiliash, we have seen many features in 1 Kgs 1 whereby the writer has villainized Adonijah. Emphasizing Adonijah's guilt is essential since it directs the reader's sympathies toward Solomon and his supporters and helps to render acceptable his "removal" in 1 Kgs 2. Such villainization

---

43. So Nelson, *First and Second Kings*, 16.

44. For translation, see Benjamin R. Foster, *From Distant Days: Myths, Tales, and Poetry of Ancient Mesopotamia* (Bethesda, Md.: CDL Press, 1995), 178–96. The best discussion of the political and propagandistic features of this text is Peter Machinist, "Literature as Politics: The Tukulti-Ninurta Epic and the Bible," *CBQ* 38 (1976): 455–82.

45. Machinist, "Literature As Politics," 458.

of the enemy is but one of several characteristic features of the literature of propaganda.

In stark contrast to Adonijah's pro-active ambitions, Solomon is portrayed as a totally passive participant in the events leading up to his coronation.[46] He reportedly neither says nor does anything to promote himself and certainly engages in no direct contest with Adonijah. In fact, Solomon is not the subject of a single action verb until *after* he has been made king.[47] He is totally silent throughout the entire affair and even after his anointing speaks only two brief statements (1:52–53) until David dies (2:10). Solomon simply enjoys the results of a court intrigue (1:11–27) which prompts David's directives to make him king (1:28–35). Even as Solomon travels to be anointed as king, the aspect of the verb chosen suggests that Solomon is, quite literally, just along for the ride:

> So the priest Zadok, the prophet Nathan, and Benaiah son of Jehoida, and the Cherethites and the Pelethites, went down and had Solomon ride (*wayyarkîbû*) on King David's mule, and led him to Gihon. (1 Kgs 1:38)

The causative force of *wayyarkîbû* (cf. also 1:33, 44) almost gives the impression that David's devotees made a *reluctant* Solomon ride the royal mule. At any rate, Solomon is consistently portrayed as taking no initiative to gain the throne. As Burke O. Long so aptly describes it, "Solomon…is something of a shadow, pictured allusively—the beneficiary of Nathan's and Bathsheba's plot; the object of David's special attention; the passive recipient of monarchical favor."[48]

What are we to make of this? If it is correct—as I believe it is—to understand these first two chapters of Kings *ostensibly* functioning propagandistically, then it is reasonable to conclude that the passive portrait of Solomon was intended to exonerate him from certain suspicions surrounding his rise to power. With McCarter, I believe "there can be little doubt that Solomon began his reign in an atmosphere of public suspicion and mistrust."[49] Some must have suspected that Solomon had intentionally sought after the throne and gained it unlawfully. And that may well have been precisely what happened! It seems highly unlikely

---

46. Cf. Volkmar Fritz, *1 & 2 Kings* (Minneapolis: Fortress, 2003), 15. While this "lack of characterization" is duly noted by Walsh (*1 Kings*, 33–34), his strictly literary reading of the text does not allow him to appreciate the political and propagandistic possibilities of Solomon's reported passivity. Seow (*1 Kings*, 20) also draws attention to this contrast between Adonijan and Solomon.

47. The first reference being 1:46 in which Jonathan reports, "Solomon now sits on the royal throne."

48. Long, "Darkness between Brothers," 86.

49. McCarter, "Plots, True or False," 360.

that Solomon played no active role in the struggle for succession.[50]
Rather than the passive bystander portrayed in the text, Solomon was
likely very involved and extremely interested in this quest for kingship.
But any hint of Solomon's involvement has been completely obscured by
the narrator who instead focuses on the political maneuverings of Nathan
and Bathsheba. As Richard D. Nelson quips, "Solomon himself had
nothing to do with the tawdry deceptions that brought him there [to the
throne], *or so the narrative wishes us to believe anyway.*"[51] In this way,
1 Kgs 1 functions as a piece of political propaganda in defense of King
Solomon and is comparable to those ancient Near Eastern texts which
seek to defend usurpers against charges of illegitimacy.[52]

To be sure, this passive, non-participatory portrait of the belated crown
prince leaves the reader with some very unsettling questions. If it is not
really believable that Solomon was totally uninvolved in the process of
gaining the throne, to what degree and in what capacity was he involved,
and why does the narrator choose not to comment upon this involvement? Such silence makes one strongly suspicious of a cover-up, an
attempt to obscure dark dealings in the palace that would reflect badly on
the new king. Moreover, the extreme pliability of Solomon throughout
the narrative raises questions about what *kind* of king he will be. Is Solomon so controlled by and ingratiated to others that he will simply do
their bidding even when it is unjust or not in the interests of the nation?
While not necessarily suggesting a subversive scribe intentionally wrote
the narrative in such a way as to raise these kinds of questions, the text
remains open to these and other less pleasant readings which do, of
course, raise questions about Solomon's right to rule.

### David's Selection

As the foregoing has demonstrated, 1 Kgs 1 does not present Solomon's
accession to the throne as a willful act of self-aggrandizement. Instead,
as we shall see, the writer uses a variety of literary devices which repeatedly emphasizes David's clear intention that Solomon succeed him. Such
a pronouncement embedded in the text must have been extremely
advantageous to the young king, considerably strengthening Solomon's

50. Unless, of course, he was so young at the time as to make his participation
impracticable.
51. Nelson, *First and Second Kings*, 21 (my emphasis).
52. For example, "The Apology of Hattusili" and "The Telepinu Proclamation";
for text, translation, and commentary, see Edgar H. Sturtevant and George Bechtel,
*A Hittite Chrestomathy* (Philadelphia: University of Pennsylvania Press, 1935), 65–
99 and 183–200, respectively. See also "The Instruction of King Amen-em-het,"
translated by John A. Wilson (*ANET*, 418–19).

political position. It would have been especially useful once David passed from the scene and accusations of usurpation swirled around the land. In such a climate a text such as this would have been extremely useful, carrying a heavy propagandistic payload.

Both David's old age and impending death are repeatedly emphasized in 1 Kgs 1:1–2:12. This can easily be observed in both narrative phrases and direct discourse. David is depicted as failing physically, unable to keep warm and sexually impotent (1:1–4). He is also described as "old and advanced in years" (1:1) and "very old" (1:15). David's charge to Solomon is also prefaced with the words, "when David's time to die drew near" (2:1). When conversing with David, Bathsheba refers to that time "when my lord the king sleeps with his ancestors" (1:21; cf. 2:10) and David himself reportedly says: "I am about to go the way of all the earth" (2:2). In addition to these indications of David's old age and imminent death, the text also emphasizes his unawareness of events outside the palace, particularly the fact that Adonijah allegedly acts as king apart from David's knowledge of it, as noted earlier (1:11, 18).

Why does the narrative go to such lengths to emphasize the frailties of King David?[53] What is the function of this admittedly unglamorous portrait of the once great king?[54] One possible explanation would be that these emphases were necessary to soften the contrived and rather manipulative efforts of Nathan and Bathsheba.[55] By portraying David as old, about to die, and clueless about major events happening right outside his door, who could fault this cunning couple for encouraging David to take care of business! Despite David's earlier (?) oath, he had failed to appoint a successor. A sympathetic reading might regard Nathan and Bathsheba as mere catalysts, encouraging David to fulfill his sacred oath.[56] Besides, had Nathan and Bathsheba not taken decisive action,

---

53. I am unconvinced by Ishida's analysis ("Solomon's Succession," 181–85; cf. his "Solomon Who is Greater," 151–52) which suggests that the writer of the Succession Narrative was anti-Davidic and intentionally sought to demonstrate David's ineptness to rule.

54. At one level, this depiction of the king subverts certain tenets of royal ideology. Cf. the discussion of the frail Kirta in Knoppers, "Dissonance and Disaster."

55. Regrettably, a careful analysis of the persuasive techniques utilized by both Nathan and Bathsheba in presenting their requests lies outside the scope of this study. For a brief discussion of the artful use of repetition in 1:11–27, see Alter, *Art of Biblical Narrative*, 98–100. A fuller and extremely sensitive analysis of the masterful use of rhetoric in these speeches can be found in Walsh, *1 Kings*, 10–18.

56. Though this would seem to be contradicted (subverted?) by 1:12, which suggests that the motivation for Bathsheba's actions are political expediency and self-preservation.

Adonijah would certainly have become king, ostensibly against the explicit oath David swore by God (1:29–30)![57]

On the other hand, reading Solomon's succession as the result of an elaborate court intrigue, reportedly inspired by the court prophet Nathan —who is not portrayed as acting on divine initiative—casts a shadow over the propriety of Solomon's rise to power and allows us to explore subversive possibilities.[58] As James S. Ackerman observes,

> The court intrigue scene in 1 Kings 1 provides no authoritative warrant to signal Solomon's legitimacy to the reader. Nathan proclaims nothing in God's name to the failing king. Instead of Nathan referring to the oracle when Solomon was renamed Jedidiah (2 Sam 12:24–25), we have Bathsheba "reminding" David of an oath that the text has not narrated.[59]

Nathan's non-prophetic role in Solomon's accession combined with the highly self-interested actions of Bathsheba cast serious doubt upon the legitimacy of Solomon. And while their efforts have the intended result of prompting the aging King David to take action by naming Solomon as his successor and making arrangements for his accession, questions about the appropriateness of this transition of power linger disturbingly in the foreground.

Moreover, whether all of this reflects favorably on Solomon largely depends upon whether, unknown to many others, David had actually made a private oath to Bathsheba that Solomon should be his successor, a matter we shall consider momentarily. The first mention of this "alleged oath"[60] appears when Nathan advises Bathsheba to ask David,

---

57. It is possible that an apologetic function is served by emphasizing Adonijah's initiatives since these could be seen as the catalyst which "forced" Solomon to accede *before* the death of David, a move which was somewhat irregular and atypical.

58. The absence of 1 Kgs 1–2 from the Chronicler's work only heightens our suspicions given the Chronicler's proclivity to omit or suppress anything hostile to Solomon. In 1 Chronicles, Solomon's succession is marked by an absence of any struggle for power. Instead, David publically and repeatedly names Solomon as successor and divine designee to build the tabernacle, a project for which David has made elaborate preparations (1 Chr 22:1–23:1; 28:1–29:25). The Chronicler depicts a smooth transition which stresses considerable continuity between David and Solomon. On the rationale behind the Chronicler's fully favorable depiction of Solomon's rise, see H. G. M. Williamson, "The Accession of Solomon in the Books of Chronicles," *VT* 26 (1976): 351–61.

59. Ackerman, "Knowing Good and Evil," 55. Ackerman continues by referencing Sternberg's (*Poetics of Biblical Narrative*, 378–80) observation that the reader is invited to question the truth of a character's statement which is supposedly based upon a past event/speech that is otherwise unreported.

60. The phrase is Walsh's, *1 Kings*, 11.

> Did you not, my lord the king, swear to your servant, saying: "Your son
> Solomon shall succeed me as king, and he shall sit on my throne"? (1 Kgs
> 1:13)

Bathsheba complies, though not exactly as Nathan had instructed. She turns Nathan's question into a statement and further ups the ante by specifically recalling the divine agent by whom this oath had been sworn:[61]

> My lord, you swore to your servant *by the LORD your God*, saying: "Your
> son Solomon shall succeed me as king, and he shall sit on my throne."
> (1 Kgs 1:17)

Her words underscore the urgency of the matter. An oath was a sacred and binding obligation and its fulfillment was imperative. After listening to Nathan's appeal (1:22–27), which, incidentally, makes no reference to the oath, David calls for Bathsheba (1:28) and reportedly not only affirms her words but confirms his old oath with a new one. The king swears to do what he has sworn!

> The king swore (*šbᶜ*), saying, "As the LORD lives, who has saved my life
> from every adversity, as I swore (*šbᶜ*) to you by the LORD, the God of
> Israel, 'Your son Solomon shall succeed me as king, and he shall sit on
> my throne in my place,' so will I do this day." (1 Kgs 1:29–30)

The foregoing threefold (!) reference to David's alleged oath certainly makes an impressive statement about his intention that Solomon succeed him.[62]

Further indications of David's selection of Solomon are forthcoming as he is portrayed as actively organizing Solomon's accession, complete with support from a priest, a "prophet," and the mercenary commander, not to mention the royal mule, anointing oil, trumpet sound, and shout of acclamation! All the required accouterments for Solomon's accession are put in place. And then, lest there be any doubt about David's selection of Solomon, David reportedly speaks these words to Zadok, Nathan, and Benaiah before they set off in search of Solomon: "Let him [Solomon] enter and sit on my throne; he shall be king in my place; for I have

---

61. While divine agency would be a characteristic feature of all oaths, its explicit reference here focuses the reader's attention on the seriousness of this binding verbal pronouncement.

62. J. P. Fokkelman (*Narrative Art and Poetry in the Books of Samuel.* Vol. 1, *King David [II Sam. 9–20 & 1 Kings 1–2]* [Assen: Van Gorcum, 1981], 106–7) believes the structure of 1 Kgs 1:5–53 draws attention to the importance of David's oath (vv. 29–30) since it is the center point of what he regards as nine chiastically arranged scenes.

appointed him to be ruler over Israel and over Judah" (1:35).[63] One could not hope for a clearer narrative statement of David's intentions. And as if this were not enough, when Jonathan makes his report to Adonijah and company, he declares, "*David* has made Solomon king" (1:43). The recurring oaths, the royal installation at Gihon, and the report of Jonathan[64] all bear ample testimony to this singular fact, a fact which the writer sought to stress when writing this apparent piece of Solomonic propaganda.[65]

Yet despite the text's strong assertion that David had selected Solomon as his successor, one nagging question remains. Had David really sworn an earlier private oath to Bathsheba promising that her son Solomon would succeed him? And if not, then was not Solomon's accession to the throne vulnerable to charges of fraud, manipulation, and illegitimacy, especially when David's indulgence of Adonijah's behavior amounted to a tacit agreement that Adonijah would be the successor?

At the very least, Nathan's suggestion that Bathsheba remind David of an oath he had made regarding Solomon comes as something of a surprise. Bathsheba appears briefly in the biblical narrative in 2 Sam 11–12 and is not heard from again until she reemerges in 1 Kgs 1.[66] If she was the recipient of such an extraordinary promise, it is not recorded in the biblical text. For this reason many scholars are convinced the entire "oath story" was conceived by Nathan and communicated through Bathsheba in a manipulative attempt to secure the throne for Solomon.[67] Perhaps

63. Even if the second half of this verse is regarded as secondary, the first part, which is undisputed, makes the point nicely by itself.

64. Notice how the speech of Jonathan—an Adonijah supporter—counters suspicions that Solomon's selection resulted from clandestine dealings. Jonathan not only reports that David has made Solomon king (v. 43), he also reports that all the king's servants came "to bless" David for the choice he made (v. 47). This implies that the king's servants were responding to David's decision rather than being responsible for it.

65. Further evidence of this emphasis upon Solomon as David's legitimate successor can be discerned in the literary texture of the narrative. In this regard, see Conroy, "Literary Analysis," 54–66 (59–60), who believes this point is emphasized by the threefold telling of Solomon's enthronement (David, vv. 33–35; the narrator, vv. 38–40; Jonathan, vv. 44–45), the *inclusio* of the reference to Solomon sitting on the throne in v. 46 and v. 48, the climactic threefold use of *wĕgam* in vv. 46–48, and the similarity between Benaiah's words in v. 37 and those reported of all the king's courtiers in v. 48.

66. For an excellent discussion of the characterization of Bathsheba, see Berlin, *Poetics and Interpretation*, 23–33 (25–30).

67. This is strongly argued by Jones, *1 and 2 Kings*, 93–94; cf. Long, "Darkness between Brothers," 85, and Marcus, "David the Deceiver," 167. Alter (*Art of*

Nathan and Bathsheba simply succeed in persuading an old king suffering from ill health that he actually had once promised that Solomon would be his successor. If so, and if Solomon's "selection" was the result of a court intrigue rooted in fraud and deception rather than the fulfillment of a private oath once made by David, then a record of such events certainly could have harmed rather than helped his cause. According to Walsh,

> The crucial question, of course, is whether David actually swore such an oath or whether it is a fabrication by Nathan designed to cozen the aged king. The conventions of biblical Hebrew narrative would easily allow the narrator to make the situation clear. Yet there is no information here or elsewhere in the Hebrew Bible to answer the question one way or the other. That fact is itself significant: we are *meant* to wonder. The possibility that Nathan and Bathsheba are simply taking advantage of David's condition to promote their own candidate raises uncomfortable questions not only about their honesty but about the whole process by which Solomon becomes king.[68]

Of course, it is impossible to be certain that Nathan fabricated this oath. Despite its absence from the biblical record, it is entirely possible that David had previously made such a promise. Moreover, for the "fabricated oath hypothesis" to work, one must assume that David was either too old and decrepit actually to remember whether he had ever made such a promise, or that he was willing—now facing his impending death—to select Solomon rather than the ambitious Adonijah.[69] Yet David is portrayed as being quite alert, possessing the wherewithal to make detailed arrangements for Solomon's succession. As Charles Conroy observes, "the precision and the decisive tone that mark David's instructions in vv 28–35 do not suggest a state of advanced senility."[70] David's lucidity is especially striking in his directives to Solomon in 1 Kgs 2:5–9. Appar-

*Biblical Narrative*, 98–100) is also quite open to this possibility. For the alternative view that the oath was authentic, see DeVries, *1 Kings*, 10.

68. Walsh, *1 Kings*, 12.

69. In this latter regard, it is interesting to consider the last minute shift of King Hussein of Jordan in 1999 who, just shortly before his death, chose his eldest son Abdullah to be crown prince rather than his brother Hassan who had enjoyed that position for over thirty years!

70. Charles Conroy, *1–2 Samuel, 1–2 Kings with an Excursus on Davidic Dynasty and Holy City Zion* (Old Testament Message 6; Wilmington, Del.: Glazier, 1983), 141. Cf. Walsh, *1 Kings*, 24. Though McKenzie (*King David*, 178) thinks David probably was senile, he at least recognizes that "it is important to the apology that David is depicted as still mentally sound though physically frail. Otherwise, his designation of Solomon would be invalid."

ently, the aging king has no difficulty recalling wrongs committed against him long ago nor is he at a loss to give deathbed instructions to redress them! In my opinion, many scholars have been far too quick to accept an amnesic David unscrupulously duped by a fabricated oath while few (if any?) have considered the possibility that David may have been a willing participant in this stratagem of an earlier oath.[71]

The text seems helplessly ambiguous at this point. By never removing the uncertainty surrounding the oath's provenance, the narrator leaves open multiple possibilities. David certainly may have spoken such an oath. Yet it is also possible that David may have been deceived or at least been willing to go along with an apparent act of deception. By leaving the matter open-ended, the scribe *qua* narrator has created a text susceptible of many different readings. Such a multivalent text does not appear to be the handiwork of a skilled submissive scribe, unless totally oblivious to the less favorable reading this text allows. Rather, here we are justified in postulating the hand of a very sophisticated subversive scribe. If this is correct, it is reasonable to assume that this scribe, commissioned to produce a propagandistic text in defense of Solomon, instead chose to compose a text which superficially supported the king while simultaneously subverting the legitimacy of his rule. As we shall see, this mingling of propagandistic and subversive elements persists throughout the rest of the chapter and into the next.

### Divine Election

Complementing Solomon's selection by David as his successor is an emphasis upon the new king's divine election. References to this divine appointment can be found throughout the narrative.[72] In 1 Kgs 1–2, Solomon's divine election is referred to three times: 1:48; 2:15, 24.[73] Interestingly, in these three references, Solomon's divine election is recognized by all of the Israelite "kings" in the story, namely, David, Adonijah, and Solomon.

---

71. So, e.g., Ishida, "Solomon's Succession," 179. Jones observes a fundamental tension in the text but does not offer an explanation. Commenting on v. 32, Jones (*1 and 2 Kings*, 98) writes, "David's shrewdness in assembling such a well-chosen party of supporters contrasts with the picture of a fumbling, senile old man given in the previous verses." Again, I would suggest that the emphasis upon David's physical failings (and old age) has less to do with characterizing him as suffering from the early stages of dementia and more to do with emphasizing the urgency of the moment. Settling this issue was critical! Now was the time for action.

72. See, e.g., 1:48; 2:15, 24; 3:6; 5:7; 8:20; et passim.

73. These have all been regarded as Dtr elaborations, though this is unnecessary. It seems quite likely that both 1:48 and 2:15 belong to the original strata.

David's words are brought to us second hand through Jonathan's alarming report to Adonijah and company. He quotes David as praying, "Blessed be the LORD, the God of Israel, *who today has granted one of my offspring to sit on my throne*, and permitted me to witness it" (1:48). Adonijah reportedly concedes Solomon's divine appointment in his conversation with Bathsheba regarding Abishag when he says, "You know that the kingdom was mine, and that all Israel expected me to reign; however, the kingdom has turned about and become my brother's, *for it was his from the LORD*" (2:15). Finally, in his response to Adonijah's request, Solomon himself claims to rule by divine right when he reportedly says, "Now therefore as the LORD lives, *who has established me and placed me on the throne of my father David, and who has made me a house as he promised*, today Adonijah shall be put to death" (2:24). These references demonstrate the way in which divine election—a common characteristic of political propaganda—is used to legitimate Solomon's right rule.[74]

On the other hand, the inclusion of Adonijah's assertion that the kingdom was his and that all Israel expected him to reign seems mildly subversive since it is never challenged.[75] Apparently, he speaks the truth. The undisputed inclusion of this datum, along with David's tacit approval that Adonijah was the crown prince (1 Kgs 1:5–6; see above), accentuates the irregular nature of Solomon's accession and was, perhaps, intended to register some disapproval of Adonijah's usurpation by his younger brother.

*Solomon's Initial Restraint*

The final episode of this chapter—Solomon's dealings with Adonijah in 1:49–53—provides us with yet another opportunity to witness the interplay between propaganda and subversion. Prior to this, as I have established, Solomon has been portrayed as a passive participant in the entire royal drama.[76] Now for the first time we are allowed a glimpse into

74. This feature becomes especially pronounced in the Chronicler's account (1 Chr 22:7–10; 28:6). See Roddy L. Braun, "Solomonic Apologetic in Chronicles," *JBL* 92 (1973): 503–16 (507).

75. Cf. Marcus, "David the Deceiver," 167, and McKenzie, *King David*, 177. For an alternate reading, see Jesse C. Long, Jr., *1 & 2 Kings* (Joplin, Miss.: College Press, 2002), 76. Long contrasts Adonijah's claim that all Israel expected him to be king with 1 Kgs 1:39–40, which speaks of "all the people" following Solomon. He also believes Adonijah's claim that the kingdom was his "must reflect Adonijah's irrational, perhaps even arrogant, point of view."

76. The only action of which he is the subject is one reported by Jonathan: "Solomon now sits on the royal throne" (v. 46). Conroy ("Literary Analysis," 63)

Solomon's character and we wonder how he will deal with his powerful older brother. Will he eliminate this very real threat to his position or will he be gracious and extend mercy?

Upon hearing of Solomon's accession to the throne, Adonijah is understandably terror stricken. He is described as engaging in a flurry of activity similar to that first used to promote himself as king. In rapid succession, Adonijah rises, goes, and grabs the horns of the altar, literally hanging on for dear life.[77] From that precarious position he declares his intentions not to let go until receiving assurances from Solomon that his life would be spared.

Solomon's response, his first words in the biblical narrative, is ambiguous at best: "If he proves to be a worthy man, not one of his hairs shall fall to the ground; but if wickedness is found in him, he shall die" (1:52). While no mention is made about who gets to judge Adonijah's behavior and what exactly constitutes wickedness, at one level, this might seem a rather fair and reasonable response. Solomon is not presented as a bloodthirsty tyrant seeking to punish his presumptuous older brother. By choosing to exercise restraint, Solomon appears almost merciful. That such examples of mercy were characteristic of propagandistic literature further suggests there were similar intentions for this text.[78]

Still, there are many features of this episode generally, and Solomon's speech particularly, which cast doubt upon such a favorable interpretation. In the first place, there is no indication that Solomon's words, directed to those who initially informed Solomon of Adonijah's fear, ever reached his very anxious older brother who surely knew his days were numbered. If they did, they is no indication that these words provided much encouragement since Adonijah seems intent upon hanging on to the altar.[79] Adonijah was quite properly apprehensive of the kind of reception he might expect to receive in the throne room—or elsewhere! Such apprehensions cast a shadow over the apparent clemency proffered him by Solomon.

suggests that the shift to Solomon's more active role, particularly his "full and perfect control of events" in this final episode of 1 Kgs 1 is reinforced by the sevenfold use of his name in vv. 51–53.

77.  The use of three consecutive verbs (*qm, hlk, ḥzq*), which is a rare occurrence in Hebrew, further accentuates Adonijah's desperate flight to the altar. Compare the similar concentration of verbs in Jonah 1:3, which emphasize the prophet's futile attempt to flee from the Lord's presence.

78.  See especially "The Apology of Hattusili" in this regard.

79.  Indicated by the fact that he does not leave this position voluntarily but is "brought down" (*wayyōridûhû*) from the altar.

Second, Solomon never makes the requested oath nor does he promise not to kill Adonijah. Instead, Adonijah's survival is made contingent upon his worthiness and lack of wickedness.[80] But what characterizes a "worthy man"[81] and what constitutes "wickedness"? This is never spelled out and constitutes a rather disturbing omission given the high stakes involved. Especially disconcerting is the implication that it will surely be Solomon who gets to judge how well Adonijah is measuring up to this rather ambiguous standard of behavior![82] Given Adonijah's recent escapades and his continuing threat to Solomonic hegemony, his failure to measure up and his subsequent "removal" is thus anticipated.

Coming to the end of this analysis of 1 Kgs 1, it is necessary to register a note of uncertainty about how to interpret and evaluate the events and actions of Adonijah, Solomon, and their respective supporters. Our indecision has been fostered by the scribe's artful use of a variety of literary techniques[83] which have left us unable to make final decisions about how we are to regard the intentions and motivations of the main players in this unfolding drama. This is the beauty of subversion.

According to Long, this ambivalence is exacerbated by the use of framing repetitions in 1 Kgs 1:1, 4, 15 which he believes are artfully deployed to mark off analepsis.[84] He writes, "The intricately structured analepsis provides a sense of ambiguity to events and complicates the reader's attitudes toward them."[85] Again, we are left wondering what kind of writer would utilize such a technique? It seems doubtful that a truly submissive scribe would intentionally craft an ambiguous narrative open to multiple interpretations. A subversive scribe seems a much better fit for the evidence in hand.

---

80. While this may appear propagandistic (see above), it not very convincing since any rival to the throne would have been regarded as "unworthy" and "wicked" for just being the opposition!

81. The relationship between *ʾîš ḥayîl* (1:42) and *ben-ḥayîl* (1:52) has been much discussed. It seems best to regard this latter reference as indicating loyalty to the throne, still a sufficiently ambiguous category as to warrant Adonijah's concern.

82. Cf. Conroy, "Literary Analysis," 62; Fokkelman, *Narrative Art and Poetry*, 379.

83. One literary technique we have not considered but which may have some bearing upon how we read the text is the use of names as puns. For a suggestive study in this regard, see Moshe Garsiel, "Puns upon Names as a Literary Device in 1 Kings 1–2," *Bib* 72 (1991): 378–86, who contends that "punning upon names in this biblical story...functions as a significant literary device to enrich and intensify the plot through a correspondence between names and themes" (p. 386).

84. Burke O. Long, "Framing Repetitions in Biblical Historiography." *JBL* 106 (1987): 385–99 (394–95).

85. Ibid., 394.

## Propaganda and Subversion in 1 Kings 2:1–12

Discussions of 1 Kgs 2 are immediately complicated by its convoluted compositional history.[86] There are, for example, the intriguing "miscellanies," inserted after 1 Kgs 2:35 and 2:46, found in the Greek text but not in the MT. There are also several difficulties regarding how 2:1–12 relates to what follows in 2:13–46. Although the so-called "Testament of David" singles out three individuals for "special" treatment, namely, Joab, Barzillai (actually his sons), and Shimei (2:5–9), nary a word is said about Barzillai's sons in the following section. The appearance of both Adonijah and Abiathar in vv. 13–27 might also seem surprising since neither had been mentioned in vv. 1–12. Finally, the two-fold reference to Solomon's kingdom being firmly established (2:12, 46) seems to betray multiple stages of editorial activity. These represent just some of the challenges facing the interpreter of this material. And while we need not untangle the lengthy and complex development of 1 Kgs 2, it is helpful to be aware of these imbroglios at the outset as we embark on our investigation of propaganda and subversion in this narrative.

### David's Final Instructions (1 Kings 2:1–9)[87]

Though some uncertainty remains about the provenance of 1 Kgs 2:1–2a, there is quite broad agreement that vv. 2b–4 derive from the Dtr.[88] DeVries describes vv. 2–4 as "a thick skein of deuteronomistic phrases," and so it is.[89] Here we have one of the purest expressions of Dtr propaganda in the entire chapter. The message is clear and unambiguous. From the Dtr's perspective, the continuation of the Davidic dynasty was not contingent upon power politics or monarchical manipulation. Instead, faithfulness to Yahweh and fidelity to the law of Moses were the requisite conditions for success *and* succession! In a way reminiscent of Deut 17:18–20, we are reminded that the well-being of the king and the continuation of his line was contingent upon his strict adherence to the

86. The reader is referred to Chapter 3 of the present study which has already introduced some of the following compositional issues.

87. For a comparison of the Testament of David to two Egyptian works, "The Instruction for Merikare" and "The Instruction of Amunemhet," and a discussion of this genre as propaganda, see Leo G. Perdue, "The Testament of David and Egyptian Royal Instructions," in *Scripture in Context II: More Essays on the Comparative Method* (ed. W. W. Hallo, J. C. Moyer, and L. G. Purdue; Winona Lake, Ind.: Eisenbrauns, 1983), 79–96.

88. For a challenge to the general consensus that 1 Kgs 2:1–10 derives from disparate sources, see W. T. Koopmans, "The Testament of David in 1 Kings II 1–10," *VT* 41 (1991): 429–49.

89. DeVries, *1 Kings*, 34.

"law." As we shall see, such instructions to the king differ markedly from the self-justificatory flavor of the remainder of the chapter.

If it is correct to understand this text as coming from the hand of (a) late pre-exilic scribe(s), the intent would apparently be to persuade both king and court that faithfulness and obedience to Yahweh marked the way forward. Given the "internal religious pluralism"[90] and competing political factions in late seventh-century BCE Judah,[91] high hopes must have been pinned on propagandistic speeches like these. What gave these particular words special authority was their ostensible origin. Attributed to none less than the great King David himself, the Dtr utilized a powerful medium through which it was hoped this message would be heard and heeded.

Leaving behind the pious imperatives in the previous verses, a dissonant chord[92] is sounded as David issues a rather different set of commands

90. To borrow a phrase from Rainer Albertz, *A History of Israelite Religion in the Old Testament Period*. Vol. 1, *From the Beginnings to the End of the Monarchy* (Louisville, Ky.: Westminster John Knox, 1994), 95–99, who uses it, in part, to refer to the variegated forms of familial piety in the late premonarchic period.

91. For a convenient discussion, see Patricia Dutcher-Walls, "The Social Location of the Deuteronomists: A Sociological Study of Factional Politics in Late Pre-Exilic Judah," in *Social-Scientific Old Testament Criticism: A Sheffield Reader* (ed. David J. Chalcraft; The Biblical Seminar 47; Sheffield: Sheffield Academic Press, 1997), 341–57.

92. Contra Koopmans ("Testament of David," 447), who, on the basis of his integrated reading of the text, deems it inappropriate to regard vv. 5–9 as "a personal vendetta contrasting sharply with the emphasis upon obedience to the law." He suggests that "the beginning of David's reign is characterized by examples of executions which are intended to typify his respect for the office of the anointed rather than a desire for revenge" and argues that David is simply instructing Solomon to go and do likewise. This misses the point. The executions Koopmans has in mind, that of the Amalekite messenger who claims to have killed Saul (2 Sam 1:13–16) and the sons of Rimmon who assassinated Ishbaal (2 Sam 4:9–12), are performed immediately after the alleged misdeed has been committed. This is quite different from the situation at the beginning of Solomon's reign in which David is allegedly encouraging Solomon to settle scores from long ago! Moreover, rather than communicating "respect for the office of the anointed" as Koopmans proposes, these executions function apologetically, clearing David of any implication in the death of Saul or his successor Ishbaal. It is here that appropriate parallels between 2 Sam 1:13–16; 4:9–12 and 1 Kgs 2:5–9 can be drawn.

An equally unsuccessful attempt to ameliorate the dissonance between vv. 1–4 and vv. 5–9 is offered by Benjamin Edidin Scolnic, "David's Final Testament: Morality or Expediency?," *Judaism* 43 (1994): 19–26. Scolnic argues that David's final instructions were given in the context of a moral code rather than as a sheer act of political expediency, thus distancing the Testament of David from ancient Near Eastern apologetic literature.

to his son and successor (vv. 5–9). Three separate issues and individuals are addressed in David's parting words. In the first and last, involving Joab (2:5–6) and Shimei son of Gera (2:8–9), respectively, David appears to be seeking retribution to redress wrongs committed in the past. The medial command, to the contrary, urges kindness for Barzillai and his sons (2:7). Setting aside this apparent anomaly for the moment, it *seems* that the old king had some scores to settle, and Solomon was given instructions about how to deal with these matters. Yet, as Steven L. McKenzie points out, "There are many reasons to doubt that David really gave these orders."[93] For example, the considerable time lag between crime and punishment is extremely difficult to explain. Are we really expected to believe that David is instructing Solomon to execute Joab and Shimei for crimes committed long ago? "Punishment of this nature would be appropriate only shortly after the offense."[94] There is an additional complication. At least in the case of Joab, an army commander who had been extremely loyal to David throughout his reign, it would have been especially duplicitous of David to order his execution on account of past murders which, in all likelihood, were orchestrated by David himself—or were clearly no worse than David's order to eliminate Uriah![95]

Then again, perhaps it is misguided to understand these words in such a punitive fashion. If one argues these are the words of David, perhaps

93. McKenzie, *King David*, 178. McKenzie regards these as "contrived orders" (p. 188) and calls the order to kill Joab an "apologetic invention" (p. 179).

94. Ibid., 179.

95. Joab is specifically indicted for killing both Abner and Amasa in peacetime (2:5). On David's likely involvement in the assassination of Abner, see James C. Vanderkam, "Davidic Complicity in the Deaths of Abner and Eshbaal: A Historical and Redactional Study," *JBL* 99 (1980): 521–39 (529–33); McCarter, "Apology of David," 501; Whitelam, "Defense of David," 75; McKenzie, *King David*, 117–22; Lemche, "David's Rise," 16–17.

It is a bit more difficult to establish David's complicity in the killing of Amasa. Vanderkam briefly touches on this issue, understanding David's involvement in Amasa's death to be similar to his involvement in Abner's. He writes (p. 533 n. 38), "As the parallel with the Amasa story shows, a convenient way in which David could, without publically incriminating himself, do away with a powerful military official was to give him Joab's job after he had extracted maximal benefit from the person (2 Sam 19:10–15; 20:4–13)." See also McCarter, *II Samuel*, 432, and McKenzie, *King David*, 171–72, who also suspect David was instrumental in Amasa's murder. The clearest motive for David's desire to eliminate Amasa would appear to be the latter's active and prominent role in Absalom's rebellion (2 Sam 17:25). Given David's practice of using Joab to eliminate unwanted elements (Uriah in 2 Sam 11:14–15), it seems quite plausible that he orchestrated the execution of Amasa.

his real intention here is simply to inform Solomon of the need to eliminate both Joab and Shimei given the serious threat they posed to Solomonic hegemony.[96] By recalling their past misdeeds, David became an apologist, providing a pretense for their political execution. Following this line of reasoning, Jeffrey S. Rogers believes that "David's counsel is not that of an embittered, impotent old king seeking personal revenge, but that of a supreme political strategist whose dying charge to his son and successor consists of specific instructions by which to ensure the stability of the kingdom, even if it is necessary to betray old loyalties and revoke old oaths."[97] While this initially seems plausible, it is somewhat problematic given the portrayal of David in the preceding chapter. In 1 Kgs 1, David seems to have no great interest in dynastic stability. In fact, given David's apparent lack of action, one might even accuse him of being the cause of dynastic *in*stability! If David was the "supreme political strategist" Rogers envisions, concerned with ensuring "the stability of his kingdom," one would expect a more pro-active plan regarding the choice of a successor. Once again, we are led to conclude that it seems highly unlikely that these are the words of David.[98]

It is best to regard David's instructions to "deal with" both Joab (vv. 5–6) and Shimei (vv. 8–9) as Solomonic propaganda placed on the lips of the aged king in order to justify Solomon's subsequent executions.[99] This assertion requires some support and will be developed below, as will the motivation behind this propagandistic speech.[100] Before examining each of the four episodes which constitute the remainder of the chapter, we turn briefly to consider subversion in the reference to the sons of Barzillai in 1 Kgs 2:7.

### *Subversion in the Sons of Barzillai (1 Kings 2:7)*
By the time we arrive at the end of 1 Kgs 2, we notice that Solomon has successfully carried out two of the three instructions ostensibly given

---

96. Though it is debatable how serious a threat Shimei actually posed.

97. Rogers, "Narrative Stock," 410.

98. While Rogers ("Narrative Stock," 412) does attribute vv. 5–9 to a Solomonic scribe, he nevertheless believes the words originated with David.

99. As Perdue ("Testament of David," 91–92) writes, "the propagandistic utility of the text, that is, placing the responsibility for executing two dangerous rebels on the shoulders of David, is in keeping with the shaping of the entire narrative which is designed to legitimate Solomon's accession to the throne over his older brothers." Cf. Seow, *1 Kings*, 26–29, who attributes non-Dtr portions of the royal testament to a "pro-Solomonic apologist."

100. See the discussion at 1 Kgs 2:13–25 and 2:36–46 which describe the executions of Joab and Shimei, respectively.

him by David on his deathbed. Both Joab and Shimei had been executed, just as "David" desired. But nary a word is said about Solomon implementing "David's" instructions regarding the sons of Barzillai. "David" had directed Solomon to "deal loyally"[101] with these individuals since they had done the same for him when he fled from Absalom.[102] He is said to have instructed Solomon to consider the sons of Barzillai "among those who eat at your table," which probably means they were to be given a pension (1:7).[103] But insofar as we can tell, this never happens. Solomon appears uninterested in lavishing acts of kindness upon others (because he is too busy killing his enemies?).[104]

As noted earlier, scribal omissions can be subversive and that certainly seems to be the case here. "Solomon carries out without qualms the two executions David [reportedly!] urged on him in 2:5–9; but nothing is said about the generosity David recommended toward the sons of Barzillai."[105] If this text was written in favor of the king, than it seems the scribe commissioned to produce this document missed a perfect opportunity to highlight the exemplary character of this newly established king! It is better to regard this omission as evidence of subversive scribal activity.

Another possible function of the account of Barzillai's loyalty in v. 7 is that it provides "structural contrast" to the *disloyalty* of both Joab and Shimei.[106] If so, then the inclusion of this episode functions as yet another propagandistic tool to intensify the evils of Joab and Shimei, making their elimination even more justifiable. Such an interpretation *might* suggest that Solomon's failure to carry through on "David's" instruction regarding the sons of Barzillai is inconsequential. On the other hand, it

101. Jones' (*1 and 2 Kings*, 52) rejection of v. 7 as original on the basis that the concept of loyalty (*ḥesed*) "introduces a strange element" is unacceptable. *Ḥesed* figures prominently in the Succession Narrative. See 2 Sam 9:1, 3, 7; 10:2; 16:17; cf. 15:20.

102. See 2 Sam 17:27–29; 19:31–40.

103. So Montgomery and Gehman, *Kings*, 90; Jones, *1 and 2 Kings*, 109; Nelson, *First and Second Kings*, 23–24.

104. This seems especially telling given David's pro-active efforts to deal loyally with Mephibosheth from the house of Saul (2 Sam 9). For an alternative reading, see Brueggemann, *1 Kings*, 29, 41, who believes David was counseling Solomon to retain the favor of Barzillai who is representative of the landed class and necessary for a "consensus government." According to Brueggemann, Solomon's apparent decision to ignore Barzillai signals a new direction in his governing practices.

105. Walsh, *1 Kings*, 68.

106. DeVries, *1 Kings*, 32. This requires understanding the murders Joab committed as acts of disloyalty against David: "You know also what Joab son of Zeruiah did to me (*lî*)…" (2:5). If, however, *lî* should be rendered "*for* me," a rather different picture emerges!

could be a testimony to the incredible dexterity of our subversive scribe, able to use the very same item to support and subvert the king simultaneously.[107]

A rather different interpretation of the importance of Barzillai the Gileadite's placement at 2:7 has been offered by Provan who questions whether we as readers are intended "to take David's words at face value."[108] Ultimately, he concludes we are not. Instead, he believes the author is inviting us to hear these words in the larger Samuel–Kings context, a context which raises questions about whether David's concern to remove blood-guilt was simply a smokescreen masking the real reason for wanting Joab out of the picture. He writes,

> The general impression throughout, indeed, is of a fairly sordid story of power-politics thinly disguised as a morality tale. So tortured are the attempts, however, to convince us that the men who died did so because they deserved it, that we cannot but be aware of their speciousness. We are invited to be suspicious, and to ask what the real reason for David's advice about Joab and the others really was.[109]

Since Adonijah posed the biggest threat, he needed to go first. According to Provan, both Joab and Shimei were also eliminated for political reasons, particularly due to the threat they (and others like them) posed to a united Israel under Solomon. Joab was too closely associated with the traditional southern Judean elements while Shimei posed at least a symbolic threat from the North on account of his Saulide connections. Both kinds of "dangerous elements" needed to be removed if Solomon was to experience peace. Provan appears to regard the insertion of Barzillai as suggesting programmatic instructions for Solomon. He queries, "Is it possible that the passage has been structured precisely so as to present Solomon with an ideal (peaceful community), and to suggest to him what kind of people from David's past—on both sides of that past—have to be removed if this ideal is to be attained (i.e. those likely to disrupt peaceful community)?[110]

While I agree that the appeal to bloodguilt is simply a foil covering the real motivation for "David's" advice that Solomon deal "wisely" with

107. Most commentators read positive motives into David's instructions regarding the sons of Barzillai. While it is possible that his directives were intended to keep the Gileadites on a short leash under close surveillance (so DeVries, *1 Kings*, 36) it seems more likely that they reflect a continuation of the trend begun in 2 Samuel which portrays David as a man who keeps his obligations, at least to some.

108. Provan, "Why Barzillai?," 108–12.

109. Or whether this actually was *David's* advice! Ibid., 113.

110. Ibid., 115.

Joab and Shimei, I am less than convinced by Provan's argument regarding the significance of Barzillai the Gileadite.[111] Rather than viewing the presence of "David's" instructions to Barzillai in 2:7 as a cipher for Solomon's peaceable kingdom, which is not impossible, I have argued that the absence of its fulfillment in the narrative conveys a subversive message intended to indict rather than inspire trust in the new king.[112] Solomon carries out the executions, but he does not carry through with the rewards.

That said, we are now ready to look more closely at Solomon's execution orders in 1 Kgs 2:13–46. According to Claudia Camp, "indeterminacy governs the first two chapters of 1 Kings."[113] As we shall see, this seems especially true of 1 Kgs 2:13–46.

### Episode 1:
#### Adonijah's Deadly Desire (1 Kings 2:13–25)[114]

The account of Adonijah's elimination is the first of four stories which report how the kingdom came to be "firmly established" in Solomon's hand (1 Kgs 2:12, 46). This first episode neatly divides into two major scenes, which narratologically can be described as: Adonijah's risky request (2:13–18) and Solomon's rapacious response (2:19–25). As the text portrays it, Bathsheba plays a central role in both scenes.[115] In the first, she (gladly?) agrees to convey Adonijah's risky request for Abishag to Solomon, perhaps because this provides a potential basis for eliminating him! In the second, she makes the request to the king and receives Solomon's emotive response, a response which has deadly results for the hopeful groom. One can only imagine Adonijah's disappointment when a weapon-wielding Benaiah appears at his doorstep instead of the attractive Abishag!

111. Unfortunately, Provan invests most of his time discussing why we ought not take David at his word and makes only the most laconic statements in regards to Barzillai.

112. Notice that Provan's thesis fails to address the issue of why the fulfillment of this instruction is never recorded in 1 Kgs 2 or elsewhere in the narrative.

113. Camp, *Wise, Strange and Holy*, 156.

114. The lack of instruction regarding Adonijah in the testimony of David (2:5–9) has led some to conclude that this episode represents a later addition. This is unwarranted since the final episode in 1 Kgs 1 adequately prepares the reader for Adonijah's imminent execution. I therefore concur with the majority of scholars who regard the account as original, with some Deuteronomistic redaction (e.g. 2:24).

115. This is especially emphasized by McKenzie, *King David*, 181–83. The centrality of Bathsheba in this incident raises some suspicions about the justness of Solomon's actions, a point explored further below.

Assuming Adonijah's request is not a literary fiction[116]—and that is a big assumption—how should we evaluate it? It seems better to regard this as a calculated risk rather than an act of utter stupidity.[117] As Adele Berlin observes, "Abishag's position is ambiguous. She has not actually had intercourse with David, so that Adonijah may think he has a right to ask for her."[118] While this is possible, one wonders how much Adonijah knew about David's sex life (or lack thereof). Moreover, if taking the concubine(s) of a king was viewed in Israel as tantamount to claiming the kingship,[119] requesting Abishag was very risky business. Even if Abishag may not technically been part of David's harem—since David reportedly never had intercourse with her—and may have been regarded as "available," it seems that such a request would still have been regarded as highly suggestive and suspicious. As Berlin observes, "Abishag, after all, had been in King David's bed, and Solomon therefore has every right to interpret or misinterpret Adonijah's request as threatening his own position. This is his opportunity to rid himself of the opposition, and he loses no time in taking advantage of it."[120]

Of course, it is highly debatable whether Adonijah's request should be construed as an open bid for the throne.[121] Given his previous fear of Solomon, it seems incredulous that he would make such a bold move. It is also unclear why Adonijah would have made such a request through Bathsheba rather than directly to Solomon.

116. McKenzie (*King David*, 181) regards the entire episode as "an apologetic invention to justify Solomon's execution of his half-brother."

117. Contra J. P. Fokkelman, *Reading Biblical Narrative: An Introductory Guide* (trans. Ineke Smit; Louisville, Ky.: Westminster John Knox, 1999), 71–72.

118. Berlin, *Poetics and Interpretation*, 29.

119. McCarter (*II Samuel*, 300) contends that "entering the royal harem was a way of claiming the throne." This point is generally assumed in the literature though it is difficult to substantiate. The relevant biblical passages are 2 Sam 3:6–11; 12:8; 16:20–22. The final passage is especially suggestive since it reports Absalom sleeping with his father's concubines in an attempt to strengthen his hold on the throne he had just recently usurped. The classic study of this issue is Matitiahu Tsevat, "Marriage and Monarchical Legitimacy in Ugarit and Israel," *JSS* 3 (1958): 237–43; cf. Jon D. Levenson, "1 Samuel 25 as Literature and History," *CBQ* 40 (1978): 11–28 (26).

120. Berlin, *Poetics and Interpretation*, 29, following Fokkelman, *Narrative Art and Poetry*, 394.

121. As Fokkelman (*Narrative Art and Poetry*, 396) observes, "There is nothing which indicates that Adonijah still truly seeks to obtain the throne." Gunn and Fewell (*Narrative in the Hebrew Bible*, 154) raise the possibility that Adonijah's request may have been motivated by a desire to have a witness to what had transpired on that fateful day (cf. 1 Kgs 1:15) though this seems rather implausible and no less risky. What could Abishag say that would really convince anyone?

Bathsheba's attitude to Adonijah's request is difficult to ascertain, though her initial question reveals some distrust of his intentions. "Do you come peaceably?" she asks. Adonijah reassures her that he does come in peace and proceeds to make his risky request which Bathsheba agrees to relay to the king. But did she naively transmit this message from Adonijah to the king? "Or did she, even more cunningly, anticipate Solomon's reaction and see this as a way to get rid of her son's opposition permanently?"[122] Consider, for instance, Bathsheba's reply to Adonijah in v. 18. The first word out of her mouth is "Good (*tôb*)!" But what does that mean? Does Bathsheba think that Abishag will make a nice bride for Adonijah or does she think the request is "good" since she knows it will give Solomon the pretext he needs to be rid of his older brother once and for all? DeVries recognizes this as "another of our narrator's enigmatic touches, hinting that Bathsheba's seeming good-natured compliance may have disguised her design to get rid of Adonijah."[123] Bathsheba goes on to say, "I [emphatic pronoun] will speak to the king on your behalf (*ʿālêkā*)." This too is riddled with delicious ambiguity since the preposition *ʿāl* is also capable of being translated "against,"[124] allowing us to wonder whether Bathsheba intended to speak for or against Adonijah. Finally, the emphatic pronoun noted above implies that Bathsheba is fully in control of the situation and not a mere pawn at the hands of men, as some commentators have implied.[125] Ultimately, it is impossible to be certain whether Bathsheba's ready compliance with Adonijah's request was for his benefit or hers; it is her final appearance in the biblical tradition.

It is also possible that Bathsheba manufactured this request in order to prompt Solomon to remove Adonijah since he remained a threat to Solomon's security (and therefore her own!) as long as he remained alive.[126]

---

122. Berlin, *Poetics and Interpretation*, 29.

123. DeVries, *1 Kings*, 37.

124. Consider Amos 3:1 for an excellent example of the rhetorical power of this multivalent term. Amos begins this oracle by saying, "Hear this word that the LORD has spoken against (*ʿāl*) you, O people of Israel, against (*ʿāl*) the whole family that I brought up from the land of Egypt." Despite the translation of the NRSV, a listening audience would not have known whether the following remarks were going to be favorable or unfavorable to them. This ambiguity continues in Amos 3:2a which actually tips the scales in favor of a salvation oracle. All such hopes are quickly dashed, however, in 3:2b.

125. E.g. Whybray, *Succession Narrative*, 40; cf. Montgomery and Gehman, *Kings*, 92.

126. While I am willing to allow Bathsheba a major role in Adonijah's downfall, I can hardly agree with McKenzie's assertion (*King David*, 181) that "this text

If this were the case, vv. 13–18 would be a literary fiction while vv. 19–21 would record the fabricated request Bathsheba actually made to Solomon.[127] In any case, there is no indication that Solomon seeks independent verification of Bathsheba's message. Nor does he bring Adonijah in for questioning. His guilt is simply accepted.

Whatever Adonijah's intentions in reportedly asking for Abishag, the text describes Solomon as viewing his request in the worst possible light since he regards it as an open bid for the throne.[128] In a ferocious riposte to Bathsheba[129] Solomon wails, "And why do you ask Abishag the Shunammite for Adonijah? Ask for him the kingdom as well! For he is my elder brother; ask not only for him but also for the priest Abiathar and for Joab son of Zeruiah!" (v. 22).[130] By referring to Adonijah as Solomon's "elder brother," the reader is reminded of the danger he still poses to the new king.

The Dtr elaboration in v. 24 furthers the defense of Solomon by appealing to his divine election. Claiming to be David's divinely appointed successor, Solomon insinuates that Adonijah's intentions were dangerously subversive. Since it was Yahweh who had established him,

functions partly as an apology for Bathsheba." In the first place, even assuming Bathsheba's complicity in Adonijah's execution, it is not clear to me why she would need an apology. Secondly, if the intention is a (partial) defense of Bathsheba's actions, this would seem to undermine McKenzie's understanding of this as Solomonic apologetic, since according to McKenzie, Bathsheba "was trying to help Adonijah, though Solomon would have none of it" (p. 181). If this was the intended message, it certainly does not cast Solomon in a very favorable light and would serve to subvert rather than support him.

127. It is interesting to note that in her speech to Solomon, Bathsheba never directly states that the request originated with Adonijah, though that is the way Solomon understands it (v. 23).

128. Ishida ("Adonijah the Son of Haggith," 178–79) argues that Solomon was justified in interpreting Adonijah's request in this way.

129. Note Bathsheba's request that Solomon not refuse her and Solomon's assurance that he will not (v. 20). Given Solomon's immediate disregard in vv. 22–25 for the assurance just given, we are permitted to see mild subversion at work in vv. 22–25 by suggesting that the actions of Solomon (or perhaps those of kings generally) are unpredictable and that his (or their) words are untrustworthy.

130. As it presently stands in MT, the text is questionable and probably corrupt. According to Burney (*Kings*, 20; followed by Jones, *1 and 2 Kings*, 113), the versions support "…ולו אביתר הכהן ולו יואב" which can be rendered "*And on his side* are Abiathar, the priest, and Joab…" (cf. Jones, *1 and 2 Kings*, 113). In any case, this verse indicates that Solomon continued to view both Abiathar and Joab—two rather influential individuals who must have enjoyed a wide public following—as enemies (co-conspirators?). This explains why they are both dealt with expediently in the following two episodes.

placed him on David's throne, and given him a "house," Adonijah's actions were contrary to the divine will. Viewed from this perspective, Solomon's swift and severe response is entirely understandable and justified.[131] His actions were necessary to eliminate the threat to the divine promise and to insure dynastic stability.

Solomon's declaration that "Adonijah has spoken this word against his life!"[132] places the blame squarely upon the "victim," a motif which recurs throughout each of the four episodes in vv. 13–46. This recurring emphasis, that each "evildoer" was being punished for his own misdeeds, appears to be the work of a submissive scribe. In Adonijah's case, his unfortunate end is presented as though it were the result of his own personal folly and ambition. Nevertheless, the unlikelihood that Adonijah ever made such a risky request for Abishag's hand in marriage coupled with the questionable intermediary role given to Bathsheba in this episode raises certain suspicions about Adonijah's culpability, or lack thereof! One wonders, in fact, whether the presumed crown prince was really guilty as charged or whether this story was simply concocted to villainize him and thereby clear the way for his expedient removal. That the narrative is open to such a reading and even seems to invite it in certain ways causes us to wonder if we have not once again found the artful touch of subversion interwoven into the fabric of this very clever text.

### Episode 2:
### Abiathar's Exile to Anathoth (1 Kings 2:26–27)

Having dispensed with Adonijah, Solomon calls the priest Abiathar to account. Abiathar, who had been a long-time supporter of David, was associated with the old Israelite sanctuaries at Nob and presumably Shiloh. He made (what turned out for him to be) the unfortunate decision of siding with Adonijah in his short-lived bid for the throne (1:7, 19, 25). This put Abiathar in direct conflict with Solomon, who had the support of Zadok, the Jebusite (?) priest who was associated with the sacred space in Jerusalem. Although no charges are brought against him, Abiathar is described by Solomon as someone who deserves death. Nevertheless, Solomon dismisses Abiathar from the priesthood and commutes his

---

131. Contra Kang (*Persuasive Portrayal of Solomon*, 130) who believes "the narrator's portrayal of Solomon's action in killing Adonijah as a sudden but decisive act seems calculated to provoke a reaction of horrified reprehension from the reader."

132. My translation. The NRSV's "has devised this scheme" is a very interpretive rendering of the Hebrew *dibber…ʾet haddābār hazzê*.

sentence to exile in Anathoth,[133] some four miles away (v. 26a).[134] The king's leniency is ostensibly predicated upon Abiathar's former service to David.[135] In particular, Abiathar is reportedly spared because he had carried the ark before David[136] and had endured all the hardships which David had endured (v. 26b).[137]

On the surface, it appears that the reader is supposed to be impressed by Solomon's clemency. As noted, the king spares Abiathar's life even though he *is said* to deserve death *(kî ʾîš māwet ʾāttâ)*. In this instance, Solomon is portrayed as a king who remembers the past loyalties and former services of his subjects and allows these positively to influence his present decisions on their behalf. For Abiathar, this literally meant the difference between life and death! Solomon's actions are further justified by the Dtr elaboration at the end of v. 27. By banishing Abiathar, Solomon was "fulfilling the word of the LORD that he had spoken concerning the house of Eli in Shiloh."[138] This is the closest we come to the practice of *vaticinia ex eventu* in the Solomonic narrative.[139] The

133. I have chosen to use the expression "exile in Anathoth" throughout for convenience sake (cf. Walsh, *1 Kings*, 55–56), though it might be more accurate to speak of Abiathar's *forced retirement* from the Jerusalemite priesthood and the concomitant command that he return home and (presumably) stay there!

134. It is often said that Abiathar's exile rather than his execution suggests that he did not represent a particularly dangerous threat to Solomon. It seems equally possible to suppose that Abiathar's importance and influence made it politically expedient to remove his priestly privileges rather than his head.

135. Since Joab rendered more extensive service to David than Abiathar, it is reasonable to conclude that the real rationale for the priest's preservation was on other grounds.

136. This is never reported in the books of Samuel (contrary to the NRSV translation of 2 Sam 15:29!). As Walsh (*1 Kings*, 55) suggests, it is possible that he was one of several persons thus engaged when David brought the ark to Jerusalem (2 Sam 6).

137. The hardships of David which Abiathar shared would seem to refer to his flight from Saul (1 Sam 22:20–23; 23:6–14) and his raid on the Amalekites (1 Sam 30).

138. The actual prophecy is recorded in 1 Sam 2:27–36 where it is delivered to Eli by an unnamed man of God. It is reiterated in 1 Sam 3:10–14 when God speaks directly to Samuel concerning the end of the house of Eli.

139. Following G. Posener's discussion of this piece, see Mason's (*Propaganda and Subversion*, 14–15; cf. 2–3) comments on this practice in "The Prophecy of Neferti," and see John A. Wilson (*ANET*, 444–46) for translation of the text. For a contrary view which denies the text functioned as political propaganda preferring instead to see it as an attempt to persuade King Amenemhet I to take action in the eastern part of his kingdom, see Hans Goedicke, *The Protocol of Neferyt (The Prophecy of Neferti)* (Baltimore: The Johns Hopkins University Press, 1977), 3–14.

implication here is that Solomon's actions are simply the outworking of the divine will, the final result of the evils of Eli's sons. What fault could there be in Solomon's action of exiling Abiathar to Anathoth if this kind of punishment had been decreed by Yahweh himself? Who could blame the king for being a conduit of God's justice?

Despite the positive and decidedly propagandistic veneer which overlays this narrative, there are numerous unsettling features which generate suspicion about the propriety of Solomon's actions and intentions. At the most basic level one might question whether Abiathar has done anything worthy of death, as Solomon charges. Of course, if David actually had designated Solomon as his successor, and if Abiathar was aware of that choice—neither of which are in evidence—his actions would constitute treason. This seems unlikely, however, since it is hard to imagine why this would not have been recorded if Abiathar had actually committed such an egregious act. Reporting such information—were it available— would have further justified his exile to Anathoth. Thus, as Walsh asks,

> On what basis does Solomon impose the death sentence in the first place? Certainly Abiathar committed no crime by supporting the heir apparent... [I]f Solomon has no legal basis for executing Abiathar, then the death sentence is unjust, and commuting the death sentence to exile is merely a smokescreen to conceal Solomon's vindictiveness toward Abiathar for supporting Adonijah.[140]

Additionally, notice that the commutation of death is *conditional*. He tells Abiathar he will not kill him "at this time" (*bayyôm hazzê*).[141] Such an open-ended statement is reminiscent of Solomon's words regarding the anxious Adonijah in 1 Kgs 1:52. Once again, Solomon is not precluding the possibility of his execution at a later date. Moreover, Solomon makes no promises and swears no oaths (despite his penchant for this in the previous episode—2:23–24!) that would assure Abiathar that he might live out the rest of his life in peace.

Another suspicious feature of the narrative involves an interesting wordplay. Abiathar is exiled to Anathoth (*'ănātōt*) rather than executed because he shared in the hardships (*hit'annîtā*). Moshe Garsiel, who notes this "pun" and regards it ironically writes, "Solomon, indeed, spares the priest's life...but he nevertheless sends him to Anathoth, which bears a connotation of suffering."[142] Walsh likewise believes "the implication of the wordplay is that exile to 'Anathoth' is one more in the series of

---

140. Walsh, *1 Kings*, 67.
141. Cf. ibid. LXX omits the "and," thus connecting the temporal element to the Abiathar's precarious condition (i.e. you deserve death *today*).
142. Garsiel, "Puns upon Names," 385.

'hardships' that Abiathar has suffered because of his loyalty to David."[143] Features such as these temper our previous enthusiasm for Solomon as a merciful monarch, causing us to question the purity of his motives and the justice of his actions. If this reading is correct, it illustrates the very subtle ways in which a subversive scribe could encode his critique of the king in the text while simultaneously portraying this king—who commuted Abiathar's death sentence (albeit a baseless one) to life in prison—as a paragon of mercy.

## *Episode 3:*
### *Joab's Altar-Side Execution (1 Kings 2:28–35)*

It is possible that the story of Joab's altar-side execution was originally connected directly to v. 25, which records Adonijah's execution. If so, it would make it unmistakably clear exactly what "news" caused Joab to flee to the sanctuary. Informed of Adonijah's grim fate, Joab realized his life was in mortal danger on account of his open support of Adonijah (1 Kgs 2:28; cf. 1:7, 19, 25, 41).[144] Like Adonijah before him, in an appeal to old Israelite tradition Joab hung on to the horns of the altar in a desperate attempt at self-preservation.

But why did Joab need to be liquidated? Did the death of Adonijah not eliminate the threat Joab posed? Not necessarily. Ishida emphasizes the enormous power and growing influence that Joab had during the reign of David. In fact, he goes so far as to say that by the end of David's life Joab was "the *de facto* ruler of the regime."[145] Because of Joab's fierce loyalty to David, his presence had not posed a threat to the kingdom. But with David gone and Solomon on the throne, the political climate had changed.[146] Joab's popularity and power represented an enormous danger to Solomon's security.[147] If Solomon was to achieve *shalom*, he and his administration needed to rid themselves of this powerful military man once and for all. This demanded no little political savvy! Joab's long and

143. Walsh, *1 Kings*, 67. One should not demand too much of this wordplay, however, since apart from the semantic correspondence involved, there is nothing in the text to indicate that this "exile" constituted a particularly severe hardship.

144. Presumably the narrator has in mind Joab's support of Adonijah during his bid for the throne (1:7) rather than any conspiratorial involvement Joab might have had in Adonijah's reported attempt to acquire Abishag.

145. Ishida, "Solomon's Succession," 185.

146. Cf. Rogers, "Narrative Stock," 410.

147. While Ishida's ("Solomon's Succession," 186) assertion "that the target of Solomon's party was Joab's downfall" seems unnecessarily narrow, it nevertheless reflects the real threat Joab posed to Solomon.

popular tenure as commander in chief of the citizen army in Israel made his removal especially tricky. Hence the need for a propagandistic construal of the events leading up to the king's execution orders.

First, notice that Joab reportedly refuses to leave the sanctuary upon Benaiah's command but instead replies, "No, I will die here." These words, which appear to provide an apology for killing someone in the sanctuary, conveniently allow Solomon to instruct Benaiah to "Do as he has said." It would seem that Joab has decreed his own fate.

Second, and more blatant, is the attempt to exonerate Solomon by appealing to retributive justice in vv. 31b–33.[148] The emphasis upon retributive justice here is nicely illustrated at the linguistic level. For example, Joab, the one who has struck down ($p\bar{a}g\bar{a}^c$, v. 32) will himself be struck down ($p\bar{a}g\bar{a}^c$, v. 31).[149] Likewise, the blood that Joab shed will return upon his own head (v. 33). Already foreshadowed in 2:5, Joab is depicted as worthy of death for murdering Abner and Amasa.[150] What made this particularly heinous was the fact that Joab (1) murdered them in peacetime (2:5), (2) shed innocent blood (2:31), (3) did so behind David's back (2:32a),[151] and (4) eliminated two men "more righteous and better than himself" (2:32b). Having thus established Joab's guilt, the

---

148. Several scholars regard vv. 31b–33 as secondary. So, e.g., Jones, *1 and 2 Kings*, 53; Rogers, "Narrative Stock," 401–2. The material is considered suspect on thematic grounds. First, it illustrates one of the Dtr's most prominent themes, namely, retributive justice. Second, it introduces an additional rationale for Joab's death which seems peripheral to the real reason for his execution. Rogers believes the appeals to past sin in the cases of Joab and Shimei are incongruent with the narrative stock which was at pains to demonstrate that Adonijah, Joab, and Shimei were executed for their own *contemporary* misdeeds. Yet given the very tenuous nature of these alleged "misdeeds," one wonders how such a clear association would help Solomon's case. It would be more effective for Solomon's submissive scribe(s) to portray these killings as retribution for sins long past so as not to arouse suspicions that they were politically motivated. I am, therefore, inclined to agree with Knoppers who believes this material is tendentious: "the references to bloodguilt are readily understandable in a political *apologia* written during Solomon's reign" (*Two Nations*, 74). With him, I would only assign v. 33b to the Dtr.

149. On *pg^c* as a technical term for execution in legal contexts, see Robert L. Hubbard, Jr., "The Hebrew Root *pg^c* as a Legal Term," *JETS* 27 (1984): 129–33. Hubbard contends that when *pg^c* stands alone, it refers to "a series of actions" including both attacking and killing. When used in connection with *mût* (1 Kgs 2:34), *pg^c* refers to the attack while *mût* refers to the actual killing (p. 132).

150. The accounts of these murders can be found in 2 Sam 3:6–39; 20:1–13, respectively. As noted above, assigning all the guilt to Joab is unfair since David was very likely behind the assassination of Abner and Amasa (as he was with Uriah!).

151. Notice that in 2:5 Joab's actions are taken as a personal offense against David himself.

writer invites us to view Solomon's execution order as recompense for the wrongful deaths of Abner and Amasa rather than an act of political expediency.[152]

Solomon is further removed from blame in this particular incident given the *agent* of Joab's demise. As Solomon declares, "*The LORD* will bring back his bloody deeds on his own head" (v. 32). The king is portrayed as a conduit of Yahweh's justice since Joab's death is to be regarded as an act of *divine* retribution.

Finally, Solomon's instructions to bury Joab[153] also seem to reflect favorably upon the king.[154] Neither Adonijah nor Shimei received such explicit preferential treatment (cf. vv. 25, 46) despite the fact that they meet their deaths in essentially the same way as Joab, namely, at the hands of Benaiah. By making the necessary provisions to insure a proper burial for Joab,[155] Solomon may be regarded as acting honorably towards this long-standing military commander.

---

152. Additionally, the reader/hearer would be aware that in the case of Joab and Shimei, Solomon was simply carrying out the orders of his father David, a narrative feature further justifying Solomon's execution orders.

153. 1 Kgs 2:31, 34. These instructions also appear in LXX at 1 Kgs 2:29 after Solomon's execution orders.

154. Contra DeVries (*1 Kings*, 39) who regards Solomon's command as an attempt "to hide a formidable and obnoxious enemy from human sight."

155. Joab is buried *bĕbêtô bammidbar*. Cf. G^L and Peshitta's "in his tomb," presupposing *bĕqibrô* (Burney, *Kings* 25). It is unclear whether this represents "modernizing" (so Montgomery and Gehman, *Kings*, 95) or whether it reflects a different *Vorlage*. Only two other people in the Hebrew Bible are described as being buried *bĕbêtô*: the prophet Samuel, buried *bĕbêtô bārāmâ* (1 Sam 25:1), and Manasseh, buried *bêtô* (2 Chr 33:20). We can dismiss the MT's reference to Manasseh's burial as tendentious (so H. G. M. Williamson, *1 and 2 Chronicles* [NCB; Grand Rapids: Eerdmans, 1982], 395), preferring the LXX (cf. 2 Kgs 21:18) "in the garden of his house." Most commentators do not comment upon the "domestic" location of Samuel's burial. Ralph W. Klein (*1 Samuel* [WBC 10; Waco, Tex.: Word, 1983], 247), however, doubts Samuel's physical house is meant and translates it as "homeland." This seems unwarranted. There is no indication that being buried in one's own home was regarded as problematic in early Israel. Apart from the fact that Joab's house is located *bammidbar*, the only difference between his burial and Samuel's is that in the latter instance, the people mourn and *they* (3d pl.) bury the prophet, while in the former there is no public ceremony and Joab's burial is simply reported (3d sing.). For potentially negative connotations associated with *bammidbar*, see Robert Alter (*The David Story: A Translation with Commentary of 1 and 2 Samuel* [New York: W. W. Norton & Co., 1999], 382 n. 34) who cites "the medieval Hebrew commentator Gersonides" who writes, "He was buried in the wilderness, which was the home fitting for him, for it would not be meet for a man like him to be part of civil society...because he had killed men by devious means and by deception."

Still, there are several features of this narrative which create suspicions about the justness of Solomon's actions. For example, the significance of the parenthetical clause in v. 28, "for Joab had supported Adonijah though he had not supported Absalom," is ambiguous.[156] On the one hand, it may simply explain *why* Joab received the news (because he had supported Adonijah) while also highlighting his loyalty to David (because he had not supported Absalom).[157] But why emphasize Joab's loyalty to David at this point? As Robert P. Gordon observes, "The biblical writer…seems almost to put in a good word for Joab."[158] Does this imply that Joab should have received the same "leniency" proffered to Abiathar in the previous episode based on his past loyalties to David? And since this is not forthcoming, might it not stand as a critique of Solomon's politically motivated killing of this high profile army commander?

Additionally, Joab's brief exchange with Benaiah in v. 30 in which he says, "I will die here" hardly justifies Solomon's "do as he says" attitude. It is unbelievable that Joab was inviting his own execution especially within such sacred precincts! His words—if they really were his words— were surely not intended as a self-pronounced death sentence. People fled to the sanctuary to escape death not seek it! Instead, Joab's response appears to be an attempt to invite Solomon to broker some kind of agreement with him, since he thought (hoped!) Solomon would not defile the sanctuary by ordering an execution at the altar.[159] Unfortunately for Joab, Solomon had different ideas.[160] Solomon's readiness to execute Joab— even while hanging on to the horns of the altar in the tent of the Lord— seems subversive since it undermines the character of the king, at least from the perspective of those who regarded the altar and tent as sacrosanct. This is exacerbated by the fact that "apparently even hatchetman Benaiah has scruples over cutting Joab down at the altar."[161] At the very

156. DeVries (*1 Kings*, 39) notes that G$^L$ reads "Solomon" rather than "Absalom" and adopts that reading, erroneously in my opinion.

157. Seow, *1 Kings*, 33, following Walsh, *1 Kings*, 57.

158. Gordon, "House Divided," 102. Montgomery and Gehman (*Kings*, 94) regard it as "part-exculpation of the one-time hero of Israel."

159. DeVries, *1 Kings*, 39.

160. It is questionable whether Joab had a legitimate right to be hanging on the horns of the altar in the first place. According to the legislation in Exod 21:12–14, the altar was to be a refuge for those who had inadvertently killed someone. Was it also appropriate to use the altar for political asylum as Joab does in this instance? Whatever the case may be, it still seems that the sanctity of the altar would have mitigated against shedding human blood upon it.

161. A. Graeme Auld, *I & II Kings* (Philadelphia: Westminster, 1986), 19. Cf. Fritz (*1 & 2 Kings*, 30) who observes, "Even the usually quite violent Benaiah has

least Solomon could have ordered Benaiah to drag Joab away from the altar before killing him. What kind of king (besides Saul!) would spill blood in such a holy place?

The final verse of this episode (v. 35), which reports Benaiah's replacement of Joab, also raises some suspicions about what is really motivating Solomon's actions. As noted above, "It is difficult to believe that blood-guilt is the real reason why loyal Joab is now, at this late date, to be done away with."[162] Instead, it would seem that Solomon's dealings with both Joab and Abiathar had more to do with political housecleaning than with justice. As Kang observes, "In the view of the narrator, Joab is not punished on the basis of the morally debatable accusations of the murder of Abner and Amasa, but mainly because of his belonging to Adonijah's party."[163] Solomon is simply replacing the old guard (and potential threats to his security) with his own supporters!

In his study investigating the theme of the Succession Narrative and the rationale for Joab's death, Wesselius also regards the explicit reasons given for Joab's execution in 1 Kgs 2:31b–33 as being rather "weak."[164] His skepticism stems from the temporal distance between Joab's alleged crimes and his punishment (see above) and from a sense of uncertainty about whether the deaths of Abner and Amasa were as undeserved as the text suggests. As a result, he believes the story has been carefully crafted to demonstrate "that both kings [David and Solomon] had their own private reasons to want Joab dead."[165]

This again raises our suspicions about the nature and function of this narrative. If this text was written as court apologetic, to use McCarter's language, how can this damning transparency be accounted for? What kind of loyal state-sponsored scribe would provide such flimsy rationale for Joab's execution while simultaneously exposing Solomon's self-serving motives for eliminating this extremely powerful man? Should this be regarded as the product of a sloppy submissive scribe, trying to put the best face on a bad situation but doing a lousy job in the process? Or does it make more sense to understand this text as the work of a subversive scribe, intentionally "hiding" a critique of the king's actions in the guise of propaganda? I believe the latter. While a propagandistic veneer

tried to maintain the asylum of the sanctuary, but Solomon orders the removal and disregards the laws of the sacred realm."

162. Provan, *1 and 2 Kings*, 33. Provan regards the issue of blood-guilt "a convenient justification for his [Joab's] death" (p. 34).

163. Kang, *Persuasive Portrayal of Solomon*, 134.

164. Wesselius, "Joab's Death," 338.

165. Ibid., 344.

is undeniable in this episode, the presence of certain ambiguities and tensions which allow for alternative and less salutary readings point to significant subversive activity in this text.

## *Episode 4:*
### *Shimei's Forbidden Journey (1 Kings 2:36–46)*

As with each of the foregoing episodes, the final episode in Solomon's consolidation of power, the case of Shimei, is also fraught with ambiguity and can be read as being favorable or unfavorable to the new king. Shimei's first appearance in the biblical narrative comes on the day David fled from Jerusalem and his usurping son Absalom (2 Sam 16:5–14). A Benjaminite and a Saulide, Shimei manages to make life rather miserable for David and his loyal band of followers as they abandon the city en route to Mahanaim. Traveling on the opposite hillside, this brazen Benjaminite hurls curses, throws stones, and flings dirt at David and his companions. Shimei vigorously abuses David and interprets David's sorry predicament as divine punishment for his bloody dealings with the house of Saul. Despite such harsh treatment, David refuses Abishai's request to punish this impudent son of Gera, reasoning that he might be cursing at Yahweh's bidding. Later, after the rebellion had ended and Absalom was dead, David again refuses Abishai's request to kill Shimei in spite of the curses he had uttered against the king (2 Sam 19:16–23).[166]

There seem to be several efforts in 1 Kgs 2 to demonstrate that Solomon was not at fault for ordering Shimei's execution. First, when understood in light of "David's" final instructions not to hold Shimei "guiltless" but rather to "bring his gray head down with blood to Sheol" (1 Kgs 2:8–9), Solomon's initial dealings with Shimei seem to be quite gracious. Though "David" desired Shimei's death for the "terrible curse" which Shimei spoke against him, Solomon seems prepared to let this Benjaminite live as long as he agrees to do so in Jerusalem where Solomon can keep an eye on him. A life lived under confinement was certainly preferable to the violent death "David" had prescribed for Shimei! Solomon almost appears to be compassionate.

Second, when Solomon does order Shimei's execution, it is justified, even if on flimsy grounds, since the king is ostensibly simply carrying out the command of his father David. As Ishida puts it, "The execution of Shimei…must be regarded *not* as a token of Solomon's cold-blooded character but as one of his political achievements in a matter which

---

166. Yet, as is often noted, the presence of one thousand (!) Benjaminites (2 Sam 19:17) may have had something to do with David's apparent leniency.

David had left unfinished."[167] Solomon thus emerges as the obedient successor who fulfills his father's deathbed wishes to a tee.

Third, though Solomon is ultimately responsible for Shimei's execution, his actions are fully justified since Shimei himself had agreed to the terms of his forced stay in Jerusalem with full knowledge of the deadly consequences of disobedience: "The sentence is fair; as my lord the king has said, so will your servant do" (v. 38).[168] Solomon reminds Shimei of this agreement when, three years later,[169] he has made the forbidden journey to Gath and back (v. 42). In this way, the reader is conditioned to conclude that Shimei got just what he deserved. He knew exactly what was expected of him and exactly what would happen if he violated those expectations. Solomon was not to blame for Shimei's death, even if it was an innocent trip.

Fourth, Solomon's actions against Shimei were fully justified given the heinousness of Shimei's sins which included the charge of violating a sacred oath.[170] According to Solomon words, Shimei had not only broken faith with him, he had lied to God! This was a serious accusation. Solomon interrogates Shimei by asking,

> Did I not make you swear by the LORD, and solemnly adjure you, saying, "Know for certain that on the day you go out and go to any place whatever, you shall die"? And you said to me, "The sentence is fair; I accept." Why then have you not kept your oath to the LORD...? (1 Kgs 2:42b–43a)

It is one thing to be disloyal to the king. It is quite another to swear falsely to Yahweh! Since such religious infidelity must certainly be punished, Solomon is further removed from charges of wrongdoing in the death of Shimei.[171]

---

167. Ishida, "Solomon's Succession," 186 (my emphasis).

168. To be sure, not too much should be made of the *voluntary* nature of Shimei's response. It appears doubtful that Shimei really had any other options available to him and protests to the tune of "I'd rather remain in Bahurim" would not have been prudent. In short, Shimei's bargaining power is negligible.

169. Gordon ("House Divided," 102) believes the reference to three years serves an apologetic function when considered in light of 1 Kgs 6:1, which reports the beginning of temple construction as the fourth year of Solomon's reign. It is "as if to say that the blood-letting had all been completed before the construction work was undertaken."

170. It is, of course, impossible to determine whether Shimei ever actually made such an oath, though the agreement would probably have involved such an oath so as to give it binding power.

171. Note also that each of the executions ordered by Solomon in 1 Kgs 2 are carried out by Benaiah, effectively keeping Solomon from getting his hands dirty (2:25, 31–34, 46).

Finally, Shimei's death is portrayed as an act of retributive justice from the hand of Yahweh himself. In vv. 44–45, however, this is not connected to Shimei's broken vow or even to his boundary breaking but rather to the evil he had done to David:[172] "You know in your own heart all the evil that you did to my father David; so the LORD will bring back your evil on your own head" (v. 44). Such a statement assigns responsibility to God for Shimei's demise, leaving Solomon standing innocently in the wings, a conduit of God's justice. Or does it? According to Fritz, "The plot [of vv. 36–46a] is structured in such a way that Solomon appears cleared of any charges; however, the reader is given the impression that Solomon has had Shimei killed for a trivial reason."[173]

Several scholars have picked up on this and argued that this episode reflects badly on the king. If so, then the account of Shimei's demise should not be read solely as a piece of political propaganda. While I think those who detect subversive elements in this account are fundamentally correct, some of the rationale they offer is not especially convincing. For example, some have contended that the death penalty was connected with crossing the Wadi Kidron, not with the more general prohibition forbidding Shimei from going "any place whatever" (ʾānê waʾānâ). According to this reading, the threat of death is specifically tied to eastbound travel. Yet Shimei's travels take him southwest, to the Philistine city of Gath in search of two runaway slaves. Technically speaking, then, Shimei does *not* cross the Kidron. As Jones writes, "Shimei was not guilty of the crime punishable by death noted in v. 37a, although he had broken the more general prohibition of v. 36b."[174] Similarly, Walsh contends that the strong emphasis on Gath (five times in less than three verses), a city located to the southwest, is highly significant and provides "the key to recognizing that Solomon executes Shimei on false charges."[175] By keeping Gath at the center of the reader's attention, Walsh reasons, it stands as a recurring reminder that Shimei travels southwest rather than east and therefore does not technically violate the deadly prohibition. If such a reading were correct, it would be wildly subversive since it would undermine the appropriateness of Shimei's execution.

172. Some (e.g. Jones, *1 and 2 Kings*, 119; cf. Rogers, "Narrative Stock," 403) regard vv. 44–45 verses as secondary since they provide a duplicate explanation for Shimei's death.

173. Fritz, *1 & 2 Kings*, 30.

174. Jones, *1 and 2 Kings*, 118. Similar suspicions that Shimei's westward travels did not technically violate the command are also raised by Provan, *1 and 2 Kings*, 40, and Seow, *1 Kings*, 34.

175. Walsh, *1 Kings*, 62.

In my opinion, however, it is better to understand Solomon's reference to the Wadi Kidron as an attempt to underscore the severity of Shimei's situation. Since the Wadi Kidron was immediately adjacent to Jerusalem, the reference has less to do with the direction of Shimei's travels and more to do with emphasizing the importance of staying within the confines of the city. Solomon is informing Shimei that taking just one step outside the city will cost him his life. As such, the (recurring) reference to Shimei's travels all the way to Gath demonstrate how grievously he has broken the agreement, thereby sealing his own fate. This, of course, provides further legitimation for Solomon's execution order against Shimei.

Still, it is possible that the mere inclusion of this episode functioned subversively to the hearers/readers by exposing Solomon's hardline attitude toward those factions which were unsympathetic to the house of David. Notice that Shimei is placed under strict "house arrest" in Jerusalem even though he has apparently done nothing to Solomon to warrant such severe treatment. It is possible that this confinement was intended to keep Shimei from returning to his home in Bahurim, a Benjaminite stronghold less than two miles east of Jerusalem, where he might rally dissident Saulides and cause trouble for the newly enthroned Davidide. As noted above, Shimei is ostensibly executed for breaking the "fair" agreement (vv. 42–44) which Solomon imposed on him. Still, given the non-political nature of Shimei's journey, it would seem that Shimei's elimination spoke volumes about Solomon's "zero tolerance" policy toward members of the pro-Saul party, a group which must have been viewed as at least a potential threat.

In this regard, consider also Ackerman's analysis of the Court History. He highlights the fact that it begins and ends with stories concerning Saulides, namely, Mephibosheth and Ziba in 2 Sam 9 and Shimei in 1 Kgs 2. With regard to the latter passage, he recalls the parallel episode from 1 Samuel in which David fled from his master Saul to Achish of Gath (1 Sam 21:10–15; cf. 27:2–4). From this, Ackerman argues,

> Narrative closure comes for the Saulides through a miniature reenactment of a scene from the struggle between Saul and David... Whereas in the beginning of the Court History David had attempted to create unity between north and south by integrating the Saulides into his court through the lame Mephibosheth, Solomon tries to unify the kingdom by slaying a symbolic representation of Saul.[176]

While those with Machiavellian tendencies would applaud Solomon's efforts, those sympathetic to the house of Saul would find such behavior

---

176. Ackerman, "Knowing Good and Evil," 54.

utterly reprehensible, to say the least. Therefore, the mere reporting of Shimei's execution in 1 Kgs 2:36–46—though ostensibly propagandistic, as I have argued at length above—is very damaging to the king from the perspective of those hearers/readers who would have been sympathetic to the house of Saul.

## *Conclusion*

We have covered considerable ground in this chapter. I have tried to demonstrate various ways in which 1 Kgs 1–2 resembles political propaganda written to legitimate Solomon's rise to power. In doing so I have, of course, assumed the existence of a tenth-century Solomon. Similarly, given both the lingering loyalties to the house of Saul and the general suspicion concerning Solomon's coronation over against the widely acknowledged crown prince, I have assumed that a considerable amount of controversy surrounded Solomon's accession. Granting these assumptions, it is reasonable to expect that Solomon and/or his supporters—we need not be precise here—commissioned the production of apologetic texts to defend the newly installed king. It is also possible that the impetus for these texts came from sycophantic scribes eager to please and praise their new patron. Whatever their precise origin, such texts were intended to present the "official version" of events leading to Solomon's rise and his consolidation of power. They would necessarily be at pains to paint Solomon in the best possible light. They could not, however, simply pass over questionable or objectionable incidents that were well known to the hearing/reading constituency. Instead, these events needed to be portrayed in a manner that would reflect most favorably upon the king.

Based upon my investigation of 1 Kgs 1–2, I would agree with those scholars who regard its function as propaganda, though, as argued above, I would contend that this is only *part* of its function. The propagandistic features of this narrative have been observed at various points in the text. For example, in 1 Kgs 1 it was noted that Solomon's passivity stood in contrast to Adonijah's ambitiousness, effectively removing Solomon from the suspicion that he himself took an active or aggressive role in becoming king. I also noted that Solomon is portrayed as having been selected by David and elected by God as successor to the throne. The new king apparently even acts with restraint in regard to his rival elder brother, Adonijah.

Similarly, in each of the four major episodes of ch. 2 I noted multiple ways in which the text supported Solomon's right to rule. For example,

Solomon's decision to kill Adonijah results from Adonijah's presumptuous request—whether real or fictitious—and his attempt to thwart the will of God which was, of course, that Solomon be king! King Solomon's clemency is on display in the second episode when he exiles rather than executes a priest who sided with Adonijah. His dealings with Joab are ostensibly justified on the basis of the murders this military man committed long ago. And finally, Shimei is eliminated for breaking the agreement he had made with Solomon (or rather, that Solomon required Shimei to make with him) to stay put in Jerusalem. In each of these episodes there is a concerted effort to demonstrate that each individual suffered for his own misdeeds.[177] I have argued that 1 Kgs 2 makes an intentional effort to demonstrate that Adonijah, Joab, and Shimei were responsible for their respective deaths.[178] That such an effort was necessary implies that some in the kingdom had their doubts about the propriety of these summary executions, thereby requiring some defense of Solomon's rule.

Interestingly, this propagandistic thrust is evident in multiple layers of the narrative. After Rogers isolates the Dtr elaborations, he argues that "the basic narrative stock of 1 Kings 2" should be regarded as Solomonic apologetic.[179] Yet even the Dtr elaborations seem to point in the same direction, a point convincingly argued by Knoppers, who writes, "If the author of the conclusion to the succession narrative defends Solomon's purge by citing David's testament, excusing Solomon, and impugning their opponents, the Deuteronomist defends Solomon's actions by referring to Solomon's achievements and by pointing out how pivotal Solomon is to the realization of Nathan's dynastic oracle."[180]

Yet, despite all these clear attempts to support Solomon, there is an unsettling undercurrent which runs throughout these chapters and which seems to subvert him.[181] In 1 Kgs 1 we found evidence of subversion in

177. As Rogers ("Narrative Stock," 412) observes, "In each case, the apologist is careful to point out that the deaths of the antagonists are the result of their own words and actions."

178. So also Cogan (*1 Kings*, 180) who believes "Solomon's apologist" intended "to demonstrate that the king's opponents had behaved in a manner that led to their own doom." Cogan sees through this and contends that "the use of naked force to secure the throne cannot be disguised."

179. Rogers, "Narrative Stock," 412.

180. Knoppers, *Two Nations*, 72.

181. I would emphasize that these are undercurrents, contra Fritz (*1 & 2 Kings*, 31) who contends that Solomon's killings are "portrayed as pure despotism" and that "Solomon is portrayed as a ruthless ruler who uses every possible means to remove Adonijah and his party."

the intentional ambiguity about whether David actually had made an oath to the effect that Solomon would be his successor. Questions about Solomon's legitimacy were also raised by the carefully crafted speeches of Nathan—identified as a prophet but acting on his own with no divine commission—and Bathsheba, the hopeful queen mother who conspired with Nathan to get Solomon on the throne even if that involved painting Adonijah's intentions in the darkest hues. Also subversive was the vague response Solomon gave to Adonijah at the end of the chapter, a response which left a death threat hanging over the former "crown prince."[182]

This subversive trend continued in 1 Kgs 2. We noted Solomon's apparent inaction regarding the sons of Barzillai, despite David's explicit instructions to "deal loyally" with them. We also observed three executions and one exile on very strained pretexts, making it extremely difficult to believe that the primary—much less the sole—function of the chapter was propagandistic. As Gordon observes, "It is indeed difficult, as most critics sense, to read 1 Kings ii as other than basically protective of Solomon's reputation... And yet there are indications in the chapter that this is not an unquestioning apologetic on Solomon's behalf."[183] Similarly, Provan regards the apology as being very transparent[184] and Baruch Halpern observes that "the apology hardly conceals the fact that Solomon's accession was a *coup d'etat*."[185] While I certainly agree with these sentiments, in my opinion, sufficient attention has not been given to offering an explanation of this phenomenon. Does this simply reflect the inferior product of a rather unspectacular apologist (i.e. are the subversive elements simply accidental)? Or might these undercurrents be intentionally deployed by a scribe or scribes who disagreed with royal policy?

The cumulative effect of these features, both propagandistic and subversive, results in a certain degree of textual indeterminacy in which the reader cannot be sure whether the text ultimately supports or subverts the king. This uncertainty is nicely reflected in Conroy's comments at the end of his discussion of 1 Kgs 2:

> On an attentive reading the text itself begins to reveal its ambiguity. While there is no explicit criticism of Solomon, the deadpan manner of narration in vv 13–46 may well insinuate an evaluation at variance with that of explicit theological comments. Furthermore the suspicion arises

182. "If he proves to be a worthy man, not one of his hairs shall fall to the ground; but if wickedness is found in him, he shall die" (1 Kgs 1:52).

183. Gordon, "House Divided," 102.

184. Provan, *1 and 2 Kings*, 40.

185. Baruch Halpern, *David's Secret Demons: Messiah, Murderer, Traitor, King* (Grand Rapids: Eerdmans, 2001), 396.

that David's "last wishes" (vv 5–9) might have been formulated by a Solomonic propaganda writer intent on justifying by David's authority a series of very questionable measures adopted by Solomon on his own initiative and in his own interests. One might also be inclined to question the interpretation Solomon put on Adonijah's request for Abishag—if the request was ever made (Bathsheba appears to have been the only witness). None of these insinuations and suspicions can be proved, but the reader is left with a distinct feeling of unease.[186]

As we have seen, this "feeling of unease" is achieved through the use of a variety of carefully deployed literary techniques resulting in a rather anemic apology. As Walsh writes in regard to the narrator's strategy, "On the surface he will say positive things, but between the lines he will undermine the positive picture with a series of gaps, innuendoes, and ambiguities that invite a much more critical evaluation of the king."[187] But why? What kind of writer would intentionally create such an ambiguous text? It seems the best explanation for this guarded critique is subversive scribal activity. Therefore, I would conclude that 1 Kgs 1–2 was written—at least in part—by (a) subversive scribe(s) who was/were commissioned to produce a piece of political propaganda but who, in the process of completing that assignment, took the liberty to inscribe his/their own subtle critique of the king.

Admittedly, it is difficult to determine the precise social connections such (a) subversive scribe(s) would have had. With what faction or group might such (a) scribe(s) be associated? Perhaps there were some in Solomon's court who still maintained pro-Saulide sympathies and recoiled at the elimination of Shimei. Or maybe this particular writer(s) represented a faction that respected the old covenant traditions which Solomon was perceived as violating by such actions as murdering Joab in sacred precincts. Still others might have truly believed Adonijah should have been the next king and felt bitter about Solomon's harsh treatment of the heir apparent and his supporters. Whatever the reason, the text reveals a stinging, albeit subtle, critique of Solomon's rise to power. To attribute such a complex and variegated text solely to "Solomon's apologist" is, in my opinion, reductionistic and misleading. The account is far more sophisticated than that, bearing evidence of serious subversion cautiously cloaked in the guise of propaganda—exactly what one would expect of a subversive scribe.

186. Conroy, *1–2 Samuel, 1–2 Kings*, 145.
187. Walsh, *1 Kings*, 47; cf. 65.

Chapter 5

## SELECTED EXAMPLES OF SUBVERSION IN 1 KINGS 3–11

*Stories can be subversive, a means of criticizing dominant patterns of thought and institution. Indeed, at times, to narrate an implicitly subversive story is the only safe way for social criticism to be spoken and heard.*

—David Gunn and Danna Fewell[1]

In the previous chapter, my analysis of 1 Kgs 1–2 demonstrated how this ostensibly propagandistic material appears to "hide" many subversive elements. For the remainder of the Solomonic narrative (1 Kgs 3–11), the focus will primarily be restricted to those features which function subversively despite the preponderance of propagandistic elements found throughout these chapters. Consequently, the format of this chapter will be episodic in nature, concentrating on only a handful of selected examples which are meant to be illustrative rather than exhaustive. It is hoped this restricted focus will allow us then to draw some broader conclusions about the nature and function of scribal subversion in the Solomonic narrative.

### Political Partnership (1 Kings 3:1–3)

First Kings 3:1–3 is clearly an ambiguous passage, one which simultaneously reflects favorably and unfavorably on Solomon (or the Solomon tradition). As Kang puts it, "3:1–3 is neither simply positive nor only negative about Solomon, but portrays Solomon in both positive and negative ways."[2] In the MT, 1 Kgs 3 begins with an intriguing note about Solomon's political marriage to an Egyptian princess.[3] Presumably, this

---

1. Gunn and Fewell, *Narrative in the Hebrew Bible*, 1–2.
2. Kang, *Persuasive Portrayal of Solomon*, 200–202 (quote from p. 200).
3. In the Greek, the miscellanies 2:46[a-l] occur in lieu of MT 3:1. MT 3:1 is represented in the Greek at 5:14[a] with two significant differences, both of which serve to enhance our appraisal of the king. First, it does not have the opening clause of MT

marriage would have been evaluated differently depending upon who was reading/hearing the text. Some audiences would certainly have regarded this marriage as a great accomplishment for Solomon, one that reflected no small achievement given Israel's relative size and stature *vis-à-vis* Egypt.[4] Others would have found such an alliance highly problematic.[5] The prophetic tradition, for example, routinely excoriated kings for making foreign alliances, not least those involving Egypt![6] Likewise, as 1 Kgs 11:1–13 makes abundantly clear, the Dtr viewed intermarriage with foreigners as the fast track to apostasy.[7] By reporting this potentially ambiguous item without providing explicit narrative evaluation, the door is left open to various interpretations, some of which reflect positively on Solomon and others which do not.[8] While it is impossible to determine whether a scribe intentionally reported this political union with subversive intent, it is undeniable that its presence in the text would have had a corrosive effect on Solomon (or the Solomon tradition) by those who deemed such a union inappropriate for an Israelite king.

The report of Solomon's marriage to an Egyptian princess is immediately followed by a list of building projects undertaken by the king. It is tempting to regard the *ordering* of building projects in 1 Kgs 3:1 as subversive since it might suggest a critique of Solomon's misplaced

3:1, which informs us that Solomon *became* Pharaoh's son-in-law (*wayyitĕḥattēn sĕlōmoh ʾet parʿōh*), a phrase that clearly suggests Solomon's subordinate role in the relationship. Secondly, when listing Solomon's building projects, $G^B$ places the construction of the Lord's house before Solomon's, disallowing the insinuation that Solomon did not have his priorities straight.

4. See Abraham Malamat, "A Political Look at the Kingdom of David and Solomon and its Relations with Egypt," in Ishida, ed., *Studies in the Period of David and Solomon*, 189–204 (197–99).

5. As Auld (*I & II Kings*, 21–22) observes, "It is not easy to decide why it is exactly here that we are told in all brevity (v. 1) of Solomon's marriage to Pharaoh's daughter. Is it a token of the establishment of his kingship (2:12, 46)? Or is it a whispered anticipation of the theme of chapter 11…? Does it hint at Solomon's international prestige; or was the marriage a means by which Pharaoh retained some leverage on the politics of the southern Levant?"

6. E.g. Isa 30:1–7; 31:1–3.

7. For discussion of the Dtr's view of intermarriage, see Gary N. Knoppers, "Sex, Religion, and Politics: The Deuteronomist on Intermarriage," *HAR* 14 (1994): 121–141, and idem "Solomon's Fall and Deuteronomy," in *The Age of Solomon: Scholarship at the Turn of the Millennium* (ed. Lowell K. Handy; Leiden: Brill, 1997), 392–410 (394–401).

8. See Lasine, "The King of Desire," 89–90, for a discussion of the indeterminate nature of this reference to Solomon's Egyptian marriage. See also Hays ("Narrative Subtlety," 152, 161) who critiques Lasine and believes the mention of this marriage is intended to reflect negatively on Solomon.

priorities: self (palace), God (temple), others (wall around Jerusalem).[9] Still, it is difficult to ascertain whether many ancient Israelites would have found such an arrangement disturbing, despite the possibility that some later tradents may have been troubled by it.[10] Clearer elements of critique launched against Solomon (or the Solomon tradition) do emerge, however, upon closer inspection of 1 Kgs 3:2–3 despite a propagandistic veneer.

### *Propaganda in 1 Kings 3:2–3*

Most critics regard vv. 2–3 as an attempt to ameliorate the embarrassment caused by Solomon's cultic activities at the Gibeonite "high place" (v. 4). According to the Dtr, all sacrificial worship outside Jerusalem was strictly forbidden. Especially onerous to the Dtr were the "high places" (*bāmôt*), "illicit" shrines regarded as stumbling blocks to pure Yahwistic faith. Given their aversion to such inappropriate cultic contexts, some explanation for Solomon's sacrifices at Gibeon was absolutely essential if the story of his divine dream was to be included in the Dtr's history.

Jones proposes that v. 3, which reassures the reader that Solomon was a devout Yahwist who followed in the footsteps of his father David, was appended for this purpose as an initial attempt to exonerate the king from charges of religious heterodoxy.[11] In his opinion, the effort was rather ineffective since it "merely set side by side two unrelated sentences."[12] The verse simply stated that Solomon loved the Lord *and* offered incense

---

9. From this perspective, vv. 1–3 suggest an unhappy correlation between Solomon's failure to make temple building his number one priority and the people's wayward worship (due to their lack of a temple). Eslinger (*Into the Hands*, 130–31) adopts this line of reasoning to argue, unconvincingly in my estimation, that Solomon's focus on building his personal palace stands as a serious allegation against the king. Cogan (*1 Kings*, 189) believes those who find a critique of Solomon in the reference to his Egyptian wife and the ordering of his building projects "may be overreading."

10. Such discomfort *may* account for the different ordering of Solomon's construction projects in the Greek text (see n. 3 above). It is possible that Greek translators transposed the order of the first two items in their *Vorlage*, giving the temple priority. If so, this change would seem more a reflection of their own religious sensibilities than of some earlier scribe's attempt at subversion. It is equally possible that the OG represents a different textual tradition altogether. Thus, one cannot assume MT's priority or that the differences were intentional changes by the translator.

11. Jones, *1 and 2 Kings*, 122. Carr (*From D to Q*, 13) contends that v. 3 should be understood as a typical Dtr regnal evaluation which is partially a critique, offering only qualified praise of Solomon.

12. Jones, *1 and 2 Kings*, 122.

at the high places without explaining the apparent incongruity.[13] This necessitated further clarification which was later supplied by v. 2. Regarded by many as a gloss on v. 3,[14] this verse makes it explicit that Solomon was sacrificing at the Gibeonite *bāmâ* rather than the Jerusalemite temple only because the latter had not yet been built.[15] Although this does not totally excuse Solomon—since Jerusalem did have the ark of the covenant and was, therefore, not lacking a sanctuary—it does put a positive spin on an otherwise unacceptable activity. Solomon apparently makes the best of a less than ideal situation.

If this analysis is correct, these verses might be considered propagandistic insofar as they exonerate the king from suspicions of religious heterodoxy while implicitly revealing the Dtr's ideology of the temple as the only legitimate place of sacrificial worship. This notion is further strengthened by the description of Gibeon as "the principal high place" (*habbāmâ haggĕdôlâ*).[16] In the absence of a proper temple, Solomon journeys to the most prominent *bāmâ* and only there offers sacrifices.[17] This king was not just worshiping on any high hill or under any green tree! He went to the most celebrated sacred spot in the region. In this way, the Dtr appears to put the best face possible on Solomon's sacrifices at Gibeon, making the king's otherwise inexcusable actions palatable.

*Subversion in 1 Kings 3:2–3*
Despite this propagandistic veneer, several features suggest a subversive undercurrent running throughout these verses.[18] As Seow observes, "it is

13. This apparent incongruity would be ameliorated, however, if these high places were considered Yahwistic, which many evidently were.

14. The adversative particle *raq* which stands as the beginning of v. 2 supports reading v. 2 as a gloss on v. 3, since the presence of the particle is otherwise unexplainable. For a careful discussion of this gloss, see Carr (*From D to Q*, 26–27, 82–85) who believes v. 2 neutralizes the qualified praise of Solomon in v. 3b and justifies Solomon's actions on the basis of the fact that everyone had to sacrifice outside Jerusalem before the construction of the temple (see esp. p. 82).

15. See Jones, *1 and 2 Kings*, 122, and references there to which Gray, *I & II Kings*, 113–14, and Montgomery and Gehman, *Kings*, 103, might also be added.

16. Cf. DeVries, *1 Kings*, 51, who believes this explanatory clause has "an apologetic purpose."

17. Note the Chronicler's attempt to obviate this tension by placing the tent of meeting in Gibeon (2 Chr 1:3, 13; cf. Lev 17:8–9; 1 Chr 16:39; 21:29)! Roddy L. Braun (*1 Chronicles* [WBC 14; Waco, Tex.: Word, 1986], 193–94) finds unconvincing the evidence marshaled by Williamson (*1 and 2 Chronicles*, 131) used to support the suggestion that this otherwise unknown tradition may have been part of the Chronicler's *Vorlage*.

18. Provan (*1 and 2 Kings*, 44–46) is suspicious of virtually everything in these verses and regards them as highly critical of the king.

peculiar that Solomon should seek to worship at the high places or the particular one in Gibeon, for the ark, the very symbol of the Lord's presence, was in Jerusalem, as v. 15 confirms... Solomon cannot be easily exonerated for having gone to that great high place."[19] Thus, even though Solomon sacrificed at a very prominent *bāmâ*, it was still a *bāmâ*! We are left to wonder whether the reference to the ark of the covenant of the Lord was intentionally included (added?) to emphasize the inappropriateness of such non-centralized sacrifices, especially when the ark itself already stood in Jerusalem![20]

Above we noted the possibility that the ordering of construction projects in v. 1 might be intentionally subversive, designed to indict Solomon for his misplaced priorities. Whether or not that reading is accepted, it is possible to read v. 2 in such a way that would make a similar accusation. If one does not assume the foregoing redactional reconstruction, it is possible to take v. 2 "to mean that the people were sacrificing at the local high places precisely because of Solomon's delay in building the Temple."[21] This would make Solomon guilty of gross negligence prolonging the people's non-centralized worship.

Ironically, another source of subversion in this passage may be found in the seemingly laudatory evaluation given Solomon in v. 3a. As noted above, many scholars regard v. 3 as the Dtr's initial and rather inept attempt to introduce the story of Solomon's Gibeonite dream. To be sure, the verse does not fully ease our discomfort with Solomon's trip to Gibeon since the first half emphasizes the king's Yahwistic devotion while the other half comments on his religious aberrations! That a later scribe apparently felt the need to add an explanatory gloss at v. 2 further confirms the ambiguity this introduction engendered. But why must v. 3 therefore be regarded as the result of clumsy editorial work? Might not this be a prime example of a subversive scribe at work? At the very least it demands closer scrutiny.

We are told in v. 3 that "Solomon loved the LORD." It would seem that such an expression must surely be understood as a positive theological evaluation of the king,[22] echoing, as it does, the great commandment of

19. Seow, *1 Kings*, 39.
20. Presumably the tent of meeting was also there. Its singular reference in the Solomonic narrative occurs in 1 Kgs 8:4 where it is described as being incorporated into the temple along with the ark and sacred vessels.
21. Seow, *1 Kings*, 37 n. 23; so also Provan, *1 and 2 Kings*, 45.
22. DeVries' (*1 Kings*, 48) suggestion that the reference to Solomon loving Yahweh be understood as "a corrective to the notice about the king's suspect marriage" in 3:1 is plausible, especially if the Dtr is attempting to neutralize anything that might be construed as unfavorable to the characterization of the king in the early

Deut 6:5. What makes this ascription even more striking is the simple fact that no other person in the entire Hebrew Bible receives such a commendation. Yet, upon closer inspection, we have reason to question whether this evaluation actually helps or hurts the reputation of the king.

Consider the fact that there are only five occurrences of the verb *ʾāhab* in 1–2 Kings, all of which occur in the Solomonic narrative (1 Kgs 3–11). Of these five, Solomon is the subject of three.[23] In addition to the reference at hand, the last chapter speaks twice of Solomon's love (11:1–2). There we discover that the object of his affection is not Yahweh, however, but a wife—actually quite a number of them! Worse still, Solomon's love is directed toward other gods. Obviously, neither of these references reflects favorably on the king. One wonders whether the narrator has intentionally ascribed this particular characteristic to Solomon at the outset to foreshadow the other loves that eventually lead to his ruin? If so, this seemingly laudatory clause suggests more about Solomon's problematic passions than about his piety.[24] "At the very least," writes Provan, "Solomon's love for God, even at this early stage in his career, was not entirely whole-hearted."[25]

The narrator also characterizes Solomon as one "walking in the statutes of his father David" (3:3; cf. 11:4), a clause which seems to emphasize further Solomon's Yahwistic devotion.[26] It may be significant, however,

---

part of the narrative. Such an effort would surely qualify as propaganda. Of course, for this to work, one must assume that the intended audience would have felt some discomfort with Solomon's marriage to an Egyptian princess.

23. 1 Kgs 3:3; 11:1, 2. The other references include Hiram's "love" of David (5:1) and Yahweh's love for Israel (10:9), mentioned by the queen of Sheba.

24. Alternatively, it could be argued that this feature of the narrative simply highlights the contrast between Solomon's early obedience and his later apostasy, assuming it is appropriate to speak of the characterization of Solomon in this fashion. Still, the brevity of the evaluative statement raises certain questions about its supposed positive function. A more comprehensive statement, something along the lines of, "Solomon loved the LORD *his God with all his heart*," would have been more effective, though perhaps that is asking too much of the text at this point.

25. Provan, *1 and 2 Kings*, 45–46.

26. Walsh ("Characterization of Solomon," 488) believes this phrase reflects negatively on Solomon and concludes that "the phrase '*ḥuqqôt* of David' refers not simply to the obedience to Yahweh which David urged on Solomon but to the blood-thirsty political expediency he recommended as well." He bases this argument on the absence of any *positive* references to walking in the statutes of another human being throughout the entire Hebrew Bible, citing as examples 2 Kgs 17:19, Ezek 20:18, and Mic 6:16, to which could be added 2 Kgs 17:8. This should be rejected for two reasons. First, while these are all negative examples, there is nothing inherently wrong with "walking in the statutes" of another individual. It was only problematic if the exemplar was evil. This is surely not the case in regard to David (cf. 11:4!).

that the narrator does not write, "Solomon did what was right in the sight of the LORD." Given the frequency with which this particular evaluative clause is attributed to many other Jerusalemite kings, beginning with David himself,[27] its absence here seems especially striking.[28] Such restraint may be intentionally subversive, designed as a critique of the king.

## *Sacred Sleep (1 Kings 3:4–15)*

The account of Solomon's Gibeonite dream[29] has routinely been regarded as political propaganda intended to legitimate Solomon's kingship.[30] What has not often been noted, however, is the manner in which the conversation that transpires between God and Solomon subverts certain aspects of royal ideology. First, Solomon admits that he does not know how to go out or come in (3:7), an expression related to military leadership.[31] In other words, Solomon admits that he does not know how to

Second, the exception clause (*raq*...) in the second half of v. 3 requires reading the preceding narrative comments positively (so Waltke and O'Connor, *Biblical Hebrew Syntax*, 670).

27. David (1 Kgs 14:8; 15:5); Asa (1 Kgs 15:11); Jehoshaphat (1 Kgs 22:43); Jehoash (2 Kgs 12:2); Amaziah (1 Kgs 14:3); Azariah (2 Kgs 15:3); Jotham (2 Kgs 15:34); Hezekiah (2 Kgs 18:3); Josiah (2 Kgs 22:2).

28. In fact, when we arrive at the end of the narrative Solomon is specifically indicted for *not* doing what was right in the sight of Yahweh (11:33). Cf. Ahaz (2 Kgs 16:2).

29. Two monographs devoted to this passage are Helen A. Kenik, *Design for Kingship: The Deuteronomistic Narrative Technique in 1 Kings 3:4–15* (SBLDS 69; Chico, Calif.: Scholars Press, 1983), and Carr, *From D to Q*.

30. See, e.g., Siegfried Herrmann, "Die Königsnovelle in Ägypten und in Israel," *Wissenschaftliche Zeitschrift der Karl Marx-Universität Leipzig* 3 (1953–54): 51–62. He is followed by Jones, *1 and 2 Kings*, 122–23, 25; Gray, *I & II Kings*, 117–23; Long, *1 Kings*, 66; Carole Fontaine, "The Bearing of Wisdom on the Shape of 2 Samuel 11–12 and 1 Kings 3," *JSOT* 34 (1986): 61–77 (63–64); Nelson, *First and Second Kings*, 34; Seow, *1 Kings*, 39–41; idem "Syro-Palestinian Context." For a departure from this consensus, see Knoppers, *Two Nations*, 82, who argues that the dream account's main purpose is *not* Solomonic legitimation, since this was already established in chs 1–2. Instead, Knoppers contends that the narrative function of the dream is to establish "the particular contours of his [Solomon's] reign" which revolve around his wisdom, wealth, and fame.

31. Argued convincingly by Kenik (*Design*, 108–14) who (p. 108 n. 137) notes that elsewhere this expression denotes freedom of movement (Josh 6:1; 1 Kgs 15:17; Jer 37:4). Cf. Anton van der Lingen, "BW'-YṢ' ('To Go Out and To Come In') as a Military Term," *VT* 42 (1992): 59–66 (65–66). He translates the final portion of 1 Kgs 3:7 as, "I do not know how to go to war successfully as a commander" (p. 66).

lead the people in battle. Interestingly, he is never equipped by God to do so. Is such an omission a critique of warfare generally and/or the king as military commander more specifically? Perhaps.[32]

Second, consider the vision of kingship embedded in these texts. Would this have supported or subverted "business as usual" in the palace? Though Nelson does not refer to the rhetoric of subversion, his interpretation of this passage seems to reflect our understanding of this concept.

> In Solomon's dream at Gibeon…two competing patterns of kingship are set before the reader: a kingship of glory and a kingship in the spirit of Deuteronomy. Solomon chooses the second pattern.
>
> What Solomon does not ask for are the trappings of glory and worldly success that made up much of the royal ideology: long life (Ps. 72:15), riches (Ps. 21:3, 5; 72:15–16), and death to the opposition (Ps. 21:8–12). It was just this pattern for kingship that Deuteronomy warned against (Deut. 17:16–17), as had Samuel (I Sam. 8:11–18). These glories would be part of Solomon's kingship (chaps. 3–10), but only as God's gifts, rewards for Solomon's proper focus on an entirely different pattern for kingship.[33]

It would seem that the nature of Solomon's request—and God's response—challenges the royal assumption that the acquisition of wealth and the elimination of potential enemies is the incontrovertible prerogative of kings and kingship.

Notice that in both of the instances we have examined thus far, the subversive undercurrent is not intended to topple the institution of the monarchy. Rather, it offers a selective critique of particular aspects of the royal machinery. By targeting specific elements, the Dtr was able to craft a text which simultaneously honors the office of the king while critiquing certain predominant assumptions about monarchical power and privilege.

Third, as noted above, God seems pleased that Solomon had not requested long life, riches, or the death of his enemies. After giving Solomon what he did ask for, God promises to also give him what he did not ask for, namely, riches, honor, and a long life, the latter being

Van der Lingen cites only four passages in the Hebrew Bible in which he believes this word-pair does not function in a military sense (Deut 28:6, 19; 2 Kgs 11:8//2 Chr 23:7; Jer 37:4; Ps 121:8). In this instances, the expression is better understood as referring to movement across a threshold, be it the sanctuary or the city gate.

32. For an alternative understanding, see Knoppers, *Two Nations*, 82 n. 46, who believes that this negative expression has been intentionally chosen to demonstrate that "the deity's gifts will enable Solomon to rule effectively without recourse to war."

33. Nelson, *First and Second Kings*, 31.

conditional upon faithful and obedient living (3:11–14). The one thing Solomon is not granted from the menu of options in v. 11 is the lives of his enemies. Might this stand as a subtle critique upon Solomon's actions in 1 Kgs 2? Gordon believes this omission may be "some kind of oblique commentary" and regards it "a fair question whether the narrative itself is implying criticism of the earlier killings."[34]

Given the redactional complexity of this passage, it seems that this "critique" would only emerge at a later stage in the text's transmission since the explicit reference to those things Solomon did not ask for (v. 11) appear to come from the Dtr.[35] This immediately raises the question of why a redactor hundreds of years removed from Solomon would be motivated to critique him covertly, unless of course Solomon were understood as a cipher for a contemporary king or for kingship generally. If so, we might speculate that a subversive scribe deployed this clever critique cautiously to voice his disapproval with a current king's elimination of enemies, political or otherwise.

### Wood for Wheat (1 Kings 5:15–26 [Eng. 5:1–12])

A somewhat different kind of subversion is lurking in the commercial agreement forged between Solomon and Hiram as Solomon prepares to build the temple.[36] While there is a considerable amount of propagandistic material in this section, it is misguided to assert that the Dtr "has skillfully composed this narrative to make Hiram look like Solomon's servant and vassal."[37] On the contrary, Hiram is neither a passive nor a subordinate partner in the negotiation process but bargains from a position of power, looking out for his own interests.[38] This becomes clearly evident upon closer inspection of Hiram's careful response to Solomon's initiatives, a response which suggests that this Israelite king is not the preeminent power broker in the region.[39]

34. Gordon, "House Divided," 103.
35. For a careful discussion of the redactional history of this passage, see Carr, *From D to Q*, 7–30.
36. For historical studies exploring international dealings between Israel and Tyre, see, conveniently, Jeffrey K. Kuan, "Third Kingdoms 5.1 and Israelite–Tyrian Relations During the Reign of Solomon," *JSOT* 46 (1990): 31–46, and note especially the references given on pp. 43–44 nn. 22–24.
37. DeVries, *1 Kings*, 80.
38. In fact, the LXX clearly portrays Hiram as the suzerain since he sends his servants to anoint Solomon (1 Kgs 5:15).
39. Brueggemann (*1 & 2 Kings*, 77–79) regards negatively the very partnership between Solomon and Hiram since it represents "entry into a world of trade and commerce viewed as fundamentally alien to the covenantal identity of Israel" (p. 78).

Since Solomon needs timber for his temple, he proposes the following to the Tyrian king: (1) he will send his servants to join Hiram's woodcutters in Lebanon, and (2) he will pay Hiram whatever wages are set for his servants (1 Kgs 5:20). While Hiram's response appears to be overwhelmingly favorable (5:21–22), Hiram is not about to allow Israelites to march into Tyrian territory and cut down *his* trees! Therefore, he modifies Solomon's original proposal in two significant ways which effectively diminish the international stature of Solomon.[40] First, he denies Solomon's request that Israelites be sent to Lebanon to cut cedars[41] alongside the Sidonians.[42] Though specific reasons are not forthcoming, such an infiltration of Israelites into Tyrian territory would have been objectionable for the potential threat it would have posed to national security and the possible loss of logging secrets.[43] Second, Hiram rejects the idea that Solomon will pay the wages of Hiram's servants (albeit to Hiram). Instead, he stipulates that Solomon's payments will meet his (Hiram's) needs and provide for his household (5:23). This ameliorates any confusion about who is really paying Hiram's servants, and keeps Solomon from having any influence over them whatsoever. These contractual alterations diminish the image of Solomon by revealing his inability to set the terms of the agreement.

Moreover, while both parties benefited from this "wood for wheat" relationship, it certainly seems Hiram got the better deal since importing staples and exporting luxury goods is a clear sign of economic strength.[44] Given this unbalanced trade agreement,[45] some have detected a note of

---

This seems unnecessarily suspicious, in my estimation, and Brueggemann himself concedes that it is unclear whether such an "ominous" signal is intended by the text.

40. Emphasized by Jones, *1 and 2 Kings*, 156–57, and Walsh, *1 Kings*, 96–97; idem, "Characterization of Solomon," 491.

41. Brueggemann's (*1 & 2 Kings*, 87) contention "that cedar is likely a coded signal...for financial extravagance and for glad cooperation with non-Israelite forces (Hiram) who do not understand Yahweh or take Yahwism with any seriousness," seems too imaginative.

42. Hiram says that his own servants would do the logging and transport the wood down the coast where Solomon's servants could then take the logs by land to Jerusalem. This would effectively keep Israel out of Tyrian territory. Admittedly, this is difficult to reconcile with the claim in 1 Kgs 5:14 that Solomon sent men to Lebanon. Walsh ("Characterization of Solomon," 491 n. 37) speculates that this may be an exaggeration, similar to that found in 9:19, which makes the extraordinary claim that Solomon even has buildings erected in Lebanon!

43. Cf. 1 Kgs 5:6b.

44. Jobling, "Forced Labor," 62.

45. David C. Hopkins ("The Weight of the Bronze Could Not Be Calculated: Solomon and Economic Reconstruction," in Handy, ed., *The Age of Solomon*,

irony in both Hiram's and the narrator's comments about Solomon's wisdom in this passage (vv. 7, 12).[46] Thus, despite certain tendencies in this passage which portray Solomon as the consummate organizer and administrator who is preparing to build a great temple for Yahweh,[47] the text does not suppress elements which reveal Hiram's power at the negotiating table.

Hiram's ability to modify the terms of the agreement and the economic advantage he presumably derived from the deal suggest he is the more powerful partner in this relationship. This seems to be corroborated by Solomon's annual payments to the king of Tyre for two decades (5:25; cf. 9:10–11). Specifically, 5:25b says that Solomon gave the wheat and fine oil to Hiram "year by year" (*šānâ běšānâ*). This expression (or close equivalent) occurs eleven times in the Old Testament.[48] By itself, this phrase seems innocuous enough. What makes its usage here so intriguing is the simple fact that both of the other occurrences of this expression in Kings refer to bringing tribute (1 Kgs 10:25; 2 Kgs 17:4). Was the reader to understand Solomon's annual Tyrian payments in like fashion?[49] Walsh thinks so and argues that the very *nature* of the payment is suggestive of Solomon's vassalage. Accordingly, Hiram's tacit denial of Solomon's proposal to pay the laborers and his demand that Solomon send food for his household puts the Israelite king "in a position *vis-à-vis* Hiram comparable to that of Solomon's own vassals toward Solomon."[50]

If such a characterization of the king was intended, the effect is a covert critique of the king in an otherwise ostensibly propagandistic text. While care is taken not to allow these less favorable items to overshadow the propagandistic portrait of the king so carefully developed throughout the rest of the temple narrative (1 Kgs 5:1–9:9), subversive elements nonetheless remain in evidence. The resulting effect is twofold: the

300–11 [307]) believes "the exchange of timber, gold, and skilled labor for agricultural products suggests the kind of unbalanced exchange that takes place between a more developed and less developed society." He also cites Solomon's yearly payments and the failure of these to satisfy Hiram (9:12) as evidence that the Tyrian king is the superior partner in this business arrangement.

46. So Walsh, "Characterization of Solomon," 492; Jobling, "Forced Labor," 66.

47. So Victor (Avigdor) Hurowitz, *I Have Built You an Exalted House: Temple Building in the Bible in Light of Mesopotamian and Northwest Semitic Writings* (JSOTSup 115; Sheffield: JSOT Press, 1992), 221; followed by Knoppers, *Two Nations*, 87 n. 60.

48. Deut 15:20; 1 Sam 1:7; 7:16; 1 Kgs 5:11; 10:25; 2 Kgs 17:4; 2 Chr 9:24; 24:5; Neh 10:34, 35; Esth 9:21; cf. 1 Sam 1:3.

49. Kuan ("Third Kingdoms 5.1," 36–37) answers this in the affirmative, following the same line of reasoning developed here.

50. Walsh, "Characterization of Solomon," 491. See 1 Kgs 4:21–24.

casual reader is left with a distinctly favorable impression of Solomon as the supremely wise, divinely elected king who builds by divine decree, while the attentive reader is able to discern the scribal subversion operating within the text, subversion which undermines Solomon and which demonstrates that this Israelite monarch was decidedly inferior to his Tyrian counterpart.

### Levying Laborers for Lebanon (5:27–32 [Eng. 5:13–18])

Although 1 Kgs 5:27–32 is generally regarded as originating from a different source than the preceding material just explored,[51] many commentators believe both sections have much the same function, namely, to glorify Solomon. An initial reading of 5:27–32 reveals that Solomon is undertaking an impressive project of epic proportions. The enormity of this project is emphasized in two ways, through manpower and materials. First, we are informed of Solomon's huge labor force. There are 30,000 woodsmen in Lebanon and five times as many stonecutters in the hill country (vv. 13–15), not to mention the 3300 supervisors over all the work (vv. 13–16)! The statistics given in this section are obviously an exaggeration of whatever the historical reality might have been. As Nelson observes, "The effort to impress is obvious in the huge numbers."[52] Yet this is precisely what we expect of royal propaganda where impressions rather than numerical accuracy are most important.[53] One can almost hear the narrator saying, "Just look how many people it took to prepare the raw materials necessary for building the temple!" With a work force of this magnitude that has expended so much energy in the preparatory phases of the project, the audience is conditioned to expect nothing less than a truly fabulous temple.

Second, specific attention is given to the quality of stones that would be used to build the foundation of the temple. Not your ordinary run-of-the-mill fieldstones, these stones are quarried and are described as "great," "costly," and "dressed" (5:31). Not only the quantity of workers but the quality of materials signals the beginnings of a great work in

---

51. Jones (*1 and 2 Kings*, 153) refers to these materials as "a series of addenda."
52. Nelson, *First and Second Kings*, 42.
53. For a useful discussion of hyperbole in the Solomonic narrative, see K. Lawson Younger, Jr., "The Figurative Aspect and the Contextual Method in the Evaluation of the Solomonic Empire (1 Kings 1–11)," in *The Bible in Three Dimensions: Essays in Celebration of Forty Years of Biblical Studies in the University of Sheffield* (ed. D. J. A. Clines et al.; JSOTSup 87; Sheffield: JSOT Press, 1990), 157–75 (157–66).

progress. Once apprised of these particulars, it would seem the only appropriate response would be to stand with mouth agape, utterly amazed and absolutely astonished at the magnitude and splendor of this monumental construction project.

Still, one wonders if this common reading of the text is completely satisfactory. Let us return for a moment to consider Solomon's enormous labor force: 30,000 in Lebanon and 150,000 in the hill country. We are told that the timber cutters were forced to spend a third of the year away from home, with groups of 10,000 working in rotating shifts. They spent one month in Lebanon and two at home before returning to Lebanon to repeat the cycle. Though Terence Fretheim believes that "allowing them two months at home for every month at work was probably viewed as generous," that assessment may be overly sanguine.[54] It is difficult to imagine how anyone forced to work away from home four months out of the year would view that arrangement as "generous." In any case, no such routine was established for the laborers (*nōśēʾ*) and stonecutters (lit. diggers—*ḥōṣēb*) in the hill country. They were permanent "workers" (i.e. slaves!).

The involuntary nature of these assignments is stressed by the introductory clause in v. 27: *wayyaʿal hammelek šēlōm mas mikkol yiśrāēl*. Likewise, the reminder in v. 31 that the people quarried "at the king's command" seems superfluous and does little more than reinforce the forced nature of their work. Additionally, the presence of Adoniram over the timber cutters and the 3300 supervisors over those in the hill country would suggest that some compulsion was necessary to keep workers at these physically demanding and time-consuming activities.

How can such an arrangement of corvèe labor ultimately reflect positively upon the king? Has the Dtr inadvertently shot himself in the foot by including such statistics or might a better explanation be to posit intentional elements of subversion in this material? It is at least possible—if not probable—that these texts betray serious discomfort with the royal practice of conscription.[55] While such a critique could hardly have been overtly registered against the royal establishment, it could be communicated through literary subversion and may betray the hand of a subversive scribe.

54. Terence C. Fretheim, *First and Second Kings* (Louisville, Ky.: Westminster John Knox, 1999), 38.

55. The vigorous effort in 1 Kgs 9:20–22 to make it unmistakably clear that all of the forced laborers spoken of in that context were non-Israelites betrays the fact that some in ancient Israel regarded the practice of conscripting Israelites to be deeply troubling.

*Solomon's Temple Dedication Prayer (1 Kings 8:46–53)*

Turning briefly to Solomon's temple dedication prayer,[56] we may be able to detect some subversive undertones in the seventh stanza (vv. 46–53).[57] In the opening line of the final part of this prayer, Solomon begins with these words: "If they sin against you—for there is no one who does not sin." At one level, this statement seems mildly subversive of Solomon himself. If there is no one who does not sin, that would include Solomon! Such speech is surely not typical of royal ideology. J. G. McConville believes these words "in the mouth of Solomon, are pregnant, foreshadowing their egregious fulfilment in himself, and hinting at the momentous consequences for the nation of the sin of the king in particular."[58]

Looking at the books of Kings *in toto*, and noting the "ambivalent" ending in Kings insofar as it regards the nation's future, McConville also thinks that "Kings may be saying that hope for the future should not be reposed in any institution or mode of government."[59] If so, he believes "this would explain the non-royal terms of the hope contained in 1 Kgs viii 46–53."[60] In other words, given the monarchy's failure as evidenced by the exile, and with no hope proffered that the people might return home from exile, this text seems to say that Judah's future does not rest on a political structure or Davidic king.[61] In this way, the passage subverts the royal establishment by registering a sense of disillusionment with it.

The interesting question here as it relates to our study is whether such a critique of the monarch and monarchy was offered during the pre-exilic period or whether it came later. If we assume the former, it would seem to represent a rather risky example of scribal subversion since the monarchy was still intact and certainly would have frowned upon such implicit criticism. On the other hand, if it can be demonstrated that this portion of the prayer stems from the exile or later, it still reflects a critique of the

---

56. For a sustained, albeit unconvincing, attempt to read the entire prayer as subversive, see Eslinger, *Into the Hands*, 155–81.

57. For a study of propaganda in 1 Kgs 8, see Gary N. Knoppers, "Prayer and Propaganda: Solomon's Dedication of the Temple and the Deuteronomist's Program," *CBQ* 57 (1995): 229–54.

58. J. G. McConville, "1 Kings VIII 46–53 and the Deuteronomic Hope," *VT* 42 (1992): 67–79 (73).

59. Ibid., 78–79.

60. Ibid., 79.

61. As McConville points out, unlike Deut 30:1–10, a passage which holds out the hope of a return from exile, 1 Kgs 8:46–53 offers a far more modest proposal. See ibid., 71–77 (76), and cf. Deut 4:25–31.

royal establishment, though it does so from a safer distance. Unfortunately, the provenance of these verses is extremely difficult to determine, rendering a clear decision one way or the other virtually impossible.[62]

## Subversion Circumscribing Royal Power
## and Prerogatives (1 Kings 9:1–9)

After Solomon's temple dedication prayer, Yahweh appears to the king a second time (1 Kgs 9:1–9). Commentators are divided over whether this passage reflects positively or negatively upon the king. According to Nelson, "The first appearance of Yahweh in 3:4–14 sets his seal of approval upon the succession of Solomon to the throne and points forward to future wisdom and riches. The second appearance actually has much the same purpose."[63] Yet many scholars regard this as one of the first passages to critique the king—albeit implicitly—given the warning that Israel will be cut off and cast out and the threat that the temple will reduced to a heap of ruins if Solomon (and/or his successors) forsake the Lord (9:6–9). As Provan puts its, "This second appearance of God marks the endpoint of Solomon's upward mobility and points us ahead to disaster."[64] How might such differing assessments be explained? I believe it best to regard this text, like many we have investigated thus far, as an admixture of propaganda and subversion.

According to Mason, "The most obvious element of Deuteronomic 'subversion' is to be found in their attitude towards the monarchy in Israel."[65] Since this attitude will be studied more extensively below,[66] I need only mention one aspect here, the Dtr's insistence that the king is not above the law. Indeed, according to the Deuteronomic law of the king, it's the other way around! Deuteronomy 17:18–20 reads:

> When he [the king] has taken the throne of his kingdom, he shall have a copy of this law written for him in the presence of the levitical priests. It shall remain with him and he shall read in it all the days of his life, so that he may learn to fear the LORD his God, diligently observing all the words of this law and these statutes, neither exalting himself above other

---

62. See, conveniently, Knoppers, "Prayer and Propaganda," 106–8, and the references there.

63. Richard D. Nelson, *The Double Reaction of the Deuteronomistic History* (JSOTSup 18; Sheffield: JSOT Press, 1981), 74.

64. Provan, *1 and 2 Kings*, 83.

65. Mason, *Propaganda and Subversion*, 75.

66. The so-called "law of the king" in Deut 17:14–20 will later be examined in light of the activities of Solomon described in 1 Kgs 10:26–11:8.

members of the community nor turning aside from the commandment, either to the right or to the left, so that he and his descendants may reign long over his kingdom in Israel.

Mason regards this view of a Torah-tethered king as "entirely subversive to the sacral views of monarchy expressed in royal psalms and 'pro-Davidic' propaganda."[67] For the Dtr, neither Solomon nor his successors simply ruled by divine fiat. Their divine right to rule was conditioned by their level of obedience to the covenant. It was to be guided and governed by strict adherence to Yahweh's commands.

This seems to be the message of vv. 4–5, as the focus shifts from temple to king:

> As for you, if you will walk before me, as David your father walked, with integrity of heart and uprightness, doing according to all that I have commanded you, and keeping my statutes and my ordinances, then I will establish your royal throne over Israel forever, as I promised your father David, saying, "There shall not fail you a successor on the throne of Israel."

Like 1 Kgs 2:4 and 8:25, these verses again conditionalize the continuance of the Davidic dynasty upon obedience to Torah.[68]

It seems clear that the seeds of subversion are planted in 1 Kgs 9:4–5 and similar passages in the Solomonic narrative and Kings which qualify the monarch's absolute power and prerogatives. The promise of a perpetual Davidide on the throne of Israel is contingent upon royal loyalty to Yahweh. In this way, the text subverts the royal ideology by bringing "Solomon and the monarchy under the Torah."[69]

## Hiram's Dissatisfying Cities (1 Kings 9:10–14)

The account of Solomon's cession of twenty cities follows the "second" divine appearance to Solomon and ostensibly occurs at the end of the twenty-year period which saw the completion of the temple–palace complex. If there is some actual historical basis in Solomon's cession of these cities—an assumption which seems quite probable since it is

67. Mason, *Propaganda and Subversion*, 78.

68. Contra Nelson (*Double Redaction*, 100–105) who argues for reading "throne of Israel" as a reference to the Northern kingdom. Cf. Richard Elliot Friedman, "From Egypt to Egypt: Dtr[1] and Dtr[2]," in *Traditions in Transformation: Turning Points in Biblical Faith; Essays Presented to Frank Moore Cross, Jr.* (ed. Baruch Halpern and Jon D. Levenson; Winona Lake, Ind.: Eisenbrauns, 1981), 167–92 (175–76).

69. Brueggemann, *1 & 2 Kings*, 122.

difficult to imagine why someone would otherwise invent such a story—then this text appears to be a classic case of royal propaganda, attempting to put the best spin possible on what is arguably a disastrous turn of events (i.e. losing territory).[70]

First, notice how the relative worthlessness of these properties is emphasized in a variety of ways, presumably suggesting that their loss of land was no big deal. After Hiram had inspected the cities, it is reported that "they did not please him" (v. 12b). This negative evaluation is reinforced through the use of direct speech when Hiram asks Solomon, "What kind of cities are these?," a question which insinuates he is not especially happy with his new acquisitions (v. 13a).[71] Finally, there is an etiological note referring to the region as "the land of Cabul," a designation which may be rendered, "as nothing" (v. 13b).[72] By repeatedly emphasizing the low quality of this territory, it seems the writer is attempting to convince his audience that it is no great loss since it was, after all, basically uninhabitable swampland![73] As Fritz observes, "The note about Hiram's disapproval serves as an excuse for Solomon. He may have transferred Israelite settlements to a foreign ruler, yet they were just inferior places Israel could afford to give up."[74]

A second indication of propagandistic intention in this text relates to the price paid for the property. If we are correct in understanding the 120 talents of gold[75] as payment for these twenty cities,[76] it would seem that

70. Surely many in Israel would have regarded the loss of land as an alarming development, not least of which those who woke up the next morning to find themselves living in Tyrian territory!

71. Kuan's ("Third Kingdoms 5.1," 39) argument that Hiram's displeasure may have been due to the situation (i.e. Solomon running out of cash to pay tribute) rather than any dissatisfaction with the quality of the cities themselves is not convincing.

72. There has been considerable discussion of the meaning and significance of *kābûl*. Some attempts have been made to identify it with an actual location near Acco (Josh 19:27). Others have searched for alternative etymological explanations suggesting translations such as "mortgaged" (Gray, *I & II Kings*, 224; Jones, *1 and 2 Kings*, 214), "March-land" (Montgomery and Gehman, *Kings*, 205), and "fettered" (Provan, *1 and 2 Kings*, 88). It is also possible that Cabul (*kābûl*) represents an auditory corruption of "boundary" (*gābûl*), witnessed in the LXX by *orion* (so DeVries, *1 Kings*, 130; cf. Walsh, *1 Kings*, 121 n. 1).

73. Though I disagree with Jones' (*1 and 2 Kings*, 212) contention that vv. 12–13 are a later addition, he is correct in noting that they reflect an attempt to justify the king's actions by emphasizing that these cities were of little value.

74. Fritz, *1 & 2 Kings*, 107.

75. The relationship between the gold which accompanied Hiram's shipments of timber (9:11) and this 120 talents (9:14) is unclear.

76. *Pace* Knoppers (*Two Nations*, 128) who regards this as tribute.

the reader/hearer should be impressed by the huge amount of gold that Solomon, a shrewd negotiator, secured for such worthless real estate. Although the exact weight of this gold is indeterminable,[77] it is, by any standard, an enormous amount of money! People were to be awed by Solomon's remarkable business savvy which allowed him to broker such a great deal.[78] As Nelson remarks, "Hiram paid more than four metric tons of gold for these worthless hamlets! The partisan Judean audience must have gleefully appreciated how Solomon beat at his own game this king of a merchant nation. The intention is once more to underline the wisdom of Solomon."[79]

The ability to take so unfavorable an incident—Solomon's sale of cities—and spin it in such a way that it actually magnifies rather than maligns the king, appears to be the work of a highly committed submissive scribe. This seems particularly true if this text (in more or less its present form) was crafted during the reign of Solomon in an attempt to defend the king against those who might have (good) cause to question his ability to rule well. As such, this little text would shine as a classic example of royal propaganda. In any case, the text as we now have it seems intent on glorifying the king.

Despite these efforts to cast the king's cession of cities in the best possible light, it is difficult to escape completely the feeling that somehow, regardless of the amount of gold Solomon receives, this sale still reflects poorly on the king.[80] Some believe this text criticizes Solomon for dealing

---

77. Gray (*I & II Kings*, 224) gives a range of 45–130 lbs/talent.

78. Whether or not Hiram ever actually gave Solomon gold is beside the point. DeVries (*1 Kings*, 132) finds the idea that Hiram sent Solomon gold "entirely fanciful" and Jones (*1 and 2 Kings*, 214) regards the 120 talents of gold as "extraordinarily large and very dubious." For an attempt to demonstrate the historical plausibility of the vast amounts of gold which reportedly flowed into Solomon's kingdom, see Alan R. Millard, "Does the Bible Exaggerate King Solomon's Golden Wealth?," *BAR* 15/3 (1989): 20–29, 31, 34. By adducing numerous literary parallels to great quantities of gold from a variety of ancient Near Eastern sources, Millard's answer to the question raised by the title is, "Not necessarily." Yet his attempt to use these parallels to establish a plausible argument that Solomon might have been as rich as the text suggests fails to consider that all such reports may have been used for propagandistic purposes rather than accurate accounting.

79. Nelson, *First and Second Kings*, 63–64; cf. idem, *Double Redaction*, 74. Similarly, Knoppers (*Two Nations*, 124), who concedes the text is somewhat ambiguous, nevertheless believes that "if the negotiations slight anyone, it would seem to be a king who receives worthless compensation, but still dispatches an enormous amount of tribute and continues to cooperate with Solomon in matters of trade."

80. The Chronicler's account (2 Chr 8:1–2) initially seems to support this notion since it *appears* to turn the Kings account on its head. As the Chronicler has it, rather

unjustly or in "bad faith" in his (apparently successful) attempt to gyp the Tyrian king by selling him shoddy cities.[81] Yet this is difficult to substantiate given our lack of knowledge about the actual circumstances that gave rise to the sale of these cities.

If there is criticism to be found here—which seems quite likely—it is to be found in the simple description of Solomon parting with Israelite property. As Walsh puts it, "Solomon may get an excellent price for the territory, but the bottom line is that Solomon gives up land."[82] One wonders how any audience, pre-exilic or otherwise, could regard this as exemplary? Giving away a piece of the "promised land," regardless of whether this transfer of territory was politically or economically motivated, must have been deeply disturbing to many in Israel. Israelite law strictly regulated the sale of land, disallowing it to be sold to another Israelite in perpetuity.[83] Understandably, there was no legislation on the books about giving away or "selling" land to a foreign king since such a thing was utterly unimaginable! As Jones puts it, "The loss of territory was a heavy blow for Israel, and this account contributes indirectly to the negative assessment of King Solomon."[84]

than selling cities to Hiram/Huram, Solomon receives cities from Hiram/Huram! Since we know the Chronicler was loath to include anything in his work that might tarnish the reputation of Solomon, it would appear that he simply reworked his *Vorlage* to craft a text more favorable to the king. Such an explanation becomes problematic, however, when one recognizes that the Chronicler often assumes the reader's familiarity with the stories of Samuel–Kings. It is doubtful, then, that the Chronicler could have gotten away with such blatant revisionism. Omitting stories is one thing; completely rewriting them is quite another. For an evaluation of this position and for other explanations, see Williamson (*1 and 2 Chronicles*, 227–29) who argues that the Chronicler's account is based on a corrupt *Vorlage*. See also Raymond B. Dillard, *2 Chronicles* (WBC 15; Waco, Tex.: Word, 1987), 62–64) who regards the Chronicler's account as a sequel to Kings, thereby easing the apparent tension by harmonizing the two accounts.

81. So Parker, "Repetition," 23–24; idem, "Philosopher King," 84.

82. Walsh, *1 Kings*, 122. Cf. Parker, ("Philosopher King," 84) who believes "any sale of land, no matter how remunerative, affects the land's integrity and undermines the promise of the Torah."

83. "The land shall not be sold in perpetuity, for the land is mine; with me you are but aliens and tenants" (Lev 25:23). Although Lev 25:18–34 presumably postdates the DtrH, it certainly reflects some of Israel's most ancient convictions about retaining the land, believed to be theirs by divine behest.

84. Jones, *1 and 2 Kings*, 213. See also Hays ("Narrative Subtlety," 171) who believes the "subtle criticism explodes into a scathing critique when read within the context of the rest of 1–2 Kings, particularly 1 Kings 16," the story of Ahab's improper acquisition of Naboth's vineyard.

This loss of land appears especially troublesome when read against the divine threat issued a few verses prior which warns that the punishment for Israel's apostasy will be precisely that, the loss of land![85] And while Walsh's contention that "Solomon's readiness to sell off what Yahweh himself bestowed...foreshadows a disastrous destiny for the nation" may be unwarranted,[86] it is difficult, as mentioned, to imagine how any ancient Israelite audience could view relinquishing land favorably. One might even say that giving land away to foreigners symbolically suggests a reversal of the settlement, that period remembered as the time when Israel gained land by taking it away from foreign peoples. A text crafted with such intentional ambiguity, supporting the king on the one hand while subverting him on the other, certainly looks like the kind of product we have come to expect from a scribe writing subversive praise. overtly exonerating the king while covertly excoriating him.

### *The Queen of Sheba's Words of Praise (1 Kings 10:6–9)*

Given the brevity of the account describing the queen of Sheba's visit, it is noteworthy that approximately one third of the narrative is devoted to the queen's speech (vv. 6–9). Her words affirm Solomon's greatness (vv. 6–7), celebrate the good fortune of those who benefit from Solomon's wisdom (v. 8), and praise Solomon's God for putting him on the throne (v. 9). The queen's words certainly look like the product of a submissive scribe and are, in certain respects, reminiscent of Hiram's extravagant speech in 5:7. Particularly striking is the strong affirmation that Solomon rules by divine design, a key component of royal propaganda. The queen declares, "Blessed be the Lord your God, who has delighted in you and set you on the throne of Israel! Because the Lord loved Israel forever, he has made you king to execute justice and righteousness" (10:9).

By this point in our study we have grown accustomed to finding subversion disguised in the cloak of propaganda. Thus, it comes as no great surprise to discover numerous scholars wondering if there might be criticism embedded in these words of praise. Fretheim believes "the witness of the queen of Sheba may also contain an implicit critique, particularly her statement about the divine purpose in making Solomon king:

---

85. As Kang (*Persuasive Portrayal of Solomon*, 199) puts it, "Solomon's giving of the cities (9:11–13) is an ominous presage in the context of Yahweh's warning against the loss of the land (9:7)."

86. Walsh, *1 Kings*, 122.

to execute justice and righteousness."[87] He asks, "Is this really the narrator *speaking in a subversive way* about the absence of justice and righteousness in the rule of Solomon (note that v. 8 mentions only his wives and servants, not the people generally)?"[88] Similarly, Brueggemann wonders if these words stand as a challenge to the Solomonic enterprise. Although he recognizes that the queen's mention of "justice and righteousness" may simply reflect her knowledge of "conventional rhetoric," he suspects it is far more ominous.[89] He writes, "One can imagine that in all the palaver of trade negotiations with pleasant behavior, cleverness, and many cocktails, when the queen said 'justice and righteousness' there came an embarrassed silence in the room."[90] Eslinger is also convinced that these words do not reflect well on the king. He emphasizes the way in which they stand in tension with vv. 4–5. In these verses which describe the salutary effects of Solomon's wisdom, Eslinger emphasizes the lack of any evidence that Solomon executes justice and righteousness. He finds this noteworthy and regards the speech as a "piece of dramatic irony" which "contrasts markedly with the actual results of Solomon's reign, which have just been foregrounded in vv. 4–5."[91] As Walsh puts it, this "mention of 'justice'…sounds more like a reminder to Solomon of his duty than a praise of his deeds."[92]

Understood this way, there is good reason to believe the reference to doing "justice and righteousness" was intended as a covert critique of Solomon's failure to satisfy this most basic monarchical obligation. After all, it is hardly an act of flattery to broadcast someone's "job description" if the purpose in doing so is to reveal how far short they fall of fulfilling it! Putting this critique on the lips of a foreigner, one who is ostensibly praising the king, seems a most effective disguise. While the queen's words appear favorable toward Solomon, they contain a subtle, stinging indictment. And regardless of whether one believes this critique was launched against a "historical" Solomon, it would have served a similar function during the reign of any king who neglected this fundamental royal responsibility.

87. Fretheim, *First and Second Kings*, 60.

88. Ibid. (my emphasis). Provan (*1 and 2 Kings*, 87) also emphasizes the restricted benefactors of Solomonic wisdom.

89. Brueggemann, *Kings*, 134. Hays ("Narrative Subtlety," 172) follows Fretheim and Brueggemann.

90. Ibid., 139.

91. Eslinger, *Into the Hands*, 151.

92. Walsh, *1 Kings*, 131. See also Long (*1 & 2 Kings*, 146) who writes, "By the creative use of structural irony, Solomon is exposed as a self-indulgent leader who has lost sight of his divinely ordained role as shepherd of Israel."

*Solomon and the Law of the King (1 Kings 10:26–11:8)*

One additional example of scribal subversion must occupy our attention before we are ready to draw some final conclusions. This concerns 1 Kgs 10:26–11:8 and its relationship to the so-called "law of the king" in Deut 17:14–20, a passage noted above. By all accounts, Deut 17:14–20 is wildly subversive, severely delimiting the powers and prerogatives of the king.[93] Here the institution of the monarchy is envisioned as more of a concession rather than a divine mandate. Although the people are allowed to appoint a king of God's choosing (v. 15), this royal designee's duties and responsibilities are seriously circumscribed. There is, for example, no mention of the king's role in the cult, nor is there any emphasis on the king's special mediatory role between the people and God, both regarded as common functions of ancient Near Eastern kings. Also missing is any notion of the king as God's vice-regent on earth, with the attendant responsibilities of bringing order from chaos, mediating fecundity to the people, and doing justice and righteousness. Instead, the Deuteronomic vision of the king assigns the monarch one simple task: reading Torah "all the days of his life" (v. 19). Moreover, the king is expressly forbidden from acquiring (*rābâ*) lots of horses (especially from Egypt), lots of wives, and lots of wealth (vv. 16–17). Such restrictions are unique and find no direct parallels in ancient Near Eastern literature.

These three restrictions are especially interesting for our study since 1 Kgs 10:26–11:8 seems to imply that Solomon violates all three of them! "Solomon gathered together chariots and horses…[m]ade silver as common as stones, and…[l]oved many foreign women" (10:26, 27; 11:1). Given such striking similarities, it is understandable that many interpreters have concluded that the Solomonic materials have been carefully arranged to correspond to the prohibitions of the law of the king, thereby severely critiquing Solomon's kingship.[94] As such, Solomon is viewed as the antithesis of the *Deuteronomic* ideal of kingship.

93. See Mason, *Propaganda and Subversion*, 75–79.

94. So Parker, "Repetition," 23; idem, "Philosopher King," 85; Eslinger, *Into the Hands*, 152–53; Walsh, *1 Kings*, 137–38; Provan, *1 and 2 Kings*, 87–88. See especially Sweeney ("Critique," 615–17) who finds additional correlations between Solomon's misdeeds and the law of the king, and Brettler ("Structure") who suggests that 1 Kgs 9:26–11:10 is comprised of three parts (9:26–10:25 [wealth], 10:26–29 [horses], and 11:1–10 [wives]) which should be labeled "Solomon's violation of Deut. 17.14–17" (p. 97). For a contrary view which argues that the law of the king predates Solomon and most likely arose in conjunction with "the inception of the monarchy," see Baruch Halpern, *The Constitution of the Monarchy in Israel* (HSM 25; Chico, Calif.: Scholars Press, 1981), 225–32.

Some have argued, however, that it is problematic to see a critique of Solomon's kingship in these verses since there are competing visions of the monarchy expressed in the Deuteronomic law of the king and the Deuteronomist's presentation of the reign of Solomon.[95] As Knoppers observes,

> For the deuteronomic authors, the monarchy is an institution which has the capacity to compromise or even threaten Israel's distinctive national identity. But the Deuteronomist does not view the monarchy as an inherently dangerous institution. According to the Deuteronomist, Israel finally achieves its promised rest and receives its central sanctuary in the time of King Solomon.[96]

The "Deuteronomic authors" to which Knoppers refers are those responsible for Deut 17:14–20 and the Deuteronomic code generally. They should be distinguished from the Dtr(s), who utilize(s) this work but feel(s) free to modify it and even subvert it in the interests of articulating a different vision of kingship from that found in Deut 17. From the Dtr's perspective, the acquisition of horses, wealth, and wives was unproblematic.[97] Even so, while the Dtr might not consider the kingly acquisition of such "items" condemnatory, there were others in ancient Israel—such as the Deuteronomic authors and like-minded individuals—who certainly did!

Given these considerations, it would seem that a passage such as 1 Kgs 10:26–29 carries especially high subversive potential. Although the acquisition of many horses and much wealth might have appeared rather innocuous to one set of readers, to others it epitomized the shortcomings and failings of the monarchic system they had come to know. And while such a passage would undoubtedly have been regarded as praising Solomon by some,[98] for others, like those standing in the tradition of 1 Sam 8 and Deut 17, it sounded an alarm. For these individuals, such a passage would have reflected negatively on kingship generally and the Solomonic tradition specifically by accentuating certain problematic practices so typical of the monarchy and monarchic power.

---

95. Gary N. Knoppers, "The Deuteronomist and the Deuteronomic Law of the King: A Reexamination of a Relationship," *ZAW* 108 (1996): 329–46.

96. Knoppers, "Deuteronomist and the Deuteronomic Law," 341.

97. As Knoppers ("Deuteronomist and the Deuteronomic Law," 337) asks, "If the Deuteronomist considered it illegitimate for kings to hoard silver, gold, wives, or horses, why does he not criticize rulers according to these criteria?"

98. Donald D. Schley, "1 Kings 10:26–29: A Reconsideration," *JBL* 106 (1987): 595–601 (601), believes "this pericope, along with 1 Kgs 10:23–25, comprises a eulogy on Solomon and his glory."

Chapter 6

CONCLUSIONS

*The account of Solomon's reign...is full of the fancy of propaganda. The legend of his piously asking God for "wisdom," the kind of astute arbitration in the matter of two prostitutes both claiming parentage of a child, the account of his wealth, the splendour and extent of his empire, his literary gifts, the international reputation he built for himself, all these are of the stuff of ancient Near-Eastern royal court literature. He is fortunate in having had the first real court in Israel and so the first official team of "PR" scribes.*

—Rex Mason[1]

*While we can find no explicit right of protest in the monarchic period, it is reasonable to assume that dissent did occur—occasionally in public, much more frequently in private, and probably not seldom hidden in the text.*

—Douglas Knight[2]

In his commentary on 1–2 Kings, Terence Fretheim includes a brief excursus on 1 Kgs 2:1–46 titled, "Politics as Usual and Narrative Justification." As part of that excursus Fretheim writes,

The considerable effort made to defend Solomon's motives suggests that the narrator would not approve such political activity as a matter of course. It may even be that the narrator has introduced subtle reservations into the account, for example, Benaiah's misgivings regarding the violation of sanctuary for Joab (2:28–30), Bathsheba's support of Adonijah's request and Solomon's angry and peremptory reneging on his promise to her (2:19–24), and Shimei's seemingly innocent violation of the agreement with Solomon (2:39–43). The narrator seems to have introduced enough ambiguity into the account of Solomon's actions to stop the reader

1.   Mason, *Propaganda and Subversion*, 46.
2.   Douglas A. Knight, "Political Rights and Powers in Monarchic Israel," in *Ethics and Politics in the Hebrew Bible* (ed. Douglas A. Knight and Carol Meyers; Semeia 66; Atlanta: Scholars Press, 1995), 93–117 (105).

from simply adopting an unquestioning stance toward what he has done. Such narrative ambiguities are also present in the narratives that follow (e.g., 3:1–3; 4:6; 5:13–14 on forced labor). *One wonders why the narrator found it necessary to be critical in relatively subtle ways* (some scholarly claims to find much negative comment about Solomon tend to forget this point).[3]

In various ways this study, with its theory of scribal subversion, has provided an answer to Fretheim's unanswered query. The reason scribes "found it necessary to be critical in relatively subtle ways" was because they sometimes wanted to criticize the very patrons for whom they worked! Such an undertaking was exceedingly risky and potentially costly. Subtlety was required when scribes wanted to write a critique transparent enough to be "seen" by like-minded intellectuals (or those they hoped to persuade), while at the same time carefully hidden from those who would find it objectionable. The use of ambiguity at key moments in the Solomonic narrative, making it difficult to determine whether the text supports or subverts the king, seems suggestive of the kind of literary subversion one might expect from the hand of a subversive scribe.

It is now time to draw this investigation of 1 Kgs 1–11 to a close by discussing some of the conclusions supported by my reading of the text. First, in contrast to many previous studies which have bifurcated the Solomonic narrative into one section that praises Solomon and another that criticizes him, this study suggests that support for and, more specifically, subversion of the king runs throughout much of the narrative. This means that the text is markedly more complex and nuanced than a simple two-part division suggests, and this casts doubt on efforts to determine precisely where praise stops and criticism begins.

Second, I have argued that many of the ostensibly propagandistic texts in 1 Kgs 1–11 contain a subversive undercurrent that can often be detected below the surface. This intriguing characteristic accounts, in part, for such widely divergent assessments of the Solomonic narrative. Those who view Solomon more positively put their emphasis on the propagandistic elements while those who take a more negative view of the king focus on the subversive undercurrents scattered throughout the narrative.

Third, given the preponderance of what might be called "subversive laced propaganda" at various points in the Solomonic narrative, it seems best to explain these particular texts as the product of a scribe(s) who

---

3. Terence E. Fretheim, *First and Second Kings* (Louisville, Ky.: Westminster John Knox, 1999), 27 (my emphasis).

used propaganda as a smokescreen for subversive ends.[4] Such covert measures used to disguise a critique of the king and/or the royal ideology were absolutely necessary for tethered scribes working for the state or closely supervised by it. Allowing for the presence of subversive scribal activity in the Solomonic narrative provides a reasonable explanation for some of the literary tensions and ambiguities found therein. In the history of biblical studies, such tensions—in the Solomonic narrative and elsewhere—have been explained in any one of a number of ways: sophisticated redactional analyses, the combination of different sources, or even just slopping editing. While not wishing to deny any of these eventualities, subversive scribal activity—a feature of literary production which has not been systematically explored before—throws an additional explanation into the mix, one that should be considered seriously when discussing this material.

In fact, this premise, that subversive scribes were actively working in the palace/temple during the monarchic period, signifies a major theoretical contribution of this study, one which I believe could be profitably applied to other portions of the Hebrew Bible. It seems fair to say that there were probably some scribes who were always content to be submissive, happily writing whatever they were told to write. And it is equally possible that there were some scribes who were constantly trying to find ways to subvert their patrons. But it is equally probable that there were scribes who vacillated between these two options based upon the particular situations and circumstances in which they found themselves. Moreover, it seems quite likely that as power changed hands in the court or temple, a scribe who normally tended to be submissive might feel compelled to be subversive, or vice versa, depending upon the new policies and persons involved.

To be sure, any application of this model must be undertaken with due caution. As Holter reminds us, "There always is a danger of doing *eisegesis* rather than *exegesis*, in the interpretation of texts supposed to have concealed meanings and undertones."[5] One must be careful not to find subversion where it would never have been apprehended by ancient intellectuals. Reading against the grain is a useful strategy for detecting subversive elements, but it can become ridiculous, missing the real point(s) of the story by imposing readings upon the text neither recognizable by attentive hearers/readers nor imagined by the original

4. To be sure, not every propagandistic text contains subversive elements. Certain texts seem to be "pure" propaganda (e.g. 1 Kgs 5:9–14 [Eng. 4:29–34]); 10:14–22).

5. Holter, "Serpent in Eden," 111.

writers.[6] The possibility of this kind of interpretive excess, however, should not discourage us from considering the presence of subversive scribal activity in these—and other—texts. Moreover, since this study has demonstrated a wide range of potentially subversive readings that would have been available to ancient readers, even if some remain unconvinced that there is *intentional* scribal subversion in certain instances, the possibility of these texts being perceived subversively still remains. As Huffmon notes, "The nature of subversion is that it can hang around, even undetected, for a long time."[7]

Fourth, by emphasizing the nature and range of scribal activity, this study has demonstrated the importance of taking the social impulses behind the production of the text into account when trying to ascertain its meaning. In the wake of the antagonism between literary critics and historical critics, "the question of the social production of literature has been ignored."[8] This is unfortunate and deprives the biblical scholar of a valuable resource for investigation into the production and consumption of biblical texts since "literature is not the result of some disembodied process but is intimately linked, both in its inception and reception, to the complexities of the social process."[9]

Few scholars have attempted to describe the social location of the author(s) of the Solomonic narrative beyond simply attributing it more or less to the Dtr.[10] Three relatively recent essays in Lowell Handy's volume *The Age of Solomon* which are specifically categorized as "sociological approaches" to the narrative are disappointing in this regard.[11] Only one of these writers, Neils Peter Lemche, even raises these sociological queries so critical for understanding the role and function of the

6.   I am not suggesting that there is only one meaning to a text or that some "original" meaning is automatically the most important. But I am saying that texts did (and do) mean something and that understanding the "writer's" original intentions is a valid line of inquiry, though obviously not the only one. For a helpful discussion of these issues, which lie beyond the scope of this study, see John Barton, *Reading the Old Testament: Method in Biblical Study* (rev. and enl. ed; Louisville, Ky.: Westminster John Knox, 1996).

7.   Huffmon, "Gender Subversion in the Book of Jeremiah," 253.

8.   Keith W. Whitelam, "Between History and Literature: The Social Production of Israel's Traditions of Origin," *SJOT* 2 (1991): 60–74 (64). By revealing propagandistic and subversive elements in the text via both the historical-critical method and a literary-critical approach, I would suggest that these two approaches need not be as antagonistic or as mutually exclusive as some scholars contend.

9.   Ibid., 65.

10.   A constructive effort to address this issue was attempted in the second part of Chapter 2 of the present study.

11.   Handy, ed., *The Age of Solomon*, 252–335.

Solomonic narrative. Yet, these are quickly brushed aside in pursuit of an extended discussion of "social archaeology."[12] Moreover, what he does manage to say regarding the producers of this text is hardly satisfying. He writes,

> The place to look for the milieu of the production of such a narrative (a quest which is truly a historical one) would probably be among a literary elite not only used to writing various sorts of official documents but also interested in written literature; the demand would be that this group would be in possession of the leisure time which enabled it to pursue *such utterly non-productive interests*. Literature in this sense is certainly a luxury and would reflect a fairly complex society with an extended scribal class.[13]

While I agree that the Solomonic narrative originates with the literary elite, it seems highly unlikely that it reflects "utterly non-productive interests" or that it was created by scribes who had nothing better to do than sit around and describe the Solomonic kingdom in "fairy tale" form, to use Lemche's language.[14] Instead, I have argued that the use of concealed subversion suggests that some portions of the Solomonic narrative were crafted by (a) clever scribe(s) hoping to disseminate destabilizing messages to (a) restricted audience(s). Despite the impossibility of ascertaining exactly what motivated a particular scribe to resort to this or that form of subversion, the fact that such activities entailed considerable risk indicates some sort of productive purpose for such writing.[15]

Fifth, this study has demonstrated that while propaganda serves as a cloaking device for subversion, there is no solitary way in which subversion is deployed within that framework. Instead, the subversive scribe had many options from which to choose. In the foregoing analysis of the Solomonic narrative we observed techniques such as ambiguity (e.g. David's previous oath) and the use of strategic omissions (e.g. no kindness offered to the sons of Barzillai despite "David's" words). Sometimes, such as the reporting of the executions in 1 Kgs 2, it seemed that paper-thin propaganda itself was a tool of the subversive scribe. Other times subversion impulses came through direct speech (e.g. Hiram's ability to ultimate set the terms of the wood for wheat exchange in 1 Kgs 5). Additionally, it was noted how a simple statement of "fact" could have subversive potential. Such seemed to be the case in the mention of

12. Neils Peter Lemche, "On Doing Sociology with 'Solomon,'" in Handy,ed., *The Age of Solomon*, 312–35 (314).

13. Ibid., 313 (my emphasis).

14. Ibid.

15. For discussion, see the section in Chapter 2 entitled "The Aims and Possibilities of Literary Subversion" (pp. 65–66).

Solomon's cession of cities in 1 Kgs 9:10–14 since those who firmly believed the land was to be held in perpetuity would have found such a sale highly disturbing. In short, subversive techniques/methods could and did come in many shapes and sizes.

Sixth, although I have not been concerned about precisely classifying different "types" of subversion *vis-à-vis* what was being undermined, this study of the Solomonic narrative would suggest the presence of considerable variety. At times the subversive scribe seemed to be attacking the very legitimacy of Solomon's right to rule. On other occasions, we observed examples of "character subversion" as Solomon's stature was diminished by accentuating his religious aberrations or his international weakness. There were also several instances in which royal ideology itself was subverted by those holding competing visions of the nature and function of the monarchy. In these examples, there were subversive impulses aimed at critiquing prevailing practices of the royal establishment while articulating a theological vision of the monarchy which places it under the rule of Torah. These assorted categories, though orbiting around king and state, demonstrate subversion's heterogeneity and its ability to be corrosive at a variety of levels.

Finally, my analysis of 1 Kgs 1–2, in particular, suggests that this portion of the Solomonic narrative—ostensibly written as a piece of political propaganda but riddled with many subversive elements—most likely had its origins during the reign of Solomon.[16] While the need to compose a defense of Solomon's consolidation of power early in his reign makes perfect sense, it becomes much more difficult to explain the rationale for such an apologia in the late seventh century BCE or any subsequent period. While my position allow room for significant redactional activity to have taken place at later points in the process of transmission, the impetus for writing 1 Kgs 1–2 at least in some for seems most appropriate in the turbulent transition of power in tenth-century Israel. As such, these findings challenge certain revisionist assumptions which posit Solomon and the Solomonic era as fictional creations of the Persian/Hellenistic Periods.

---

16. My argument is not, however, dependent upon a tenth-century date. The subversive elements retain their force even if the text was composed much later. Additionally, it should be noted that I am not only speaking of 1 Kgs 1–2 here. Matters related to the composition and date of the remainder of the Solomonic narrative are considerably more complex and room should be allowed for many scribal hands over a significant period of time.

## Areas for Further Study

Throughout this study I have devoted considerable attention to the fascinating interplay between propaganda and subversion and have attempted to demonstrate a variety of ways in which propagandistic writing might serve as a cloaking device for subversive scribal activities. This process has raised several other potentially fruitful areas for further study which should be noted. First, more attention could be given to the implications of this study *vis-à-vis* the Dtr. Second, more attention could be focused on the complex issue of method, namely, how to determine whether something is propagandistic[17] or subversive. Third, the concept of submissive and subversive scribal activity developed in this study could be applied to other portions of the Hebrew Bible, especially those which have previously been thought to function primarily as political propaganda. It would be interesting to determine the degree to which these texts might also betray evidence of scribal subversion. Fourth, questions related to textual indeterminacy and scribal intentionality could be explored further. While some attention was given to these matters in Chapter 2, more could be done to assist readers with these complex theoretical questions as they relate to biblical texts. Finally, it would be important, especially to faith communities concerned about issues of divine inspiration, to consider how such texts might still function authoritatively if originally written for propagandistic and subversive purposes.

## A Final Word

In closing, I end with the words of J. A. Brinkman, whose sentiments capture much of what I have been attempting in this study:

> In essence, we read what the scribes wrote, with their selectivity, distortions, fabrications, and slant, in their words, and with their rhetorical emphases. Our task in interpreting these texts is perhaps not so much to reconstruct the singular "event history"…which offered the occasion for writing—though this too may be a legitimate occupation for the historian—as to understand the broad range of the message, both overt and subliminal, communicated through the scribal formulation. It is important to be aware of and to appraise the scribal filter through which the information comes to us.[18]

This is what I have attempted to do by exploring the Solomonic narrative through the optics of propaganda and subversion.

17. See, for example, the brief discussion in McKenzie, *King David*, 44–45.
18. Brinkman, "Through a Glass Darkly," 36.

# BIBLIOGRAPHY

Abegg, Martin, Jr., Peter Flint, and Eugene Ulrich. *The Dead Sea Scrolls Bible: The Oldest Known Bible Translated for the First Time into English*. New York: Harper-Collins, 1999.

Abrams, M. H. *A Glossary of Literary Terms*. 4th ed. Montreal: Holt, Rinehart & Winston, 1981.

Ackerman, James S. "Knowing Good and Evil: A Literary Analysis of the Court History in 2 Samuel 9–20 and 1 Kings 1–2." *JBL* 109 (1990): 41–60.

Ackroyd, Peter R. "The Succession Narrative (So-Called)." *Int* 35 (1981): 383–96.

Albertz, Rainer. *A History of Israelite Religion in the Old Testament Period*. Vol. 1, *From the Beginnings to the End of the Monarchy*. Translated by John Bowden. Louisville, Ky.: Westminster John Knox, 1994.

Alter, Robert. *The Art of Biblical Narrative*. New York: Basic Books, 1981.

—*The David Story: A Translation with Commentary of 1 and 2 Samuel*. New York: W. W. Norton & Co., 1999.

Amit, Yairah. *Hidden Polemics in Biblical Narrative*. Translated by Jonathan Chipman. Leiden: Brill, 2000.

Anderson, A. A. *2 Samuel*. WBC 11. Dallas: Word, 1989.

Ash, Paul S. "Solomon's? District? List." *JSOT* 67 (1995): 67–86.

Auld, A. Graeme. *I & II Kings*. Philadelphia: Westminster, 1986.

Bal, Mieke. *Death and Dissymmetry: The Politics of Coherence in the Book of Judges*. Chicago: University of Chicago Press, 1988.

Baines, John. "Literacy and Ancient Egyptian Society." *Man* 18 (1983): 572–99.

Barré, Lloyd M. *The Rhetoric of Political Persuasion: The Narrative Artistry and Political Intentions of 2 Kings 9–11*. CBQMS 20. Washington, D.C.: Catholic Biblical Association of America, 1988.

Bar-Efrat, Shimon. *Narrative Art in the Bible*. Tel Aviv: Sifriat Poalim, 1979. Repr., JSOTSup 70. Sheffield: Almond Press, 1989.

Bartlett, F. C. "The Aims of Political Propaganda." Pages 463–70 in *Public Opinion and Propaganda*. Edited by Daniel Katz, Dorwin Cartwright, Samuel Eldersveld, and Alfred McClung Lee. New York: Holt, Rinehart & Winston, 1954.

Barton, John. "Dating the 'Succession Narrative.'" Pages 95–106 in *In Search of Pre-exilic Israel: Proceedings of the Oxford Old Testament Seminar*. Edited by John Day. JSOTSup 406. London: T. & T. Clark, 2004.

—*Reading the Old Testament: Method in Biblical Study*. Rev. and enl. ed. Louisville, Ky.: Westminster John Knox, 1996.

Bellis, Alice Ogden. *Helpmates, Harlots, and Heroes: Women's Stories in the Hebrew Bible*. Louisville, Ky.: Westminster John Knox, 1994.

Berlin, Adele. *Poetics and Interpretation of Biblical Narrative*. Bible and Literature Series 9. Sheffield: Almond Press, 1983. Repr., Winona Lake, Ind.: Eisenbrauns, 1994.

—ed. *Religion and Politics in the Ancient Near East*. Bethesda, Md.: University Press of Maryland, 1996.

Berlinerblau, Jacques. "Ideology, Pierre Bourdieu's *Doxa*, and the Hebrew Bible." Pages 193–214 in *The Social World of the Hebrew Bible: Twenty-Five Years of the Social Sciences in the Academy*. Edited by Ronald A. Simkins, Stephen L. Cook, and Athalya Brenner. Semeia 87. Atlanta: Scholars Press, 1999.

—"Preliminary Remarks for the Sociological Study of Israelite 'Official Religion.'" Pages 153–70 in *Ki Baruch Hu: Ancient Near Eastern, Biblical, and Judaic Studies in Honor of Baruch A. Levine*. Edited by Robert Chazan, W. W. Hallo, and L. H. Schiffman. Winona Lake, Ind.: Eisenbrauns, 1999.

—"The Present Crisis and Uneven Triumphs of Biblical Sociology: Responses to N. K. Gottwald, S. Mandell, P. Davies, M. Sneed, R. Simkins and N. Lemche." Pages 99–120 in Sneed, ed., *Concepts of Class in Ancient Israel*.

—*The Vow and the "Popular Religious Groups" of Ancient Israel: A Philological and Sociological Inquiry*. JSOTSup 210. Sheffield: Sheffield Academic Press, 1996.

Berquist, Jon L. *Judaism in Persia's Shadow: A Social and Historical Approach*. Minneapolis: Fortress, 1995.

Bledstein, Adrien Janis. "Is Judges a Woman's Satire of Men Who Play God?" Pages 34–54 in Brenner, ed., *A Feminist Companion to Judges*.

Bleiberg, Edward. "Historical Texts as Political Propaganda during the New Kingdom." *Bulletin of the Egyptological Seminar* 7 (1985–86): 5–13.

Blenkinsopp, Joseph. *Sage, Priest, Prophet: Religious and Intellectual Leadership in Ancient Israel*. Louisville, Ky.: Westminster John Knox, 1995.

—"Theme and Motif in the Succession History (2 Sam. XI 2ff) and the Yahwist Corpus." Pages 44–57 in *Volume du Congrès: Genève, 1965*. VTSup 15. Leiden: Brill, 1966.

Bodner, Keith. *David Observed: A King in the Eyes of His Court*. HBM 5. Sheffield: Sheffield Phoenix Press, 2005.

Booth, Wayne C. *A Rhetoric of Irony*. Chicago: University of Chicago Press, 1974.

Braun, Roddy L. *1 Chronicles*. WBC 14. Waco, Tex.: Word, 1986.

—"Solomonic Apologetic in Chronicles." *JBL* 92 (1973): 503–16.

Brenner, Athalya, ed. *A Feminist Companion to Judges*. The Feminist Companion to the Bible Sheffield 4. Sheffield: JSOT Press, 1993.

Brettler, Marc Zvi. "Biblical Literature as Politics: The Case of Samuel." Pages 71–92 in Berlin, ed., *Religion and Politics in the Ancient Near East*.

—"The Book of Judges: Literature as Politics." *JBL* 108 (1989): 395–418.

—*The Creation of History in Ancient Israel*. London: Routledge, 1995.

—"The Structure of 1 Kings 1–11." *JSOT* 49 (1991): 87–97.

Brinkman, J. A. "Through a Glass Darkly: Esarhaddon's Retrospects on the Downfall of Babylon." *JAOS* 103 (1983): 35–42.

Brueggemann, Walter A. *1 & 2 Kings*. Smyth & Helwys Bible Commentary. Macon, Ga.: Smyth & Helwys, 2000.

—"The Prophet as a Destabilizing Presence." Pages 49–77 in *The Pastor as Prophet*. Edited by Earl E. Shelp and Ronald H. Sunderland. New York: Pilgrim, 1985.

—*The Prophetic Imagination*. Philadelphia: Fortress, 1978.

—*Theology of the Old Testament: Testimony, Dispute, Advocacy*. Minneapolis: Fortress, 1997.

—"'Vine and Fig Tree': A Case Study in Imagination and Criticism." *CBQ* 43 (1981): 188–204.

Bryce, Trevor. *The Kingdom of the Hittites*. Oxford: Clarendon, 1998.

Burney, C. F. *The Book of Judges with Introduction and Notes and Notes on the Hebrew Text of the Books of Kings with an Introduction and Appendix*. New York: Ktav, 1970. Reprint of *Notes on the Hebrew Text of the Books of Kings with an Introduction and Appendix*. N.p., 1903.

Camp, Claudia V. *Wise, Strange and Holy: The Strange Woman and the Making of the Bible*. JSOTSup 320. GCT 9. Sheffield: Sheffield Academic Press, 2000.

Carlson, R. A. *David, the Chosen King: A Traditio-Historical Approach to the Second Book of Samuel*. Uppsala: Almquist & Wiksells, 1964.

Carr, David McLain. *From D to Q: A Study of Early Jewish Interpretations of Solomon's Dream at Gibeon*. SBLMS 44. Atlanta: Scholars Press, 1991.

—"The Politics of Textual Subversion: A Diachronic Perspective on the Garden of Eden Story." *JBL* 112 (1993): 577–95.

Carroll, Robert P. "Rebellion and Dissent in Ancient Israelite Society." *ZAW* 89 (1977): 176–204.

Clements, Ronald E. *Abraham and David: Genesis 15 and its Meaning for Israelite Tradition*. Naperville, Ill.: Alec R. Allenson, 1967.

—ed. *The World of Ancient Israel: Sociological, Anthropological and Political Perspectives*. Cambridge: Cambridge University Press, 1989.

Cogan, Mordechai. *I Kings*. AB 10. New York: Doubleday, 2001.

Conroy, Charles. *1–2 Samuel, 1–2 Kings with an Excursus on Davidic Dynasty and Holy City Zion*. Old Testament Message 6. Wilmington, Del.: Glazier, 1983.

—"A Literary Analysis of 1 Kings I 41–53, with Methodological Reflections." Pages 54–66 in Emerton, ed., *Congress Volume: Salamanca, 1983*.

Cosgrove, Charles H., ed. *The Meanings We Choose: Hermeneutical Ethics, Indeterminacy and the Conflict of Interpretations*. JSOTSup 411. London: T. & T. Clark, 2004.

Crenshaw, James L. "Education in Ancient Israel." *JBL* 104 (1985): 601–15.

—*Education in Ancient Israel: Across the Deadening Silence*. New York: Doubleday, 1998.

—"Method in Determining Wisdom Influence Upon 'Historical' Literature." *JBL* 88 (1969): 129–42.

Cross, Frank Moore, Jr. *Canaanite Myth and Hebrew Epic: Essays in the History of the Religion of Israel*. Cambridge, Mass.: Harvard University Press, 1973.

Crown, A. D. "Messengers and Scribes: The ספר and מלאך in the Old Testament." *VT* 14 (1974): 366–70.

Culley, Robert C., and Robert B. Robinson, eds. *Textual Determinacy: Part One*. Semeia 62. Atlanta: Scholars Press, 1993.

Davies, Eryl W. *The Dissenting Reader: Feminist Approaches to the Hebrew Bible*. Hants, UK: Ashgate, 2003.

Davies, G. I. "Were there Schools in Ancient Israel?" Pages 199–211 in Day, Gordon, and Williamson, eds., *Wisdom in Ancient Israel*.

Davies, Philip R. *In Search of "Ancient Israel"*. 2d ed. JSOTSup 148. Sheffield: Sheffield Academic Press, 1995.

—"Is there a Class in this Text?" Pages 37–51 in Sneed, ed., *Concepts of Class in Ancient Israel*.

—*Scribes and Schools: The Canonization of the Hebrew Scriptures*. Louisville, Ky.: Westminster John Knox, 1998.

—"The Social World of the Apocalyptic Writings." Pages 251–71 in Clements, ed., *The World of Ancient Israel*.

Day, John, Robert P. Gordon, and H. G. M. Williamson, eds. *Wisdom in Ancient Israel*. Cambridge: Cambridge University Press, 1995.

Delekat, Lienhard. "Tendenz und Theologie der David-Salomo-Erzählung." Pages 22–36 in *Das ferne und nahe Wort*. Edited by F. Maass. BZAW 105. Berlin: Topelmann, 1967.

Demsky, Aaron. "Scribe." Pages 1041–43 in vol. 14 of *Encyclopaedia Judaica*. 16 vols. Jerusalem: Keter, 1971.

Dever, William G. *What Did the Biblical Writers Know & When Did they Know It? What Archaeology Can Tell Us about the Reality of Ancient Israel*. Grand Rapids: Eerdmans, 2001.

DeVries, Simon J. *1 Kings*. WBC 12. Waco, Tex.: Word, 1985.

Dillard, Raymond B. *2 Chronicles*. WBC 15. Waco, Tex.: Word, 1987.

Dutcher-Walls, Patricia. "The Social Location of the Deuteronomists: A Sociological Study of Factional Politics in Late Pre-Exilic Judah." Pages 341–57 in *Social-Scientific Old Testament Criticism: A Sheffield Reader*. Edited by David J. Chalcraft. The Biblical Seminar 47. Sheffield: Sheffield Academic Press, 1997. Repr. from *JSOT* 52 (1991): 77-94.

Ellul, Jacques. *Propaganda: The Formation of Men's Attitudes*. Translated by Konrad Kellen and Jean Lerner. New York: Knopf, 1968.

Emerton , J. A., ed. *Congress Volume: Jerusalem, 1986*. VTSup 40. Leiden: Brill, 1988.

—*Congress Volume: Salamanca, 1983*. VTSup 36. Leiden: Brill, 1985.

Empson, William. *Seven Types of Ambiguity*. 2d ed. New York: New Directions, 1947.

Eslinger, Lyle. *Into the Hands of the Living God*. JSOTSup 84. Sheffield: Almond Press, 1989.

Exum, J. Cheryl. *Fragmented Women: Feminist (Sub)versions of Biblical Narratives*. Valley Forge, Pa.: Trinity, 1993.

Fishbane, Michael. *Biblical Interpretation in Ancient Israel*. Oxford: Clarendon, 1985.

Flanagan, James W. "Court History or Succession Document? A Study of 2 Samuel 9–20 and 1 Kings 1–2." *JBL* 91 (1972): 172–81.

Fokkelman, J. P. *Narrative Art and Poetry in the Books of Samuel*. Vol. 1, *King David (II Sam. 9–20 & 1 Kings 1–2)*. Assen: Van Gorcum, 1981.

—*Reading Biblical Narrative: An Introductory Guide*. Translated by Ineke Smit. Louisville, Ky.: Westminster John Knox, 1999.

Fontaine, Carole. "The Bearing of Wisdom on the Shape of 2 Samuel 11–12 and 1 Kings 3." *JSOT* 34 (1986): 61–77.

Foster, Benjamin R. *From Distant Days: Myths, Tales, and Poetry of Ancient Mesopotamia*. Bethesda, Md.: CDL Press, 1995.

Foulkes, A. P. *Literature and Propaganda*. London: Methuen, 1983.

Fox, Michael V. "The Uses of Indeterminacy." Pages 173–92 in Robinson and Culley, eds., *Textual Determinacy: Part Two*.

Freedman, David Noel, ed. *The Anchor Bible Dictionary*. 6 vols. New York: Doubleday, 1992.

Fretheim, Terence C. *First and Second Kings*. Louisville, Ky.: Westminster John Knox, 1999.

Friedman, Richard Elliot. "From Egypt to Egypt: Dtr[1] and Dtr[2]." Pages 167–92 in *Traditions in Transformation: Turning Points in Biblical Faith. Essays Presented to Frank*

*Moore Cross, Jr.* Edited by Baruch Halpern and Jon D. Levenson. Winona Lake, Ind.: Eisenbrauns, 1981.

Frisch, Amos. "Structure and Its Significance: The Narrative of Solomon's Reign (1 Kings 1–12.24)." *JSOT* 51 (1991): 3–14.

Fritz, Volkmar. *1 & 2 Kings*. Minneapolis: Fortress, 2003.

Fuchs, Esther. "Marginalization, Ambiguity, Silencing: The Story of Jephthah's Daughter." Pages 116–30 in Brenner, ed., *A Feminist Companion to Judges*.

Gammie, John G., and Leo G. Perdue. *The Sage in Israel and the Ancient Near East*. Winona Lake, Ind.: Eisenbrauns, 1990.

Garbini, Giovanni. *History and Ideology in Ancient Israel*. New York: Crossroad, 1988.

Garsiel, Moshe. "Puns upon Names as a Literary Device in 1 Kings 1–2." *Bib* 72 (1991): 379–86.

Green, Barbara. *Mikhail Bakhtin and Biblical Scholarship: An Introduction*. Atlanta: Society of Biblical Literature, 2000.

Gibson, J. C. L. *Language and Imagery in the Old Testament*. Peabody, Mass.: Hendrickson, 1998.

Goedicke, Hans. *The Protocol of Neferyt (The Prophecy of Neferti)*. Baltimore: The Johns Hopkins University Press, 1977.

Goldingay, John. *Models for Interpretation of Scripture*. Grand Rapids: Eerdmans, 1995.

Good, Edwin M. *Irony in the Old Testament*. Philadelphia: Westminster, 1965. Repr., Sheffield: Almond Press, 1985.

Gooding, D. W. *Relics of Ancient Exegesis: A Study of the Miscellanies in 3 Reigns 2*. SOTSMS 4. Cambridge: Cambridge University Press, 1976.

Gordon, Robert P. "A House Divided: Wisdom in Old Testament Narrative Traditions." Pages 94–105 in Day, Gordon, and Williamson, eds., *Wisdom in Ancient Israel*.

Görg, Manfred. "Die 'Sünde' Salomos: Zeitkritische Aspekte der jahwistischen Sündenfallerzählung." *BN* 16 (1981): 42–59.

—"Das Wort zur Schlange (Gen 3,14 f.): Gedanken zum sogenannten Protoevangelium." *BN* 19 (1982): 121–40.

Gray, John. *I & II Kings: A Commentary*. OTL. Philadelphia: Westminster, 1963.

Gunn, David M. *The Fate of King Saul: An Interpretation of a Biblical Story*. JSOTSup 14. Sheffield: JSOT Press, 1980.

—*The Story of King David: Genre and Interpretation*. JSOTSup 6. Sheffield: JSOT Press, 1978.

Gunn, David M., and Danna Nolan Fewell. *Narrative in the Hebrew Bible*. Oxford: Oxford University Press, 1993.

Habel, Norman C. *The Land is Mine: Six Biblical Land Ideologies*. OBT. Minneapolis: Fortress, 1995.

Halpern, Baruch. *The Constitution of the Monarchy in Israel*. HSM 25. Chico, Calif.: Scholars Press, 1981.

—*David's Secret Demons: Messiah, Murderer, Traitor, King*. Grand Rapids: Eerdmans, 2001.

Handy, Lowell K., ed. *The Age of Solomon: Scholarship at the Turn of the Millennium*. Leiden: Brill, 1997.

Haran, Menahem. "On the Diffusion of Literacy and Schools in Ancient Israel." Pages 81–95 in Emerton, ed., *Congress Volume: Jerusalem, 1986*.

Harris, William V. *Ancient Literacy*. Cambridge, Mass.: Harvard University Press, 1989.

Hays, J. Daniel. "Has the Narrator Come to Praise Solomon or Bury Him? Narrative Subtlety in 1 Kings 1–11." *JSOT* 28 (2003): 149–74.

Heaton, E. W. *The School Tradition of the Old Testament*. Oxford: Oxford University Press, 1994.

Herrmann, Siegfried. "Die Königsnovelle in Ägypten und in Israel." *Wissenschaftliche Zeitschrift der Karl Marx-Universität Leipzig* 3 (1953–54): 51–62.

Hess, Richard S. "The Form and Structure of the Solomonic District List in 1 Kings 4:7–19." Pages 279–92 in *Crossing Boundaries and Linking Horizons: Studies in Honor of Michael C. Astour on His 80th Birthday*. Edited by Gordon D. Young, Mark W. Chavalas, and Richard E. Averbeck. Bethesda, Md.: CDL Press, 1997.

Heym, Stefan. *The King David Report*. New York: G. P. Putnam's Sons, 1973.

Holladay, William L. *Jeremiah 2: A Commentary on the Book of the Prophet Jeremiah Chapters 26–52*. Hermeneia. Minneapolis: Fortress, 1989.

Holter, Knut. "The Serpent in Eden as a Symbol of Israel's Political Enemies: A Yahwistic Criticism of the Solomonic Foreign Policy?" *SJOT* 1 (1990): 106–12.

Hopkins, David C. "The Weight of the Bronze Could Not Be Calculated: Solomon and Economic Reconstruction." Pages 300–11 in Handy, ed., *The Age of Solomon*.

Hubbard, Robert L., Jr. *The Book of Ruth*. NICOT. Grand Rapids: Eerdmans, 1988.

—"The Hebrew Root *pgʿ* as a Legal Term." *JETS* 27 (1984): 129–33.

Huffmon, Herbert B. "Gender Subversion in the Book of Jeremiah." Pages 245–53 in *Sex and Gender in the Ancient Near East—Proceedings of the 47th Rencontre Assyriologique Internationale, Helsinki, July 2–6, 2001*. Edited by Simo Parpola and Robert M. Whiting. Helsinki: Neo-Assyrian Text Corpus Project, 2002.

Hurowitz, Victor (Avigdor). *I Have Built You an Exalted House: Temple Building in the Bible in Light of Mesopotamian and Northwest Semitic Writings*. JSOTSup 115. Sheffield: JSOT Press, 1992.

Ishida, Tomoo. "Adonijah the Son of Haggith and his Supporters: An Inquiry into Problems about History and Historiography." Pages 165–87 in *The Future of Biblical Studies: The Hebrew Scriptures*. Edited by Richard Elliot Friedman and H. G. M. Williamson. Decatur, Ga.: Scholars Press, 1987.

—"Solomon's Succession to the Throne of David—A Political Analysis." Pages 175–87 in Ishida, ed., *Studies in the Period of David and Solomon*.

—"Solomon Who is Greater than David: Solomon's Succession in 1 Kings I–II in the Light of the Inscription of Kilamuwa, King of y'dy-Śam'al." Pages 145–53 in Emerton, ed., *Congress Volume: Salamanca, 1983*.

—"The Succession Narrative and Esarhaddon's Apology: A Comparison." Pages 166–73 in *Ah, Assyria: Studies in Assyrian History and Ancient Near Eastern Historiography Presented to Hayim Tadmor*. Edited by Mordecai Cogan and Israel Ephʻal. ScrHier 33. Jerusalem: Magnes, 1991.

Ishida, Tomoo, ed. *Studies in the Period of David and Solomon and Other Essays*. Winona Lake, Ind.: Eisenbrauns, 1982.

Jackson, Rosemary. *Fantasy: The Literature of Subversion*. London: Methuen, 1981.

Jamieson-Drake, David W. *Scribes and Schools in Monarchic Judah: A Socio-archeological Approach*. JSOTSup 109. Sheffield: Almond Press, 1991.

Jobling, David. "'Forced Labor': Solomon's Golden Age and the Question of Literary Representation." Pages 57–76 in *Poststructuralism as Exegesis*. Edited by David Jobling and Stephen D. Moore. Semeia 54. Atlanta: Scholars Press, 1992.

Jones, Gwilym H. *1 and 2 Kings*. 2 vols. NCB. Grand Rapids: Eerdmans, 1984.

Kang, Jung Ju. *The Persuasive Portrayal of Solomon in 1 Kings 1–11*. Bern: Peter Lang, 2003.

Kenik, Helen A. *Design for Kingship: The Deuteronomistic Narrative Technique in 1 Kings 3:4–15*. SBLDS 69. Chico, Calif: Scholars Press, 1983.

Klein, Ralph W. *1 Samuel*. WBC 10. Waco, Tex.: Word, 1983.

Knight, Douglas A. Forward to *Prolegomena to the History of Israel*, by Julius Wellhausen. Atlanta: Scholars Press, 1994.

—"Political Rights and Powers in Monarchic Israel." Pages 93–117 in *Ethics and Politics in the Hebrew Bible*. Edited by Douglas A. Knight and Carol Meyers. Semeia 66. Atlanta: Scholars Press, 1995.

Knoppers, Gary N. "The Deuteronomist and the Deuteronomic Law of the King: A Reexamination of a Relationship." *ZAW* 108 (1996): 329–46.

—"Dissonance and Disaster in the Legend of Kirta." *JAOS* 114 (1994): 572–82.

—"Is there a Future for the Deuteronomistic History?" Pages 119–34 in *The Future of the Deuteronomistic History*. Edited by Thomas Römer. BETL 147. Leuven: Leuven University Press, 2000.

—"Prayer and Propaganda: Solomon's Dedication of the Temple and the Deuteronomist's Program." *CBQ* 57 (1995): 229–54.

—"The Preferential Status of the Eldest Son Revoked?" Pages 115–26 in *Rethinking the Foundations: Historiography in the Ancient World and in the Bible. Essays in Honour of John Van Seters*. Edited by Steven L. McKenzie and Thomas Römer. Berlin: de Gruyter, 2000.

—"Sex, Religion, and Politics: The Deuteronomist on Intermarriage." *HAR* 14 (1994): 121–41.

—"Solomon's Fall and Deuteronomy." Pages 392–410 in Handy, ed., *The Age of Solomon*.

—*Two Nations Under God: The Deuteronomistic History of Solomon and the Dual Monarchies*. Vol. 1, *The Reign of Solomon and the Rise of Jeroboam*. HSM 52. Atlanta: Scholars Press, 1993.

—"The Vanishing Solomon: The Disappearance of the United Monarchy from Recent Histories of Ancient Israel." *JBL* 116 (1997): 19–44.

Knoppers, Gary N. and J. Gordon McConville, eds. *Reconsidering Israel and Judah: Recent Studies on the Deuteronomistic History*. Winona Lake, Ind.: Eisenbrauns, 2000.

Koopmans, W. T. "The Testament of David in 1 Kings II 1–10." *VT* 41 (1991): 429–49.

Kuan, Jeffrey K. "Third Kingdoms 5.1 and Israelite–Tyrian Relations During the Reign of Solomon." *JSOT* 46 (1990): 31–46.

LaCocque, André. *The Feminine Unconventional: Four Subversive Figures in Israel's Tradition*. Minneapolis: Fortress, 1990.

Langlamet, F. "Pour ou contre Salomon? La rédaction prosalomonienne de I Rois, I–II." *RB* 83 (1976): 321–79, 481–529.

Lasine, Stuart. "Indeterminacy and the Bible: A Review of Literary and Anthropological Theories and their Application to Biblical Texts." *HS* 27 (1986): 48–80.

—"The King of Desire: Indeterminacy, Audience, and the Solomon Narrative." Pages 85–118 in Robinson and Culley, eds., *Textual Determinacy: Part Two*.

Lemaire, André. *Les Ecoles et la formation de la Bible dans l'ancien Israel*. Fribourg: Editions Universitaires, 1981.

—"The Sage in School and Temple." Pages 165–81 in Gammie and Perdue, eds., *The Sage in Israel and the Ancient Near East.*

Lemche, Neils Peter. "David's Rise." *JSOT* 10 (1978): 2–25.

—"On Doing Sociology with 'Solomon.'" Pages 312–35 in Handy, ed., *The Age of Solomon.*

Lenski, Gerhard E. *Power and Privilege: A Theory of Social Stratification.* New York: McGraw–Hill, 1966.

Levenson, Jon D. "1 Samuel 25 as Literature and History." *CBQ* 40 (1978): 11–28.

Lincoln, Bruce. *Authority: Construction and Corrosion.* Chicago: University of Chicago Press, 1994.

Lingen, Anton van der. "BW'-YŞ' ('To Go Out and To Come In') as a Military Term." *VT* 42 (1992): 59–66.

Lipiński, E. "Royal and State Scribes in Ancient Jerusalem." Pages 157–64 in Emerton, ed., *Congress Volume: Jerusalem, 1986.*

Liver, J. "The Book of the Acts of Solomon." *Bib* 48 (1967): 75–101.

Liverani, Mario. "Propaganda." Pages 474–77 in vol. 5 of Freedman, ed., *The Anchor Bible Dictionary.*

Long, Burke O. *1 Kings with an Introduction to Historical Literature.* FOTL 9. Grand Rapids: Eerdmans, 1984.

—"A Darkness between Brothers: Solomon and Adonijah." *JSOT* 19 (1981): 79–94.

—"Framing Repetitions in Biblical Historiography." *JBL* 106 (1987): 385–99.

Long, Jesse C., Jr. *1 & 2 Kings.* Joplin, Miss.: College Press, 2002.

Longman, Tremper, III. *Literary Approaches to Biblical Interpretation.* Grand Rapids: Zondervan, 1987.

Machiavelli, Nicolò. *The Prince.* Edited by Robert Maynard Hutchens. Translated by W. K. Marriott. Chicago: William Benton, 1952.

Machinist, Peter. "Literature as Politics: The Tukulti-Ninurta Epic and the Bible." *CBQ* 38 (1976): 455–82.

Magonet, Jonathan. *The Subversive Bible.* London: SCM Press, 1997.

Malamat, Abraham. "A Political Look at the Kingdom of David and Solomon and its Relations with Egypt." Pages 189–204 in Ishida, ed., *Studies in the Period of David and Solomon.*

Marcus, David. "David the Deceiver and David the Dupe." *Proof* 6 (1986): 163–71.

—Review of Yairah Amit, *Hidden Polemics in Biblical Narrative. BibInt* 12 (2004): 324–26.

Mason, Rex. *Propaganda and Subversion in the Old Testament.* London: SPCK, 1997.

McCarter, P. Kyle, Jr. *II Samuel.* AB 9. New York: Doubleday, 1984.

—"The Apology of David." *JBL* 99 (1980): 489–504.

—"Plots, True or False: The Succession Narrative as Court Apologetic." *Int* 35 (1981): 355–67.

McConville, J. G. "1 Kings VIII 46–53 and the Deuteronomic Hope." *VT* 42 (1992): 67–79.

McKenzie, Steven L. *King David: A Biography.* Oxford: Oxford University Press, 2000.

McKenzie, Steven L. and Stephen R. Haynes, eds. *To Each its Own Meaning: An Introduction to Biblical Criticisms and their Application.* Rev. and Exp. ed. Louisville, Ky.: Westminster John Knox, 1999.

McNutt, Paula M. *Reconstructing the Society of Ancient Israel.* Louisville, Ky.: Westminster John Knox, 1999.

Mettinger, Tryggve N. D. *King and Messiah: The Civil and Sacral Legitimation of the Israelite Kings*. ConBOT 8. Lund: Gleerup, 1976.

Millard, Alan R. "An Assessment of the Evidence for Writing in Ancient Israel." Pages 301–12 in *Biblical Archaeology Today, Proceedings of the International Congress on Biblical Archaeology, Jerusalem, 1984*. Edited by Janet Amitai. Jerusalem: Israel Exploration Society, 1985.

—"Does the Bible Exaggerate King Solomon's Golden Wealth?" *BAR* 15/3 (1989): 20–29, 31, 34.

Miscall, Peter D. *The Workings of Old Testament Narrative*. Philadelphia: Fortress, 1983.

Montgomery, James A., and Henry Snyder Gehman. *A Critical and Exegetical Commentary on the Books of Kings*. ICC. Edinburgh: T. & T. Clark, 1951.

Mowinckel, Sigmund. "Israelite Historiography." *ASTI* 2 (1963): 4–26.

Nelson, Richard D. *The Double Reaction of the Deuteronomistic History*. JSOTSup 18. Sheffield: JSOT Press, 1981.

—*First and Second Kings*. IBC. Louisville, Ky.: John Knox, 1987.

—"Josiah in the Book of Joshua." *JBL* 100 (1981): 531–40.

Niditch, Susan. *Oral World and Written Word: Ancient Israelite Literature*. Louisville, Ky.: Westminster John Knox, 1996.

Noth, Martin. *The Deuteronomistic History*. 2d ed. JSOTSup 15. Sheffield: JSOT Press, 1991. Translation of *Überlieferungsgeschichtliche Studien*. 2d ed. Tübingen: Max Niemeyer, 1957.

—*Könige*. BKAT 9/1. Neukirchen–Vluyn: Neukirchener, 1968.

Olley, John W. "Pharaoh's Daughter, Solomon's Palace, and the Temple: Another Look at the Structure of 1 Kings 1–11." *JSOT* 27 (2003): 355–69.

Oppenheim, A. Leo. "The Position of the Intellectual in Mesopotamian Society." *Daedalus* 104, no. 2 (1975): 37–46.

Pardee, Dennis. *Handbook of Ancient Hebrew Letters: A Study Edition*. Chico, Calif.: Scholars Press, 1982.

Pardes, Ilana. *Countertraditions in the Bible: A Feminist Approach*. Cambridge, Mass.: Harvard University Press, 1992.

Parker, Kim Ian. "Repetition as a Structuring Device in 1 Kings 1–11." *JSOT* 42 (1988): 19–27.

—"Solomon as Philosopher King? The Nexus of Law and Wisdom in 1 Kings 1–11." *JSOT* 53 (1992): 75–91.

Patrick, Dale and Allen Scult. *Rhetoric and Biblical Interpretation*. JSOTSup 82. Sheffield: Almond Press, 1990.

Penchansky, David. *What Rough Beast? Images of God in the Hebrew Bible*. Louisville, Ky.: Westminster John Knox, 1999.

Perdue, Leo G. "'Is there Anyone Left of the House of Saul…?' Ambiguity and the Characterization of David in the Succession Narrative." *JSOT* 30 (1984): 67–84.

—"The Testament of David and Egyptian Royal Instructions." Pages 79–96 in *Scripture in Context II: More Essays on the Comparative Method*. Edited by W. W. Hallo, J. C. Moyer, and L. G. Perdue. Winona Lake, Ind.: Eisenbrauns, 1983.

Polzin, Robert. *Moses and the Deuteronomist: A Literary Study of the Deuteronomistic History*. Part One, *Deuteronomy, Joshua, Judges*. New York: Seabury Press, 1980.

Porten, Bezalel. "The Structure and Theme of the Solomon Narrative (1 Kings 3–11)." *HUCA* 38 (1967): 93–128.

Pritchard, James B., ed. *Ancient Near Eastern Texts Relating to the Old Testament*. 3d ed. Princeton, N.J.: Princeton University Press, 1969.

Provan, Iain W. *1 and 2 Kings*. NIBCOT. Peabody, Mass.: Hendrickson, 1995.

—"Why Barzillai of Gilead (1 Kings 2:7)? Narrative Art and the Hermeneutics of Suspicion in 1 Kings 1–2." *TynBul* 46 (1995): 103–16.

Pury, Albert de, and Thomas Römer, eds. *Die sogenannte Thronfolgegeschichte Davids: Neue Einsichten und Anfragen*. OBO 176. Freiburg: Universitätsverlag; Göttingen: Vandenhoeck & Ruprecht, 2000.

Pyper, Hugh. S. "Reading David's Mind: Inference, Emotion and the Limits of Language." Pages 73–86 in *Sense and Sensitivity: Essays on Reading the Bible in Memory of Robert Carroll*. Edited by Alastair G. Hunter and Philip R. Davies. JSOTSup 348. Sheffield: Sheffield Academic Press, 2002.

Rainey, Anson F. "The Scribe at Ugarit: His Position and Influence." *PIASH* 3 (1969): 126–47.

Rendsburg, Gary A. "Biblical Literature as Politics: The Case of Genesis." Pages 47–70 in Berlin, ed., *Religion and Politics in the Ancient Near East*.

—"David and his Circle in Genesis XXXVIII." *VT* 36 (1986): 438–46.

Robinson, Robert B. and Robert C. Culley, eds. *Textual Determinacy: Part Two*. Semeia 71. Atlanta: Scholars Press, 1995.

Rogers, Jeffrey S. "Narrative Stock and Deuteronomistic Elaboration in 1 Kings 2." *CBQ* 50 (1988): 398–413.

Rosenberg, Joel. *King and Kin: Political Allegory in the Hebrew Bible*. Bloomington: Indiana University Press, 1986.

Rost, Leonhard. *The Succession to the Throne of David*. Translated by Michael D. Rutter and David M. Gunn. Historic Texts and Interpreters in Biblical Scholarship 1. Sheffield: Almond Press, 1982. Translation of *Die Überlieferung von der Thronnachfolge Davids*. BWA(N)T 3/6. Stuttgart: Kohlhammer, 1926.

Runions, Erin. "Zion is Burning: 'Gender Fuck' in Micah." Pages 225–46 in *In Search of the Present: The Bible through Cultural Studies*. Edited by Stephen D. Moore. Semeia 82. Atlanta: Scholars Press, 1998.

Sakenfeld, Katharine Doob. *Just Wives? Stories of Power and Survival in the Old Testament and Today*. Louisville, Ky.: Westminster John Knox, 2003.

Saldarini, Anthony J. "Scribes." Pages 1012–16 in vol. 5 of Freedman, ed., *The Anchor Bible Dictionary*.

Schley, Donald D., Jr. "1 Kings 10:26–29: A Reconsideration." *JBL* 106 (1987): 595–601.

Schniedewind, William M. *How the Bible Became a Book: The Textualization of Ancient Israel*. New York: Cambridge University Press, 2004.

Scolnic, Benjamin Edidin. "David's Final Testament: Morality or Expediency?" *Judaism* 43 (1994): 19–26.

Seow, C. L. "1 Kings 1:1–11:43: The Reign of Solomon." Pages 13–97 in vol. 3 of *The New Interpreter's Bible: A Commentary in Twelve Volumes*. Nashville: Abingdon, 1999.

—"The Syro-Palestinian Context of Solomon's Dream." *HTR* 77 (1984): 141–52.

Shenkel, James Donald. *Chronology and Recensional Development in the Greek Text of Kings*. HSM 1. Cambridge, Mass.: Harvard University Press, 1968.

Simpson, William Kelly, ed. *The Literature of Ancient Egypt: An Anthology of Stories, Instructions, and Poetry*. New ed. New Haven: Yale University Press, 1973.

Sneed, Mark R. "A Middle Class in Ancient Israel?" Pages 53–69 in Sneed, ed., *Concepts of Class in Ancient Israel.*

—ed. *Concepts of Class in Ancient Israel.* South Florida Studies in the History of Judaism 201. Atlanta: Scholars Press, 1999.

Soden, W. von. "Verschlüsselte Kritik an Salomo in der Urgeschichte des Jahwisten?" *WO* 7/2 (1974): 228–40.

Sperling, David S. *The Original Torah: The Political Intent of the Bible's Writers.* New York: New York University Press, 1998.

Sternberg, Meir. *The Poetics of Biblical Narrative: Ideological Literature and the Drama of Reading.* Bloomington: Indiana University Press, 1985.

Sturtevant, Edgar H., and George Bechtel. *A Hittite Chrestomathy.* Philadelphia: University of Pennsylvania Press, 1935.

Sweeney, Marvin A. "The Critique of Solomon in the Josianic Edition of the Deuteronomistic History." *JBL* 114 (1995): 607–22.

Sweet, Ronald F. G. "The Sage in Mesopotamian Palaces and Royal Courts." Pages 99–107 in Gammie and Perdue, eds., *The Sage in Israel and the Ancient Near East.*

Tadmor, Hayim. "Propaganda, Literature, Historiography: Cracking the Code of the Assyrian Royal Inscriptions." Pages 325–38 in *Assyria 1995: Proceedings of the 10th Anniversary Symposium of the Neo-Assyrian Text Corpus Project, Helsinki, September 7–11, 1995.* Edited by Simo Parpola and Robert M. Whiting. Helsinki: Helsinki University Press, 1997.

Taylor, Bernard A. *The Lucianic Manuscripts of I Reigns.* Vol 2, *Analysis.* HSM 51. Atlanta: Scholars Press, 1993.

Thackeray, Henry St. J. "The Greek Translators of the Four Books of Kings." *Journal of Theological Studies* 8 (1907): 262–78.

—*The Septuagint and Jewish Worship*, 2d ed. London: Oxford University Press, 1923.

Thompson, J. A. *The Book of Jeremiah.* NICOT. Grand Rapids: Eerdmans, 1980.

Thomson, Oliver. *Mass Persuasion in History: An Historical Analysis of the Development of Propaganda Techniques.* New York: Crane, Russak & Company, 1977.

Thornton, T. C. G. "Solomonic Apologetic in Samuel and Kings." *CQR* 169 (1968): 159–66.

Tov, Emanuel. "The LXX Additions (Miscellanies) in 1 Kings 2 (3 Reigns 2)." *Text* 11 (1984): 89–118.

Trebolle, Julio. "The Text-Critical Use of the Septuagint in the Books of Kings." Pages 285–99 in *VII Congress of the International Organization for Septuagint and Cognate Studies, Leuven 1989.* SBLSCS 31. Edited by Claude E. Cox. Atlanta: Scholars Press, 1989.

Trible, Phyllis. "Bringing Miriam Out of the Shadows." *BRev* 5/1 (1989): 14–25, 34.

—"Depatriarchalizing in Biblical Interpretation." *JAAR* 41 (1973): 30–48.

—"Eve and Miriam: From the Margins to the Center." Pages 5–24 in *Feminist Approaches to the Bible.* Edited by Hershel Shanks. Washington D.C.: Biblical Archaeological Society, 1995.

—*God and the Rhetoric of Sexuality.* OBT 2. Philadelphia: Fortress, 1978.

—*Texts of Terror: Literary–Feminist Readings of Biblical Narratives.* OBT 13. Philadelphia: Fortress, 1984.

Tsevat, Matitiahu. "Marriage and Monarchical Legitimacy in Ugarit and Israel." *JSS* 3 (1958): 237–43.

Vanderkam, James C. "Davidic Complicity in the Deaths of Abner and Eshbaal: A Historical and Redactional Study." *JBL* 99 (1980): 521–39.

Vanhoozer, Kevin J. *Is there a Meaning in this Text? The Bible, the Reader, and the Morality of Literary Knowledge.* Grand Rapids: Zondervan, 1998.

Veijola, Timo. *Die Ewige Dynastie: David und die Entstehung seiner Dynastie nach der deuteronomistischen Darstellung.* Annales Academiae Scientiarum Fennicae B 193. Helsinki: Suomalainen Tiedeakatemia, 1975.

—"Salomo–der erstgeborgene Bathsebas." Pages 230–50 in *Studies in the Historical Books of the Old Testament.* Edited by J. A. Emerton. VTSup 30. Leiden: Brill, 1979.

Walker, C. B. F. "Cuneiform." Pages 14–73 in *Reading the Past: Ancient Writing from Cuneiform to the Alphabet.* Written by J. T. Hooker et al. New York: Barnes & Noble Books, 1998. Repr., The British Museum Company, 1990.

Walsh, Jerome T. *1 Kings.* Berit Olam: Studies in Hebrew Narrative & Poetry. Collegeville, Minn.: Liturgical Press, 1996.

—"The Characterization of Solomon in First Kings 1–5." *CBQ* 57 (1995): 471–93.

Walsh, J. P. M. *The Mighty from their Thrones: Power in the Biblical Tradition.* OBT 21. Philadelphia: Fortress, 1987.

Waltke, Bruce K. and M. O'Connor. *An Introduction to Biblical Hebrew Syntax.* Winona Lake, Ind.: Eisenbrauns, 1990.

Walton, John H. *Ancient Israelite Literature in its Cultural Context: A Survey of Parallels between Biblical and Ancient Near Eastern Texts.* Grand Rapids: Zondervan, 1989.

Warner, Sean. "The Alphabet: An Innovation and its Diffusion." *VT* 30 (1980): 81–90.

Weber, Max. *Ancient Judaism.* Edited and translated by Hans H. Gerth and Don Martindale. Glencoe, Ill.: Free Press, 1952.

—*The Sociology of Religion.* Translated by Ephraim Fischoff. Boston: Beacon, 1963.

Weeks, Stuart. *Early Israelite Wisdom.* Oxford Theological Monographs. New York: Oxford University Press, 1994.

Wesselius, J. W. "Joab's Death and the Central Theme of the Succession Narrative (2 Samuel IX–1 Kings II)." *VT* 40 (1990): 336–51.

West, Gerald. "Reading on the Boundaries: Reading 2 Samuel 21:1–14 with Rizpah." *Scriptura* 63 (1997): 527–37.

White, Marsha. "'The History of Saul's Rise': Saulide State Propaganda in 1 Samuel 1–14." Pages 271–92 in *"A Wise and Discerning Mind": Essays in Honor of Burke O. Long.* Edited by Saul M. Olyan and Robert C. Culley. Providence, R.I.: Brown University, 2000.

Whitelam, Keith W. "Between History and Literature: The Social Production of Israel's Traditions of Origin." *SJOT* 2 (1991): 60–74.

—"The Defense of David." *JSOT* 29 (1984): 61–87.

—"Israelite Kingship: The Royal Ideology and its Opponents." Pages 119–39 in Clements, ed., *The World of Ancient Israel.*

—"The Symbols of Power: Aspects of Royal Propaganda in the United Monarchy. *BA* 49 (1986): 166–73.

Whybray, R. N. "The Sage in the Israelite Royal Court." Pages 133–39 in Gammie and Perdue, eds., *The Sage in Israel and the Ancient Near East.*

—*The Succession Narrative: A Study of II Samuel 9–20; I Kings 1 and 2.* SBT II/9. Naperville, Ill.: Alec R. Allenson, 1968.

Williamson, H. G. M. *1 and 2 Chronicles.* NCB. Grand Rapids: Eerdmans, 1982.

—"The Accession of Solomon in the Books of Chronicles." *VT* 26 (1976): 351–61.

Winters, Alicia. "The Subversive Memory of a Woman." Pages 142–54 in *Subversive Scriptures: Revolutionary Readings of the Christian Bible in Latin America*. Edited and translated by Leif E. Vaage. Valley Forge, Pa.: Trinity, 1997.

Würthwein, Ernst. *Die Erzählung von der Thronfolge Davids—theologische oder politische Geschichtsschreibung?* Theologische Studien 115; Zürich: Theologischer Verlag, 1974.

Yee, Gale. "'Fraught with Background': Literary Ambiguity in II Samuel 11." *Int* 42 (1988): 240–53.

Younger, K. Lawson, Jr. "The Figurative Aspect and the Contextual Method in the Evaluation of the Solomonic Empire (1 Kings 1–11)." Pages 157–75 in *The Bible in Three Dimensions: Essays in Celebration of Forty Years of Biblical Studies in the University of Sheffield*. Edited by D. J. A. Clines et al. JSOTSup 87. Sheffield: JSOT Press, 1990.

Zipes, Jack. *Fairy Tales and the Art of Subversion: The Classical Genre for Children and the Process of Civilization*. New York: Routledge, 1991.

# INDEXES

## INDEX OF REFERENCES

# INDEX OF AUTHORS